THE BEER ESSENTIALS

The *Spirit Journal* Guide to
Over 650 of the World's Beers

F. PAUL PACULT

NEW YORK

Library of Congress Cataloging-in-Publication Data

Pacult, F. Paul.
The beer essentials : the Spirit journal guide to
the world's beers / F. Paul Pacult. —1st ed.
p.   cm.
Includes bibliographical references.
ISBN 0-7868-8173-9
1. Beer.   I. Title.
TP577.P225   1997
641.2'3'0296—dc21   97-847
CIP

Designed by Jessica Shatan

FIRST EDITION
2 4 6 8 10 9 7 5 3 1

For Helen Ann Daniels,
who has always believed and encouraged.

THE BEER
ESSENTIALS

CONTENTS

ACKNOWLEDGMENTS

This collection of reviews has come into being over the course of seven years and with the help of many people. My first salute is to Alexander Douglas, without whose assistance, patience, and reliability *F. Paul Pacult's Spirit Journal,* the guiding light of this book, would never have been successful.

Enormous thanks to both Sue Woodley, my wife, and Richard Pacult, my brother, for their tireless proofreading and superb grammatical and stylistic suggestions.

John Riggio of *The New York Times,* who on a business trip to Boston provided the most memorable trip through an airport security checkpoint I've ever experienced.

Jim Koch, of Boston Beer Company, has been a valued supporter as well as a fountainhead of information. I'd also like to thank Boston Beer Company brewers Jim Pericles and José Ayala for contributing so generously to my brewing education.

Of the many brewpub managers, bartenders, and brewers who have been so kind and free with their time, information, and expertise, I'd especially like to point out Lon Lauterio of Mountain Valley Brew Pub in Suffern, New York; Kirby Shyer of Zip City Brewing in Manhattan; Stuart Gildred Jr. and Dave Hammel of Baja Brewing Company in San Diego, California.

Last, but certainly not least, I'd like to express my appreciation to my editor at Hyperion, Rick Kot, and to my agent, Robert Lescher, for their keen insights and for making this project a reality.

THE BEER
ESSENTIALS

INTRODUCTION

**Wine is but a single broth,
ale is meat, drink, and cloth.**
—Old English proverb

My childhood memories of growing up in Chicago in the 1950s and 1960s
are colored, in part, with the amber-gold tone of the mainstream American
lagers that were favorites in the Midwest during those meat-and-potatoes
decades. My father and uncles drank beer on a regular basis. Beer was simply a part of their lives, enjoyed with little ceremony, no fuss, no proclama-
tions. Our extended family, a naturally vigorous and gregarious bunch made
up of nine nuclear units, frequently congregated on weekends for street foot-
ball, barbecues, and nickel-and-dime poker games, most often at our house
on Chicago's far northwest side. Schlitz, Hamm's (complete with the
Hamm's bear, whose commercials sponsored the Cubs' games on WGN-
TV), Old Style, Meister Brau, Ballantine, and Pabst Blue Ribbon lagers
flowed freely, for how else were the adults supposed to wash down all the
homemade food that was available?

This handful of beer brands, whose logos I can still envision, were the
potent emblems of a rite of passage for my brother, Rick, and myself. To have
Dad offer us a sip of his Schlitz or Ballantine Ale was a big deal, for while I
didn't care that much for the taste—what kid really does?—the offer from
the old man was in and of itself the coveted reward. In my subconscious
mind, a tiny sip of beer from my father's glass meant that I was beginning
to go places.

While my dad and my uncles enjoyed their brew ice cold, my paternal
grandfather, who had been born in Europe, preferred his beer warm—*very*
warm. The bemused expression on my father's face whenever my grand-
mother heated my grandfather's beer in a saucepan still makes me laugh.
Dad looked like a minister standing in the middle of the street helplessly
watching his church burn to the ground.

Also in the scrapbook of my family's folklore was the story of my Meister Brau–loving uncle, Stanley, and his antiheroics. Everyone, including his nieces and nephews, called this gruff, kind-hearted, diamond-in-the-rough truck driver, Stash (pronounced *Stahsh*). Every summer from about 1955 to 1965, carloads of family members would convoy up to a northern Illinois recreational spot called Third Lake. We'd usually number from fifteen to twenty-five people. The entire day would be spent barbecuing, fishing, swimming, and playing cards and softball.

One summer in the early 1960s, my mother's sister, Dorothy, purchased a fancy and expensive woven wicker picnic basket of which she was especially proud. I remember her showing everyone its spiffy features—brightly colored plates and utensils, built-in holders for salt and pepper shakers and plastic cups, red-checkered napkins—as if she were boasting about a new car. On one of our more memorable Saturday picnics that season, an old-fashioned Midwest summer storm complete with ear-piercing thunder, a torrential downpour, and dangerous lightning suddenly engulfed Third Lake, forcing everyone to scramble to the nearest car for shelter. Dorothy ended up in our Chevrolet Impala with my mother, brother, and myself. When she realized that her new picnic basket was getting pounded by rain, hail, and a howling wind, Dorothy almost had to be physically restrained by my mother to stay inside the relative safety of the Chevy.

Just then, my mother said, "Oh, look, Dorothy. Stash's leaving his car and heading right for your table."

Dorothy sighed with relief. "Good old Stash. I'll bet you that he's going to rescue my picnic basket."

With the rain and wind whipping at him and lightning flashing overhead, Stash dashed to the table. Clutching his ever-present baseball cap with one hand, he opened the cooler that was standing right next to my aunt's new wicker basket with the other hand, reached in, yanked out two cans of his beloved Meister Brau lager, and scurried back to his car, leaving the basket to the elements. What made matters worse, and in retrospect even more amusing, was that Stash waved his Meister Brau can at us from his car while he cracked it open, as if triumphantly indicating his bravery in the face of the extreme conditions.

I cite these tales for one simple reason: Beer means good times to me, as it does to so many others. It signifies family, food, fun, and friends. As opposed to the pomposity with which wine and some distilled spirits are frequently consumed, beer is uncomplicated, fundamental, and straightforward. Beer appeals to just about everyone, young and old, rich or poor. While the recent surge in its popularity and market presence has been hailed, somewhat exaggeratedly, as either the "beer phenomenon" or the "beer renaissance" by some of the more excitable observers, I view its increasing acceptance as a natural and inevitable development in line with the consumer trends of the late 1990s. ·

Even though sales of popular American lagers have rarely flagged, wine became the libation king during the 1970s and 1980s. Consumers became fascinated with wine's intricacies and subtleties as well as its worldwide appeal and exotic origins. Americans began to travel as never before and often brought back the names of wines they'd enjoyed on their trips, hoping to find them or comparable vintages in their hometowns. As wine became the choice for sophisticated dining, beer stayed the blue-collar thirst slaker.

I fully and eagerly participated in the wine movement by working in a northern California winery, Sonoma Vineyards (known today as Rodney D. Strong Vineyards) from 1973 through 1982. Immediately after relocating to New York City to pursue a writing career, I was employed for two years by Morrell and Company, a carriage trade retail wine and spirits store. These employment experiences thoroughly prepared me for writing about and evaluating alcoholic beverages from all corners of the globe. By the time I was writing about and consulting full-time on these beverages in the mid-1980s, the people whose palates had come to maturity on wine were beginning to expand their sensory experiences by entering the more complex territories of port and brandy. By the late 1980s, whiskies, especially the single malts of Scotland, were coming into vogue.

Interestingly, beer sales continued to be stable all through the various changes and progressions of America's collective taste. In fact, as U.S. consumers grew more enamored with more characterful wines and spirits, the beer mavens among them started to take notice of Europe's brews, which on average are considerably more substantial than the ubiquitous American lagers. Likewise they began to experiment with the few and often difficult-to-find domestic "microbrews" and regional beers then available, such as those from California's Anchor Brewing, Oregon's Henry Weinhard, and Pennsylvania's Yuengling Brewing Company. By the end of the decade, the pioneering American microbrewers, neighborhood brewpubs, and contract brewers realized they had an opportunity to satisfy consumers who were searching for more challenging taste experiences in all categories of beverage alcohol. With an eye to their brethren from Europe, the small band of top-quality domestic brewers began offering Old World–style porters, ales, stouts, and bock beers.

By 1990 and 1991, the stampede was on as family-owned and limited-partnership breweries of all sizes started to increase nationwide, both in major metropolitan areas and medium-sized towns. The neighborhood brewery, which was commonplace in seventeenth-, eighteenth-, and nineteenth-century America, was revived. So deep has the impact of small breweries been on the beer industry as a whole that the mainstream megabrewers headquartered in the midsection of the country—the huge companies with household names like Anheuser-Busch, Miller, Coors, Pabst, and Stroh's, who for decades supplied America with the vast majority of its beer—have in the last half-decade been offering their own versions of meatier, small-batch beers and even buying into microbreweries.

As a result of the furious brewing activity both here and abroad, consumers are faced with the fortuitous prospect of having more kinds of beer to taste from more sources than ever before.

Over the last seven years in both the pages of my quarterly newsletter, *F. Paul Pacult's Spirit Journal,* and in *The New York Times Sunday Magazine,* I've discussed, reviewed, and rated hundreds of domestic and imported beers. *The Beer Essentials* is the official collection of those detailed notes and ratings, plus scores of additional beer evaluations that have never been published in any venue. *The Beer Essentials,* which I consider to be a work-in-progress, since there are so many more beers yet to evaluate, is my personal celebration of beer, of beer lovers, of the brewers with whom I've met and shared a pint, and, most important, of the memory of my Uncle Stash galloping through a July monsoon in northern Illinois to grab a couple of cans of Meister Brau—the Holy Grail found.

Speaking of Beer—
Beer's Pedigree

Blessing of your heart, you brew good Ale.
—William Shakespeare,
The Two Gentlemen of Verona

Calls for beer have been voiced by men and women for about as long as our species has been civilized. With the obvious exception of water, beer is universally recognized by historians, anthropologists, and archeologists as the oldest natural fermented beverage. Paving the way for beer's discovery was man's momentous decision to settle down into primitive agrarian communities. As our bipedal, highly intelligent noble ancestors gradually traded their nomadic existence, which was doubtless fraught with unimaginable trials and uncertainties, for the steadiness of the purposeful cultivation of crops, the seed of the story of beer germinated.

Early pottery and stone tablets, unearthed in the area of what is now southern Turkey and northern Iran and dated at approximately 3000 B.C., depict the earliest farmers as growers of grain, most likely barley. Since beer is made from the same three rudimentary ingredients as bread (grain, water, and yeast), it should come as no surprise that beer production probably developed at about the same time as bread making. Some historians believe that beer may actually have preceded bread, since the date of invention of the oven remains hidden in the mists of time.

One unknown Sumerian poet of this era wrote: "I feel wonderful drinking beer; in a blissful mood with joy in my heart and a happy liver." A commonplace Sumerian greeting went, "My sister, your grain—its beer is tasty, my comfort."

Over time the Sumerians, who are acknowledged to be both the creators of civilization as well as the originators of beer, were outpaced by the Mesopotamians and Babylonians in the art of beer making. But by then, agricultural settlements were too successful a concept to stay confined to the Middle East's so-called Fertile Crescent of the Tigris-Euphrates river valleys. Organized communities eventually spread to areas like the Nile River

Valley, where the ancient Egyptians formed one of history's most formidable and durable civilizations—a hallmark of which was masterful brewing.

In the ancient world brewing was the province of women. Indeed, the Egyptian deity of beer was Hathor, a goddess. In dynastic Egypt beer was a focal point of society and touched every stage of life from birth to death. Babies were ritualistically anointed with it, workers were remunerated with it, and tombs were stocked with it. Few cultures since have been so literally and figuratively saturated with beer.

Because they had the proper ingredients at hand, the bakers in the clay and stone settlements of Babylonia, Uruk, Alexandria, and Thebes ended up being the community's brewers, as well. Hence, it's not farfetched to argue that beer is every bit as much a food as bread. Beer, it has been stated, *is* bread in liquid form. To verify that claim, just sip on thick English stout or a husky Washington State porter and you'll immediately perceive the similarities.

Other societies in China, Greece, and even central and northern Europe became proficient in the brewing art long before Jesus walked the arid terrain of Galilee or Siddhartha sat beneath the bodhi tree in India. Artifacts found on the island of Rhum, which lies off Scotland's western coast, have led archeologists to conclude that brewing probably existed on this remote chunk of rock as long as four millennia ago.

The Romans expanded beer making as confidently as they expanded their empire throughout Europe. Their term for beer was *cerevisia,* a word constructed from *Ceres,* the Roman deity of agriculture, and *vis,* meaning "strength."

As the Roman Empire imploded, the omnipotent Roman Church, under Charlemagne, took up the banner of beer making. By around 1000 A.D., as Europe's Dark Ages were concluding, the art of brewing was safeguarded and advanced in the industrious monasteries of the Christian monks, as well as in the fortified castles and estates of the aristocracy. Many of the best beers in the world are still produced by monks, especially the Trappist Order in Belgium and Holland. The positive influence of monasteries on the evolution of beer as we know it cannot be overstated. Through trial and error the monks refined brewing into an art form and a viable trade. It is widely believed that they were the first brewers to introduce the key fourth ingredient, hops, to the brewing process in the 800s.

During the medieval period of 800–1500 A.D., beer was viewed by the general populace as a source of comfort and sustenance as well as a palatable alternative to polluted drinking water, which was commonplace as cities and towns grew in size without even rudimentary hygiene. Beer was most often consumed in the Middle Ages at roadside taverns and village public halls, which brewed their own crude ales. The era's land barons and emerging city-states, on the other hand, regarded beer as a source of revenue with which to cement, develop, and expand their holdings. The powerful sold their ales to the hoi-polloi to fund their further adventures and expansions.

In Elizabethan England, the country estates and manors of the gentry almost always had their own microbreweries or, at the very least, vast stocks of ale. In fact, the English word "butler" was derived from the manorhouse term, "buttery," which referred to the storeroom for "butts," or huge wooden casks, of ale. The keeper of the buttery was called the butler.

After the formation of the first brewing trade guild in Belgium, beer became unstoppable as a commercially viable enterprise. With the exchange of ideas and information through the network of guilds, beer production grew to be an important and innovative industry at the local level across the whole of Europe. For instance, German brewers were the first beer makers to produce their beers in the cold months, then "lager" them, which meant that they stored them in the cold caves of the Alps during the warm summer season. This method of production resulted in the clear, crisp, golden beers that are today coveted around the world.

The Germans were also the first brewers to establish brewing regulations. The landmark standards of 1487 were the foundation for the later beer purity laws, referred to as the "Reinheitsgebot of 1516," which stated that German beer could be produced from only four ingredients—malted barley, malted wheat, hops, and water. (Yeast was, of course, utilized as the catalyst for fermentation and was, in actuality, the fifth element.) It was the Reinheitsgebot declaration that informed consumers of beer that the beverages that they were drinking were of the day's highest guaranteed standards. This formalization of ingredient requirements changed brewing forever.

Eventually the guilds served as the platform for the development of regional varieties, thereby creating distinct beer identities. This individualization of beer varieties by the brewers of the British Isles and continental Europe helped establish the traditional styles of beer that we enjoy to this day.

By the time of the Renaissance, beer had become an integral element of every stratum of European culture. It was served and eagerly consumed in the lowliest dining halls as well as at the poshest costume parties hosted by the kerchief-in-sleeve elite. Beer's bounty excluded none and charmed all, from the courts of China to the castles of England. Even more than wine, beer was by the late 1500s genuinely universal.

In the remarkable three-century period of exploration from the late fifteenth century through the late eighteenth century, beer was considered an absolute standard provision on any long ocean voyage. The inventory of staples on virtually any wayfaring vessel routinely recorded three times the amount of beer to that of water because, in addition to its being a soothing beverage, beer was a natural and easily transported food rich in nutrients. With the frantic rush of colonial expansion in the sixteenth and seventeenth centuries, beer found a welcome home in the faraway New World colonies of North America. No less an historic event than the earlier-than-planned landing of the *Mayflower* was caused, in some measure, by the depleted stores of ale on board. Hoping in their original navigational scheme to land on the coast of Virginia, the Pilgrims instead had to settle for the rocky shoreline of Massachusetts in 1620 because "we could not now take time for further search or considerations, our victuals being much spent, especially our beer," according to the ship's log.

Once settlements had been established along the eastern seaboard of North America, the farmers of the New World also became its first microbrewers. The winters of New England and the mid-Atlantic region being routinely harsh, beer became an especially critical fortification against the period known as "the starving time." Consumption of beer in seventeenth-century New England was, by some reports, upwards of three quarts or more per day per person. Yet because of the strongly held religious beliefs and behavioral dictums of the Puritans and other colonists who fled Europe as a result of religious persecution, even the slightest inebriation was not tolerated. In fact, public displays of drunkenness frequently incurred extremely unpleasant disciplinary actions.

Prominent colonists and patriots were often associated with brewing. The Dutchman Peter Minuit, who had the vision to purchase Manhattan Island from the local Native Americans, founded the first known public brewery in America in 1622. Six decades later, William Penn opened the first commercial brewery in Philadelphia, making that city the focal point for brewing in the colonies. Samuel Adams, who had a hand in the instigation of the Boston Tea Party uprising in 1773, was reputedly both a Massachusetts brewer (though recent questions have arisen concerning this assertion) and a signer of the Declaration of Independence. Other colonial leaders involved with brewing included Ethan Allan, George Washington, John Adams, and Thomas Chittenden, the first governor of Vermont. Thomas Jefferson conceived and put to paper much of the Declaration of Independence in a Philadelphia tavern called the Indian Queen. After he set aside the responsibilities of nation building and governing, Jefferson experimented with homebrewing at his beloved estate, Monticello.

As the colonists pushed further west in the eighteenth and nineteenth centuries, they matched their finely honed brewing skills to the grain they were able to grow in unprecedented abundance in these long, flat, fertile valleys of the Ohio and Mississippi rivers, and the burgeoning population's beer consumption grew dramatically. It's estimated that by the midpoint of the nineteenth century approximately 1,500 domestic beers were available. However, a significant change in the style of beer was evolving during this period. The brown, thick, fortifying ales that were brewed in the colonial states of New York, Massachusetts, and Pennsylvania were gradually being replaced by lighter, crisper, gold-colored lagers made in the central states. By the turn of the twentieth century, the mainline brewing centers of the United States had become the heartland cities of Milwaukee, St. Louis, Chicago, Detroit, and Denver, where megabrewers like Miller, Stroh, Anheuser-Busch, Coors, Schlitz, G. Heileman, and Pabst flourished.

Following World War I, the temperance movement, which had been vociferously (and sometimes violently) demonstrating against all alcoholic beverages as far back as the 1840s, most prominently in the death angel figure of Carrie Nation, saw its fondest wish come true when on January 17, 1920, America's tap was temporarily turned off by an Act of Congress. Even though the infamous Eighteenth Amendment (also known as the National Prohibition Act and the Volstead Act in dubious honor of its author, Minnesota representative Andrew Volstead) had a national approval rating of a meager 20 percent, the serving or transporting of any beer, wine, or distilled spirit remained illegal in the United States until 1933, when newly elected president Franklin Roosevelt engineered the passage of the Twenty-first

Amendment, which repealed Prohibition. To his credit, FDR had realized that, in the throes of the nation's most crippling depression in history, America would not be harmed by a sip of beer. (He reportedly remarked at the execution of the repeal, "I think this would be a good time for a beer.") The country's economy likewise needed as many people back in meaningful employment as possible, and the alcoholic beverage industry could assist in that struggle.

But the consequences of nearly a decade and a half of federally imposed Prohibition were devastatingly harsh and long-lasting on the majority of American brewers. Of the 1,600 American breweries that were reportedly operating prior to the passing of the Volstead Act, less than half reopened after the amendment's repeal. And more telling, of those reopened breweries, almost 70 percent soon failed because of overall financial woes, markets that required expensive redevelopment, and costly equipment that had fallen into disrepair after over fourteen years of inactivity.

After the hostilities of World War II were brought to a close, the megabrewers in America's heartland geared up production for the lubrication of the nation's economic recovery, population explosion, and subsequent prosperity. American families moved to the outskirts of the major metropolitan areas; bought homes; drove Buicks, Fords, and Plymouths; and gulped down the ubiquitous golden lagers with comfortably familiar names like Budweiser, Miller High Life, Pabst Blue Ribbon, and Coors. Life was stable, and the beer was cold, plentiful, and reliably thirst-quenching. The marketing and advertising dominance of the coterie of megabrewers was such that their only competition came from within their own ranks.

With the occasional excursion into the world of imported beers, Mr. and Mrs. America settled in by and large for the long haul with their Bud or Miller or Pabst. The sole branching out by the mainstream beers occurred in the late 1970s and early 1980s with the introduction of the so-called "light" beers, disturbingly tasteless lagers that contained fewer calories. Here again, the marketing wizards of the megabrewers created both a supply and a demand with clever and award-winning advertising, such as the inspired early Miller Lite spots that featured a regular cast of sports legends and celebrities.

But the cultural sophistication and inquisitive tastes of Americans would eventually lead them beyond the admirably good, all-American, and serviceable lagers pumped out in swollen rivers by the big boys. The search for more complex and flavorful brews was about to begin. Next stop, the Microbrew Zone.

Microbreweries are currently classified as any brewery that annually produces fewer than 15,000 barrels of beer. I can recall my first taste of the pioneering microbrew called New Albion sometime in the middle of the 1970s. Oddly enough, that initial encounter took place at the winery at which I was working. A coworker named Augie Cruz handed me an ice-cold bottle of New Albion at one of our annual "crush" parties, which celebrated the end of the harvest. I remember being amazed at the difference between New Albion and my regular beer of that era, Coors.

New Albion was the new-fangled fizzy creation of brewer Jack McAuliffe. Showing considerable brass, McAuliffe brewed his cutting-edge beer in the old mission town of Sonoma in the heart of California's North Coast wine country. Further south in San Francisco, Fritz Maytag had already set up shop for Anchor Brewery, which has since become world-renowned for its unique Steam Beer.

The 1980s proved to be the pivotal decade for microbrewing and contract brewing in America, as these beers quickly multiplied and became an integral part of the domestic brewing landscape. The personal sacrifice, business sense, and skill of brewers like Bert Grant (Grant's) in Yakima, Washington; Jim Koch (Samuel Adams) in Boston, Massachusetts; Ed and Carol Stoudt (Stoudt's) in Adamstown, Pennsylvania; Ken Grossman and Paul Camusi (Sierra Nevada) in Chico, California; and Bill Owens (Buffalo Bill's) in Hayward, California, have ushered in the present Golden Age of beer making in America. The path trailblazed in large measure by these visionary brewers in the 1970s and 1980s is now a beer superhighway as the turn of the millennium approaches.

THE INGREDIENTS
OF BEER

Yes, hurrah the hops, and hurrah the malt,
They are life's flavor and life's salt!
—From the opera *Marta*

Understanding the manifold styles of beer immeasurably enhances anyone's drinking enjoyment. By comprehending beer's remarkably broad spectrum of colors, aromas, textures, and flavors, drinkers are able either to leisurely stroll through the world's portfolio of beer or to home in on the style that is the most satisfying to their unique taste. Tracking down the world's thousands of beers can become something of a lifelong endeavor. But, as I have found out, the discovery itself of new and different beers is where the most satisfaction lies.

Beer is among the simplest, yet most diverse of commonplace, man-made beverages. The majority of beers are produced from the building-block elements of water, malted grain (most prominently barley and, to a lesser degree, wheat), hops, and yeast. While some brewers whom I've interviewed don't readily include yeast as a key ingredient, because rather than contributing significant flavor yeast serves primarily as a the catalyst to launch fermentation, most experts in the field believe that yeast nevertheless must be considered one of the cornerstone components.

The most important ingredient of all is the one that's the most readily available on most of the planet—water. H_2O makes up over nine-tenths of the composition of any beer. The flavor impact of water, however, used to be greater than it is now, at the close of the twentieth century. Brewers in previous centuries would search for pristine water sources from which to make their beers. Once located and procured, water sources in the Old World were carefully guarded against contamination. Water in sixteenth-century England or eighteenth-century Bavaria was considered to be of the utmost importance to brewers, because if the source turned bad, it would effectively put them out of business. Today's brewers rarely have that worry, since technological advances allow them to chemically adjust and correct real or potential problems.

Interestingly, many contemporary brewing houses treat their water as a routine matter in order to ensure the continuity of taste and chemical balance. Overly hard water, or water rich in magnesium and calcium, is undesirable for lighter, golden types of beers, such as pilseners or wheat beers. Other beer styles have become distinctive primarily *because of* the water source. Three prime examples of the latter are the dry, razor-edged pale ales from Burton-upon-Trent in central England, where the water is hard because of gypsum deposits; the London area's plump, dark, and round brown ales, which are influenced by southeastern England's chalky water; and the ultracrisp lagers of Bohemia, whose local water is very low in sodium and is the foundation for smooth, almost dainty golden beers.

Barley is the grain of choice when it comes to beer making. This ancient cereal grass comes in three basic packages—two-row, four-row, and six-row—which refer to the grain's customary growing habits. Some strains of barley develop two rows of grains, which pop out of the sides of the stem. The brewers of the United Kingdom and continental Europe generally prefer to use two-row barley, because this type of fat-grained grass produces the kind of malt that's naturally more concentrated in starch than either four- or six-row. What they lose in the process, however, is enzyme counts. North American brewers, on the other hand, like six-row barley, because in addition to being easier to grow than two-row, this prolific strain is chockful of enzymes. One deficiency of six-row barley, though, is that its thicker husk contains higher levels of tannin. An increasing number of brewers in the United States are including both strains of barley in their brewing process in order to maximize the positive aspects of each while minimizing the negative.

But before barley can work its biochemical magic, it needs to be malted, a process that encourages an increase in its starch content. Malting entails the barley's first being steeped in long vats of water for forty hours, then being spread on concrete floors and allowed to partially germinate. After five days, the half-sprouted barley is dried in kilns. Malted barley's elevated starch level is next transformed into a desirable sugar level when enzymes convert starch into sugar during the mashing process. In mashing, the malted grain (now in the form of milled grist) is dumped into huge stainless steel or concrete vessels called *mash tuns* and combined with hot water (commonly around 175 degrees Fahrenheit). The soluble starches in the grain become sugars through the action of diastase, the operative enzyme. The mash is then moved to yet another vat, called the *lauter tun,* in which the liquid becomes separated from the grain solids as it filters through a grated false floor. The resulting sweet, viscous, and appealingly fragrant liquid is called *wort.*

The wort is next boiled in the brew kettle with hops. After the hop solids are removed, the wort is cooled. For the crucial fermentation stage, the duration of which is usually five to seven days, yeast is added, or in brewhouse lingo, "pitched" into the tank filled with wort. The tumultuous action of the yeast cells feeding on the wort's sugars converts them into carbon dioxide (CO_2) and ethyl alcohol.

After the yeast cells are sated and fermentation is completed, and prior to the beer's being moved to the conditioning tank for aging, the brewmaster measures its actual density. The *specific gravity*, as the density is termed, is quantified by comparing the weight of a predetermined amount of beer against the weight of an equal volume of water. The difference is the specific gravity. With the number 1.000 being used for the standard weight of water, for instance, if the beer weighs 1.035, the specific gravity of that ale or lager is listed as 1035. The higher the specific gravity, the more robust the beer. It should be noted that loftier gravity doesn't necessarily translate into better beer. There are numerous outstanding beers with lower specific gravities. Gravity is simply a yardstick of density, nothing more.

With the completion of the first fermentation, the liquid that is now unfinished beer is piped to another tank. Here, it either undergoes the process of *krausening,* in which a second fermentation is commenced, thereby giving beer its effervescence as in most microbrews, or it is merely stored, or *lagered,* for clarification. Most mainstream lagers are artificially carbonated to save time and money.

After finishing, the fermented liquid is filtered to correct haziness and then pasteurized for purity. The beer is, at last, racked, kegged, or bottled straightaway, depending on who's doing the brewing. The delicious result is beer. The entire production process from milling the barley malt to bottling or kegging consumes from three to six weeks.

Malted barley can also be roasted to influence the flavor of the beer. The darker the roast, the more profound the impact upon the taste and appearance. Brooding, chocolate-brown porters and stouts are the sturdy, robust products of chocolate or black malts, both of which have been charred.

While barley is the heavily favored cereal grain for beer production worldwide, it is not the only grain that makes good beer. Malted wheat is the foundation for Germany's illustrious *weizenbiers,* in which it commonly accounts for over half the grain used. Other cereal grains, referred to in brewer's jargon as *adjuncts,* include rice (used in some standard American lagers), corn (an ingredient of various light ales, especially), and oats (found in some superdark ales and Belgian ales). But, barley has been, is now, and, in all probability always will remain first among equals.

Hops are the zest, the attitude, the accentuation of the constitution of most beers, the ingredient that separates the beer of the last thousand years from the syrupy-sweet, thick, and, more than likely, disgusting concoctions that were quaffed before the discovery of hops as a flavoring. Initially domesticated by the Romans, who were given to munching on its tasty shoots, hops are the dried, ripe blossoms of a climbing vine *(Humulus lupulus)* from the mulberry family and are even a distant relative of *cannabis,* or marijuana. (One hops grower told me that the blossoms of hops can cast a tranquilizing effect when used as part of the stuffing in pillows.) Hops have been a flavor additive to beer since the early centuries of the Middle Ages. Some hops contribute an herbal bitterness, while others introduce a spicy, flowery quality in the aroma and taste. The influence of hops is determined by the brewmaster as much by when he or she adds the hops to the brew kettle as by the type of hops employed. When hops are blended in at the beginning or the middle of the boil, they impart bitterness to the flavor. When tossed in at the end of the boil, hops enliven the bouquet. When more hop intensity is desired, the brewer will add even more hops to the tank in which the secondary fermentation occurs. This procedure is called *dry-hopping*.

The intensity of hop influence is measured by a universally employed system known as International Bitterness Units (IBUs). The lower the IBU measurement, the more mundane and flavorless the beer. For example, that widely distributed golden lager that you had with pizza last night probably didn't register more than 12, at tops 15, IBUs. But the IBU count on the stout that you're planning on having after dinner tonight in all likelihood measures over 25, possibily even 30, on the IBU scale. The bitter, sometimes herbal, dryness that hops contribute to the aroma and flavor of beer is generated from the acid, resin, and oil compounds found in the petals of the plant as well as its blossoms, which more resemble chubby, miniature pinecones than petaled flowers in the usual sense.

Hops are grown most successfully in Great Britain, the Pacific Northwest of the United States and Canada, the Czech Republic, and Germany. Other countries with active areas of hop cultivation include Belgium, New Zealand, and, increasingly, Australia. As the global wine industry boasts its grape varieties, especially the so-called "noble" types like *cabernet sauvignon, merlot, chardonnay,* and so forth, brewers parade their hop families, including an aristocratic group known as the noble hops. Four excellent and widely employed hop varieties grown in the United Kingdom include *Fuggles, Kent Goldings, Northern Brewer,* and *Brewer's Gold.* Hops with names like *Clusters, Cascade, Galena, Willamette, Mt. Hood,* and *Chinook* are prominent in the domestic hop industry. The noble hops grown in Germany and the Czech Republic include *Hallertauer Mittelfrueh,* considered by many brewers to be the finest hop; *Hersbrucker; Saaz;* and *Tettnang.*

Invisible to the naked eye, yeast is the unicellular organism that consumes the sugars in the wort and leads to fermentation, in which the liquid's innate sugars are transformed into ethyl alcohol and carbon dioxide. The ethyl alcohol gives beer its body, power, and sense of direction, while the carbon dioxide contributes bounce, personality, and vivacity in the form of bubbles. The particular strain of yeast introduced to the wort will influence the flavor and the fundamental type the beer will become, either an ale or a lager.

Brewers take great pains to safeguard their yeast cultures for the simple reason that if the culture is contaminated or altered biochemically in any way, the chances are good that the taste of the resulting beer(s) will be different. The consequences of even a minor taste shift on an established brand are potentially catastrophic.

The top-fermenting strains of yeast (so called because the yeast cells float to the top of the fermentation vat after they have converted the innate sugars of the wort), which are responsible for the production of ale, are fast-fermenting varieties that prefer to do their handiwork in the moderate temperature range of 59–77 degrees Fahrenheit. Ales are markedly fruitier and more idiosyncratic than lagers mainly because of esters, which are a secondary result of fermentation. Esters are the aromatic compounds within ale that smell remarkably like fresh fruits, frequently orchard varieties like apples, nectarines, pears, and even tropical fruit.

Bottom-fermenting strains of yeast ferment at a much slower rate. The yeasts used in the making of lager perform best at lower temperatures, usually in the 40- to 55-degree Fahrenheit range. The reason that lagers are so razor-crisp and clean, even austere, is that bottom-fermenting yeasts produce little in the way of secondary compounds, such as esters. Sniff a sweet, ripe English brown ale right after a dry, prickly American lager and you'll immediately appreciate the difference that the type of yeast makes.

Bear in mind that these are the basic brewing steps and ingredients for ales and lagers. Each brewer pretty much follows this rudimentary blueprint and then adds his or her own personal touches that contribute to their beer's uniqueness. But no amount of scholarly definition or clinical analysis can precisely describe why beer smells, feels, and tastes so satisfying. Thankfully, there remains an element of mystery to the process . . . which is as it should be. The fulfillment of any beer comes to pass only at that enchanting moment when it meets our senses. That fact is as valid today as it was in dusty Sumerian encampments of six thousand years ago.

The Styles of Beer

And what this flood of deeper brown,
Which a white foam does also crown,
Less white than snow, more white than mortar?
Oh, my soul, can this be Porter?
—*The Dejeune*

The majestic beer pantheon contains only two fundamental categories, ales and lagers, which dominate the many thousands of barrels of beer made every day in breweries and brewpubs from Munich to Seattle. Each category has its own all-star lineup of variations within the basic theme.

Ale (A) is a beer that has evolved through the biochemical action of top-fermenting yeast. Ales ferment at temperatures that range between 59 and 77 degrees Fahrenheit.

Lager (L) is bottom-fermented and at much lower temperatures (usually between 40 and 55 degrees Fahrenheit) than ale. The name comes from the German term *lagern,* which means "to store." Records and artifacts suggest that this style of beer may have been discovered back in the Dark Ages, possibly as far back as the eighth century A.D., when ancient European brewers may have stowed away their beer in ice caves for later use. They subsequently discovered that the deliberate, very icy fermentation produced a crystalline beer, free from turbidity.

Specialty (S) *beers* are styles that are either blends of the processes that create ales and lagers or beverages that are considered beers but dwell just outside the ale and lager headings. They are the fringe beers.

Abbey/Trappist (A): The best Abbey ales come from the Trappist monasteries. These are great, buxom, and wine-like, frequently have high alcohol content, and run from brick-red to mahogany-colored. Trappist ales are especially fruity because of the presence of esters that are the result of special strains of yeast and brewing methods. Trappist ales show some sediment and are perfect for cellar aging for up to five years. There are only a half-dozen Trappist breweries in Europe today, five in Belgium and one in Holland.

Altbier, Alt (A/L): Born in German breweries, primarily in and around the city of Dusseldorf, this often pretty style of beer is colored an orange-pekoe-tea-like copper to a rich brown hue. The term *alt* means "old" in German and relates directly to the brewing process, which is more akin to the making of ale than lager. Although the fermentation is on the warm side of the scale, the Germans age alts in cold storage, like lagers, thus the A/L categorization. Alts are aromatic due to the high hop content.

Amber (A/L): An intensely fruity and hoppy style of domestic ale or lager that's the color of unadulterated tea. Though not a ponderous style, ambers can be very pleasant quaffing.

American Lager (L): The rather neutral-tasting beer type that made Milwaukee famous. Pale straw to golden in appearance, dry to off-dry, crisp and lean to the point of being flimsy, these moderate-alcohol (4–5 percent) beers are decent, if on the whole uninspiring, thirst slakers.

Barley Wine (A): Considered a subcategory of strong ale, barley wine is high in alcohol content (8–10 percent) and traditionally dark in appearance, usually a harvest-gold to medium chocolate brown. The aroma is sweet and malty, while the flavor is normally quite bitter. An acquired taste.

Bitter (A): The U.K. term used to refer to the copper-to-bronze-to-ruby-toned ales that are part and parcel of the British pub landscape. Doubtless the most common draft beer type in the land of fish and chips. Goes from being mildly bitter and astringent to the mouth-puckering level, which is labeled "ESB" (Extra Special Bitter). The alcohol level is normally 4–5 percent by volume.

Black Beer (L): An extremely dark—indeed, inky—opaque lager known for its bitter chocolate-like aroma and taste. The best examples come from Japan.

Bock, also Bok (L): This classic style of bottom-fermented beer comes in various degrees of strength and depth of flavor, running from off-dry to mildly sweet. Believed to have been developed in Einbeck, Germany, in the early thirteenth century, it is traditionally consumed in the dark months of the year. Regular bock beer has a deep tawny color and a rich fragrance. Double bock, called Doppelbock in Germany, is loftier in alcohol (6–8 percent) and thicker than regular bock. There's even an eye-popping triple bock beer available from the Boston Beer Company. A commonly held misconception is that bock beer is beer that's been at the bottom of the barrel. The "dregs" label that has been foisted upon bock for decades is totally false.

Brown Ale (A): An invention of the brewers in the north of England who flourished in the U.K.'s coal mining regions, Brown ales are stocky, firm, and on the sweet side and exhibit a high concentration of maltiness. Their low alcohol readings (4–5 percent) make them excellent chug-a-lug beers in chilly weather. Color ranges from copper-penny to coffee-brown.

Dry Beer (L): Totally uninteresting, mass-produced beers of North America that have no sweetness, scant body or texture, and about as much complexity as mineral water. Clean enough, however, to kill a hearty thirst on a July day.

ESB: See "Bitter."

Export/Dortmunder (L): Quite commonly an attractive pale lemon-yellow to a straw-gold color, this nimble, medium-bodied lager is a direct product, or a wannabe send-up, of the German city of Dortmund. The authentic Exports are noted for their inherent silkiness and crisp drinkability.

Faro (S): A very rare specialty beer that's part of the lambic family. Faros are usually golden to light amber in color, flabby in texture (an effect due frequently to the presence of residual sugar), sweet and fruity in the bouquet and flavor, and softly effervescent. Faros are doused with sugar, caramel, or molasses, or any combination of those three additives, and are frequently pasteurized to prevent the added sweetener from fermenting. Very few bottlings are available, not just in the U.S., but anywhere.

Gueuze (S): Another specialty beer, hay-gold to amber in color, that's considered a lambic because it's a marriage of old and new lambics. What makes *gueuze* (pronounced two ways, *gerzz* or *goo-zah*—take your pick) so unique, however, is the secondary fermentation it undergoes right in the bottle that's eventually purchased. That process, known in Champagne, France, as *méthode champenoise,* is the reason for its sustained effervescence. Bottle-aging for gueuze sometimes lasts as long as 6 to 9 months. It also has an abnormally long shelf life, upwards of five years, in some cases.

India Pale Ale/a.k.a. IPA (A): An underappreciated ale style in the U.S., India pale can at its best offer sublime, moderately bitter aromas and flavors of flowery hops and ripe red fruit. Appearance ranges from honey-gold to rust. The name evolved in the nineteenth century when British brewers were transporting ale to troops stationed in India and other far-flung British Empire–controlled ports-of-call. The tedious voyage around Africa's Cape demanded that a beer be robust and immune to drastic changes of climate. This wonderful variety more often than not survived the journey.

Lambic, also Lambiek (S): A top-fermented, fruit-flavored, wheat-beer style that originated in fifteenth-century Belgium in a hamlet called Lambeek. Doubtless the world's rarest beers, lambics are typically acidic and fruity, though the fruit is not usually of the ripe or succulent kind but, rather, is more green, sour, and understated. The most common types of fruit employed include raspberries, peaches, red cherries, plums, and even cranberries. In a departure from all other types of beer, no yeast is injected into the wort, and it is left to natural airborne yeasts to initiate fermentation. The brewing of lambics can, in some cases, take years.

Light Beer (L): A lager that is lower in calories than full-strength standard bottlings. Usually a gutted, vapid, shadow of a beer. Few exceptions exist.

Malt Liquor (L): Generally, a higher-alcohol beer (6–8 percent by volume) with a neutral taste and full body. Created more for a quick hit of alcohol than for any sense of character or complexity. The bottom feeder of the beer category. Please note, however, that many beers from Germany have the words "Malt Liquor" on their labels, which has nothing to do with the over-inflated, overalcoholic domestic style of beer.

Marzen/Oktoberfest, a.k.a. Vienna (L): Originated in Munich in the pre-refrigeration era, Marzen was developed as a beer that was brewed in the month of March and stored all summer long in cool caves. As a result, it's known either as Marzen or Oktoberfest. (The Oktoberfest tradition began in 1810 with the royal marriage—in October—of Bavarian Prince Luit-pold.) These are keenly malty, medium- to full-bodied lagers that are aromatic and alluring. The color ranges from a burnished orange to a dark copper.

Pale Ale (A): Some of the world's finest ales inhabit this well-populated sub-category, which evolved in the great brewing center of Burton-upon-Trent, England, in the seventeenth and eighteenth centuries. The beers them-selves are rarely pale, but in reality, more of an amber-bronze-rust hue. There's always the presence of bitterness in the underpinning flavor, with a dry to off-dry maltiness coming over the top. Bitter, which is marginally lighter than pale ale, can be included in this subcategory.

Pilsener, also Pils, Pilsner (L): Pilsener's color spans from pale straw yel-low to sunny, rich gold. This is a typically light- to medium-bodied, floral-scented, hoppy, stone-dry, and intensely malty lager that originated in 1842 in the old Bohemian town of Pilsen. The alcohol level is routinely in the 4–5 percent range. It's said that this was actually the first clear, golden beer of its kind. One of the top five styles of beer and certainly the most globally emulated.

Porter (A): Appearance-wise, porter runs a narrow corridor of color from deep amber to dark copper to black coffee, all with hints of red. Charac-terized to the point of distraction as the cruiserweight to stout's heavy-weight, porter is one of the more flavorful and deeply satisfying styles of ale, whose aromas and flavors can evoke bittersweet chocolate, coffee beans, roasted nuts, baked apples or pears, malt, and even spice. Porters' depth of flavor and appearance comes from the use of black patent malts and roasted, unmalted barley. Definitely a cool month or winter variety of ale, which should never be served too cold. Thought to have been introduced to Britain in the early eighteenth century. The name developed from the fact that train porters in England used to sell porter to passengers, who would shout out, "Porter!" when they were thirsty.

Scotch Ale/Scottish Ale, a.k.a. Wee Heavy (A): If beer has a rough equiv-alent to single-malt Scotch whisky, this is it. The best are heavily malted, full-bodied, show a deep amber-auburn hue, and offer a husky texture that fills the mouth like few other beer styles. The deep, grainy, mashy flavor and dark tone are the products of the roasted barley malt. Only a few can be found in the U.S.

Seasonal/Winter/Christmas Beers (S): Special brews have long been pro-duced for consumption during the holiday-season winter solstice. These beers, which more often than not are ales, are frequently enhanced with spices like nutmeg, cinnamon, cloves, coriander, and ginger. Appropriate for the season, of little use past then.

Smoked Beer/Rauchbier (S): Smoked beers can be either lagers or ales. The smoky aroma and flavor are derived from the drying of the barley malt in kilns. The brewers in Bamburg, Germany, fire their kilns with beechwood; American brewers employ hickory, apple, alder, and maple woods; while other brewers simply use peated malt. Admirers of single-malt Scotches from the island of Islay might take note of smoked beers for their summer drinking.

Steam Beer (S): This idiosyncratic beer combines the ale and lager brewing processes, in that it is a bottom-fermenting beer fermented at temperatures that are normally used for top-fermenting varieties. Germany has long espoused steam beers, which they call *dampfbiers,* but it's been a San Francisco brewer, Anchor, who has championed the steam beer cause in the U.S.

Stout (A): A broad subcategory of the meatiest, most complex, and darkest of top-fermented ales that includes Oatmeal, Cream, Dry, Sweet, and Imperial. More potent than porter, stouts are like a meal in themselves and in the past have been viewed as such. Stout is a beer category that one works up to rather than employs as a launching point. Stouts range in taste from dry, velvety, and roasted to sweet, thick, creamy, and chocolatey.

Strong Ale, a.k.a. Old English Ale (A): A very potent, endowed, texturally bulky ale that runs in color from pale amber to tawny and in bouquet and flavor from almond-like to fruity to creamy-sweet. Usually quite bitter to the taste and low in hops influence.

Vienna (L): See Marzen/Oktoberfest.

Wheat/Weizen/White/Weissbier/Wit (S): The majority of brewers believe that the malt made from barley grain makes the best beer. Others tout wheat beers as the finest. Wheat is, after all, the most cultivated grain (though like its cousin barley it is really a grass) on the planet. Normally light to medium in body, these golden, extremely fizzy, lower-in-alcohol beers are made mostly from wheat malt with some measure of barley malt thrown in for balance. They are commonly very tart, dry, and yeasty to the taste. Some, especially those from Europe, exhibit a lovely yellow fruit bouquet that can be immensely pleasurable. Very similar in appearance to French *pastis* such as Pernod or Ricard, one of the characteristics of wheat beers is a harmless cloudiness when chilled.

How I Evaluate Beer
and How *You* Should

**He is not deserving the name of Englishman
who speaketh against ale, that is, good ale.**
—George Burrow, nineteenth century

When people ask me how I come to take such meticulous (some say, ob-
sessive) notes for beers and ales, I usually give them an abbreviated version
of the section that follows. I even occasionally find a few noble souls who
are so genuinely intrigued by the process that I'm forced to paint the entire
canvas for them. More frequently, though, people quiz me about how *they*
should be tasting their beers and ales to be getting the most out of them. I'll
address that topic right after a blow-by-blow on how I analyze beer, because
it's better to have a good, thorough foundation before starting out. My beer
appreciation tips for average consumers are the acorn edition of the process
that I follow. If you have absolutely no interest in a professional's method
of beer evaluation, I recommend that you skip to the next section, "Now,
How You Should Taste Beer."

It's Much More Than a Matter of Taste

Over the course of a decade and a half of professional taste evaluations, I've
come to employ the same basic strategy in the sampling of beer, wine, and
spirits, with minor variations due to the different nuances posed by each
variety of alcoholic beverage. The most demanding of the three by a wide
margin is the spirits group, not so much because of its markedly higher alcohol levels than either beer or wine, as because of its overall greater complexity. Brandies, whiskies, rums, vodkas, eaux-de-vie, and wines that have
been fortified with brandy have, in general, more flesh on their bones and,
as a result, require more appraisal time. Whereas I may take as long as three
hours to deliberately evaluate eight whiskies or cognacs, I'll rate and take
detailed notes on twice as many beers in the same time period the following morning.

Whatever the libation, whatever the category, I allow all the time that is necessary to properly and thoroughly assess the character of any product. Doubtless my fastidious approach toward evaluation is a reflection of the decade I spent in the California wine industry. During that time, I came to appreciate the amount of pride and labor that goes into the making of wine. As a journalist whose focus since then has been solely on alcoholic beverages, I've purposely gotten my hands dirty by working in distilleries and breweries in order to elevate my comprehension of the production of beer and spirits to the same level as I have of wine.

The vast majority of the time I taste products for formal reviews in my private tasting facility, where every environmental condition that is conducive to concentration has been implemented. Proper light (natural daylight is the best) is a salient requirement, which is one of the reasons why I taste only in the morning, most frequently from the hours of 8:00 A.M. to 12:00 noon. The morning light on that corner of my home is optimum for discerning not only the color but the clarity of beer. I shudder at the prospect of judging the appearance of a nuanced beverage like beer by artificial light.

People sometimes chortle or gasp when they hear of my morning tasting regimen. Aside from taking advantage of the daylight, I sample beers in the morning for two other reasons: One, since on designated tasting days I refrain from eating breakfast, my palate is unadulterated and, two, being an early riser, I'm mentally keener in the early hours of the day. Taste evaluations take a prodigious amount of focus, persistence, and discipline when a taster is meticulous, so alertness, a clean, fresh palate, and mental dexterity are paramount considerations.

In the case of beer, I never evaluate more than fifteen beers on any given morning, no matter how fit I'm feeling. Palate fatigue, an often undetected spectre of sensory diminishment, is the number-one pitfall of professional tasters and quietly develops with a gradual loss of concentration. Fortunately, over the years I've come to intimately know my comfort and proficiency limits. Experience has taught me not to push them too far past their individual zeniths. It's always preferable to stop sampling too soon for the day rather than to taste two or three beers more than is prudent, because those last few entries may not be receiving one's most finely tuned attention.

Allowing that the beer samples have been stored and chilled with sufficient care (mind you, beer should never be overchilled—this means specifically that lagers are best served between 45 and 55 degrees Fahrenheit and ales at between 50 and 60 degrees), I employ a fourfold process that takes into account *appearance, smell, taste,* and *aftertaste.* I first deposit the beer properly into the glass. With the glass resting upright, I pour the beer down the center of the glass in order to allow the head of foam to emerge. I gauge the color and clarity and watch the head for approximately one and a half to two minutes. The intensity of the carbonation and bubble size should be consistent with the style of the beer.

For example, the golden beers such as pilseners or the great ales from Belgium normally display thick, white to off-white clouds of foam, while medium-weighted to heavier ales like bitter, porters, and stouts reveal beige-colored foams that vaporize quickly in comparison to pilseners. Beers with greater malt content usually have more velvety heads. I like to see heads still maintaining their volume after that initial 90–120 seconds if the style calls for longevity. When the foam geysers out of the bottle, a red flag goes up in my analytical mind because this spouting may be the sign of bacterial infection.

And then, there's the bubbles question. Large, volleyball-like bubbles that sploosh to the beer's surface can mean that the carbonation was artificially induced, while small, tightly wound, bead-like bubbles indicate in the majority of instances that carbonation occurred naturally.

One crucial note: I never fill the sampling glass more than halfway, to allow ample room for both the foam and bouquet to have their full say. Both require enough space to evolve with aeration, and the only way to let them have sufficient contact with air is to pour only half a glass, but no less than one-third.

Appearance affords me a lot of information. Additionally, because sight is the initial sensory contact, the "first impression" rule comes into play no matter how experienced the taster. Beer's color, which I personally consider to be important, though others do not, is best evaluated in daylight, but not direct sunlight. My evaluation table is pure white in order to ensure maximum exposure for each beer. The color should be within the established framework of each style.

The issue of clarity can be befuddling to beer neophytes, especially Americans and Canadians, who are accustomed to seeing beers as pristine golden beverages. The fact is that, when you hold most beers up to a daylight window or a bright light, you'll see light pass through the liquid, which will be free of suspended particles or bottom-hugging sediment. But for a few specific styles, varying degrees of cloudiness or depth of color are totally proper and are, in fact, to be expected. The brown-black opacity of an oatmeal stout or the turbidity of an ice-cold wheat beer or the minute sediment of a lambic can confuse or cause concern for the newcomer to beer. (For a more detailed explanation of what each beer style should look like, please refer to the sections titled "The Ingredients of Beer" and "The Styles of Beer.") My message is this: Before you pour a beer down the drain because you are suspicious of its appearance, first find out what the standard demeanor of the style happens to be.

If I had to rely on just one sense for evaluation purposes, it would certainly be my sense of smell. Since smell constitutes over 90 percent of our sense of taste, the odds are highly favorable that when we are charmed by the aroma of a food or a beverage we'll approve of its flavor. Take away the ability to smell, and taste virtually vanishes. My professional tasting operation temporarily shuts down whenever I suffer from a head cold or allergies. There's simply no point in trying to analyze any type of beverage when the nasal cavity or sinuses are blocked.

Smell is also the most primal of the senses. Long before our species settled into the relative reliability and stability of a civilized existence, we were hunter-gatherers, roaming the forests and plains in search of a kill or a wild fruit tree. The sense of smell of the precivilization-era humans had to be significantly sharper than ours is today for the simple reason that, the more acute all of their "long-range" senses—smell, hearing, and sight—the better their odds of survival. Today, smell is the most subtle of our senses, and so for tasting purposes, it needs to be given time to develop. That's why I spend much more time involved with the "nosing" part of any evaluation than in any of the other three areas.

My standard nosing routine is as follows: After observing the appearance, which normally takes only a minute or two, I take an initial whiff of the beer sample in order to see what's it's like right out of the bottle. Sometimes the first nosing is meek, only to gain momentum and complexity as it aerates. Other times it's feral and aggressive right out of the gate and then loses steam. Whatever the situation, a decade and a half of professional tasting has convinced me beyond any doubt that four nosing passes over a five- to ten-minute period are more than adequate for proper and thorough beer fragrance evaluation. Usually, most of my notes are jotted down during the third and fourth nosings, after the beer has been allowed ample time to evolve aromatically.

Rules of thumb all too frequently end up as broken thumbs, but there are a couple of safe bets when it comes to beer aromas. Lagers, like those from the U.S. and Canada and the pilseners of Germany and the Czech Republic, are normally quite herbaceous and/or floral in the nose, while the more potent ales, especially those from England and Belgium, are for the most part fruity and/or biscuity. Wheat beers from anywhere are, by and large, highly aromatic in a grainy, spicy (especially clove), and cracker-like way. Lambics, of course, are intensely fruity as a rule.

The next step is sipping a small amount. Not more than a half-ounce is really necessary for the first tasting. At this point, the tongue feels the density of the carbonation as well as monitors the entry impressions, such as harshness/smoothness, sweetness/tartness, fruitiness/graininess, plumpness/thinness, floweriness/bitterness, and so on. Just as in wine evaluation, it's advisable to leave the lips parted just a crack in order to lightly inhale while the beer rests on the tongue. This procedure allows oxygen to mingle with the beer, thereby further stimulating its aromas and flavors. After approximately twenty to thirty seconds of palate saturation, I spit the beer out into a spittoon. This tasting process is repeated a total of three to four times over a period of five to ten minutes.

(Note: I spit after every sampling whether I'm evaluating three beers or twelve beers that particular morning. Whereas some experts swallow, I choose not to for the sake of maintaining focus. In my opinion, everything one needs to know about any beer can be ascertained without swallowing as long as one repeats the identical evaluation procedure. Consistency and concentration are the key components of any professional taster.)

While the "palate entry" is important, it's at the "midpalate" point—that suspended moment right before swallowing—that the beer really shows what it's made of. At this juncture the sensitivity of the muscle that we call the tongue enters the picture. The tip of the tongue determines the level of sweetness, while the sides identify sourness and saltiness. The very back of the tongue detects any bitterness, which usually comes from the hops. Most beers either flourish or fizzle by the midpalate stage. It's the rare beer that can recover its composure if it fails the test posed by the midpalate.

After spitting out the final taste, all that's left is to evaluate the "finish," the aftertaste that remains on the palate. Some finishes linger, while others disappear. The finish sums up the entire tasting experience. While I personally don't believe that the finish alone can make or break a beer, it occasionally does influence the bestowal or the withdrawal of a rating star. The overwhelming majority of beers are judged more by the aroma and the flavor than by the appearance or the finish.

On average, I take a minimum of ten and as long as twenty minutes to evaluate every beer in my tasting facility. I write my notes in longhand while tasting, then transfer them later onto my computer. If a beer tastes horrible, I'll always give it the benefit of the doubt and pop open a second bottle if it's available, which is why I always like to have two examples of every brew. Speaking of which, I prefer to sample beer from bottles rather than aluminum cans. Call me persnickety, but I sincerely believe that beer tastes better when poured out of glass than out of metal.

I shop for and purchase well over three-quarters of the beers I evaluate. Whenever possible, I check the freshness dating, though regrettably not every brewer has the guts or the foresight to clearly indicate that vital information. Beer is a delicate beverage that in most instances does not age well in the bottle past eight to ten months. Beer is also notoriously sensitive to ultraviolet light, which is why the world's best brewers bottle their beers in brown glass. Freshness is everything to beer. Freshness is everything to beer evaluation.

Now, How You Should Taste Beer

In conducting beer tastings around the country I find that the issue of evaluation for average beer drinkers inevitably pops up at some point during the proceedings. Here's the procedure I recommend for everyday beer lovers who want to intensify and amplify their beer-drinking experiences:

Like a professional's methodology, the casual beer drinker's tasting format should utilize the four senses of sight, smell, taste, and touch. When pouring the beer, quickly note the color, strength, and length of the effervescence. Also, look for purity and clarity, unless it's a weiss-white-wheat beer, which should display some cloudiness especially if it's very cold. There's no need to spend more than ten to fifteen seconds on a beer's appearance for the casual imbiber.

Next, whereas I spend ten minutes nosing a beer over the course of four separate passes, you shouldn't spend more than a minute sniffing it over two brief passes. Fill just half of the glass. The first pass immediately following the pour will, in most cases, impart a lot of information with regard to style and purity to your sense of smell. Be forewarned, though, that some beers take time to come around after being cooped up in a bottle for a while. It's not unusual for a beer to require a few seconds of aeration to blow off chemical or stale smells. So, be patient. If you note an odor that seems a trifle off right after the beer hits the glass or if there's very little aroma, allow it a grace period of a quarter- to a half-minute to adjust to its new surroundings. Go back and take another deep whiff, with your nose just above the foam. Note if it's fruity or grainy, bitter or sweet, piquant or delicate.

After nosing, taste it by taking about an ounce into your mouth, but rather than swallowing straightaway, let the beer rest on your tongue for about ten seconds. This momentary period of suspension permits the beer to coat the entire palate. Then swallow. Those first few seconds after the beer has traveled down your throat is the point at which the most flavor will be discerned. Just as you did when nosing the beer, determine the most obvious flavor characteristics first: grainy/fruity, sweet/bitter, salty/sour, piquant/delicate. Don't forget your sense of touch. What is the texture like? Is it creamy and thick, or watery and thin? Is there any harshness, or is it smooth?

Next, in the faint echoes of the aftertaste, attempt to define those soft pulses of taste. Those are the secondary, or background, flavors. What is the residual flavor like in the throat and on the tongue? Note the aftertaste's properties, which always end up mirroring by levels of degree the midpalate point of the taste. Is the aftertaste weak or strong?

The primary and secondary flavors combined with the texture and finish create the whole mouth presence. This entire tasting procedure should take only about one minute.

So, with the appraisal of the appearance taking you fifteen seconds, analysis of the aroma requiring sixty seconds, and your evaluation of the flavor, texture, and finish consuming about another sixty seconds, figure on giving a beer a semi-thorough assessment in less than two and a half minutes. It should prove a very agreeable way of spending 135 seconds.

As you develop your four senses in analytical terms and as you collect more data from which to draw for future beer tastings, you'll discover that your appreciation for the finer points and nuances of the brewing art deepen not only your enjoyment, but the enjoyment of those around you.

THE BEER ESSENTIALS RATING SYSTEM

**Of beer an enthusiast has said that it could
never be bad, but that some brands might
be better than others . . .**
—A. A. Milne

By nature I'm skeptical of ratings systems, whether they involve one person's opinion or the consensus of a group of people. Ultimately what any rating really means is, did you like the thing in question or not? I've found over the years of conducting beer, wine, and distilled-spirits tastings around the nation that even people with little acumen for judging alcoholic beverages know quality when they sample it. They may not have the ability to explain to me why they like or dislike a beverage, but, in general, they more often than not have a firm viewpoint and frequently express it.

I've disagreed with critics of movies, live theater, restaurants, cars, and alcoholic beverages often enough over the years to know that it's my opinion that counts the most with me, and that at the heart of criticism is pure subjectivity. My *Webster's Collegiate Dictionary* defines "criticize" as "to consider the merits and demerits of and judge accordingly." I prefer the definition of "evaluate," which is "to determine the significance, worth, or condition of usually by careful appraisal and study." I think of myself as more of a professional evaluator than a critic. I've always made it clear to readers of my newsletter, *F. Paul Pacult's Spirit Journal,* that the reviews and ratings are solely my own and no one else's and should be taken as such. I don't believe that anyone's judgment should be taken as final on any subject.

Nonetheless, value judgments by experienced people can be of assistance to consumers in terms of saving both time and money. I've used the five-star rating system for the past four years in the newsletter. I originally began with a 100-point evaluating system, but I was never quite sure what the real difference was between an 82 and an 83 score or, worse, if anyone really cared. I concluded that the 100-point system was too fine a measuring device and, to my way of thinking, too silly and picayune. Although it remains the most widely employed scoring format for rating alcoholic beverages, I believe the process has gone totally haywire when ratings like 88+ start being meted out by critics. That type of hairsplitting serves only to prop up the ego of the critic. Coming to my senses, I bagged the 100-point system for the more benign five-star system, which, I'm delighted to say, was warmly received by the majority of my subscribers. It's the only scoring system that I use in reviews for any publication, not just the *Spirit Journal.*

The greater share of the beers reviewed in *The Beer Essentials* fall within the two- to four-star range. Very few beers have received five stars, because I believe that genuine excellence—the type of distinction that defines a style—is rare and, as such, should not be dealt with in a cavalier manner. I also feel the same is true of one-star ratings, a judgment I give to relatively few beers. I hold that unless a beer is almost undrinkable or doesn't at all meet the established criteria of its category, it shouldn't be saddled with a one-star branding. Finally, I regard my rendering of the five-star rating system as a "benefit of the doubt" kind of format and I don't apologize for it. My spleen is vented to my satisfaction in the detailed reviews.

★ **Disappointing:** The quality of this beer is either below the established-category average standards or too far outside the category's long-standing quality criteria. Therefore, it is **not recommended.**

★★ **Average:** A beer of mediocre quality whose characteristics meet but do not exceed or enhance the established standards of its category. Though this ordinary beer may be perfectly acceptable and satisfactory to some consumers, it is **not recommended** by the author.

★★★ **Above Average:** This well-made beer carries the **recommendation** of the author. It's a beer that displays better than average quality within the established standards of its category and, as such, has a very good chance of satisfying the tastes of most consumers.

★★★★ **Superb:** A **highly recommended** beer whose attributes, in the opinion of the author, are of such exemplary quality and character that they far exceed the established standards of the beer's category. An outstanding product that is worthy of a search-and-seizure mission.

★★★★★ **Classic: Highest recommendation.** That rare, highly distinguished, distinctive, idiosyncratic, and/or classical beer that represents a benchmark within its category. This beer presents a standard against which its peers can be judged. A beer of extraordinary quality, scope, and character that transcends price.

(I do not utilize half stars, because I find them half-full.)

MATCHING BEER
WITH FOOD

**Dost thou think, because thou art virtuous,
there shall be no more cakes and ale?**
—William Shakespeare, *Twelfth Night*

The temptation in writing a guidebook like this is to wander away from the premise, which is the simplicity of beer, and to delve into unnecessarily complex and intricate serving recommendations with regard to cuisine. But with the introduction in the last decade of so many new (at least to American consumers) styles of beer from both domestic and foreign brewers, merely asserting that "crisp lagers go well with pizza, and full-bodied ales pair up best with pork chops" is unhelpfully facile. Surprisingly, in the late 1990s there remain beer writers who, I'm sure in all sincerity, still tell their readers that beer's versatility enables it to be paired with any kind of fare. This type of outdated information woefully shortchanges the topic and helps to keep beer well behind wine in circles of fine dining.

In view of the recent expansion of the beer playing field, some fundamental yet flexible guidelines with regard to complementary beer and food combinations are, most definitely, in order for the purpose of bringing knowledge and, as a result, far greater enjoyment to the unenlightened. With increasing numbers of restaurant beer lists reading like *War and Peace* and more chefs cooking with beer in watering holes across the nation, background data on enhancing beer and food combinations can only make the average consumer's sensory experience more fulfilling.

Since it's been acknowledged for centuries that beer *is* food, beer and food are more easily matched than wine and food. For starters, think "like with like." Beer is made from grain, water, and yeast, the identical ingredients as are found in bread. Thus, it's no surprise that, first and foremost, beer so admirably teams with meals and dishes that involve starch-based components, such as sandwiches, pizza, pasta, potatoes, and breaded meats, fowl, or fish. Beer and bread are nearly one and the same and, therefore, in many instances walk down the aisle of cuisine in harmony.

Serving properly matched beers throughout an entire meal is a practice much more prevalent in Europe than it is in the U.S. In the face of wildly different variations in beer styles (smoked beers, fruit beers, porters, and stouts, to name a few of the more exotic), less intrepid American cooks and diners, due to unfamiliarity with the subtleties of the styles, still tend to reach for the relative safety of the wine list rather than the beer menu. But, there's recently been a change in the wind. Whereas the overwhelming majority of consumers serve only one or two types of beer for any festivity that involves food, chefs around the U.S. are becoming increasingly cognizant of a definite pecking order in the service of beer throughout a meal. While beer may not yet be the focus of service rituals as elaborate as those for its grape-based cousin, as one is exposed to more styles of beer it becomes apparent that certain beers are best enjoyed with certain "like" foods and at specific times during a meal.

PREPARING THE PALATE

In many parts of the world, light, dry white wine or fino sherry is customarily served before a meal because they each prime the appetite. Prior to eating a main course, you want a beverage that will cleanse your palate, not overburden it with sweetness, smokiness, or maltiness. In the case of beer, the more agile styles with noticeable degrees of dryness, such as ESB (Extra Special Bitter), pale ale, most American lagers, and even some of the very dry wheat/weisse beers, frequently make ideal before-dinner quaffs.

Among my favorite aperitif suggestions are:

- Ballantine IPA
- Celis White
- Dixie Blackened Voodoo Lager
- Geary's Pale Ale
- Grant's Weis Beer
- Nor'Wester Hefe Weizen
- Pete's Wicked Lager
- Spanish Peaks Black Dog Pale Ale
- Wit White
- De Troch Chapeau Gueuze Lambic (Belgium)
- Erdinger Weissbier Hefetrub (Germany)
- Foster's Lager (Australia/Canada)
- Grolsch Premium Lager (Holland)
- Haake Beck N/A (Germany)
- Liefmans Goudenband Lambic (Belgium)
- Niagara Falls Eisbock Ice Beer (Canada)
- Pinkus Home Brew Wheat Beer (Germany)
- Royal Oak Pale Ale (England)
- Samuel Smith's Lager (England)

HEARTY MAIN COURSES AND DISHES

For entrée dishes of meat, fish, fowl, rice, or vegetables that are dressed in sauces, the key to successful matching lies in the constitution of the sauce.

Spicy sauces, like those from Mexico, some areas of China, India, and Thailand, are much better paired with razor-sharp, medium- to full-bodied lagers and bitter ales than with any type of wine. The prickly brushfires set by hot peppers in the mouth are best complemented and controlled by dryness and bitterness, as opposed to sweetness.

Beer suggestions for spicy, hot, or chili-pepper-oriented main courses include:

- Samuel Adams Boston Lager
- Brooklyn Brewery Lager
- Dock Street Bohemian Pilsener
- Jack Daniel's 1866 Classic American Ale
- Pig's Eye Pilsener
- Red Hook ESB
- Saranac Golden Pilsener
- Stegmaier 1857 Lager
- Stoudt's Golden Lager
- Wild Boar Classic Pilsner
- Corona Extra Pilsener (Mexico)
- Dos Equis XX (Mexico)
- Fuller's London Pride Ale (England)
- Gambrinus Lager (Czech Republic)
- Heineken Lager (Holland)
- Kingfisher Indian Lager (England)
- Pilsner Urquell (Czech Republic)
- Radegast Original Lager (Czech Republic)
- Singha Lager (Thailand)
- Tsingtao Pilsener (China)

In the case of sweeter, yet still tangy sauces, such as Mexican molè, tomato-based pasta sauces or pizza bases, and the spicy sweet-sour sauces of China, I recommend the following lagers and ales, which have the character to stand up to thicker, sweet-leaning sauces:

- Baderbrau Bock
- Catamount Bock
- Gritty McDuff's Best Brown Ale
- Jack Daniel's 1866 Classic Amber Lager
- Negra Modelo (Mexico)
- Beck's Dark Pilsener (Germany)
- Caledonian Amber Ale (Scotland)
- Double Diamond Burton Ale (England)
- Old Growler English Ale (England)

For the millions of chili lovers, porter makes the best beer companion both in terms of drinking accompaniment and cooking. Beer is a must in any great chili, whether the chili is made with or without meat. My wife's vegetarian recipe, Sue's Bonfire Chili, always includes Samuel Adams Honey Porter. The depth of the dark ale flavor plus the slightly sweet kiss of honey have helped make her chili a favorite with our friends. In fact, the recipe was published in *The New York Times Magazine*.

Other excellent ingredient choices for chili are:

* Geary's London Style Porter
* Erdinger Weissbier Dunkel (Germany)

In the U.S., the warm-weather months of June through September are the time when the hallowed ritual of backyard barbecuing is at its peak. However, the smoky, roasted flavors and aromas that are part and parcel of the "Q" experience can lay waste to most golden lagers.

If you want to absolutely wow your guests at the barbecue table, serve:

* Alaskan Smoked Porter
* Nor'Wester Blacksmith Porter
* Rogue Smoke Rauch Style Ale
* Aecht Schlenkerla Rauchbier (Germany)

These four lush, piquant, and individualistic ales, all of which gain their intense smokiness from deeply roasted barley malt (like and like), also go remarkably well with smoked ham, turkey, trout, and sausages.

Beef, lamb, and game entrées almost always require an ale that can stand up to the textural complexity of meat without overshadowing the often subtle flavors found in London broil, Porterhouse steak, lamb chops, rack of lamb, or braised venison. Substantial ales from England, in particular, accompany and embellish meat dishes in especially fine form. Try:

* Adnams Nut Brown Ale (England)
* Bateman's XXXB (England)
* Brakspears Henley Ale (England)
* Newcastle Brown Ale (England)
* Samuel Smith's Nut Brown and Pale Ales (England)
* Whitbread Traditional Pale Ale (England)
* Young's Ram Rod Pale Ale (England)

I'd even include the great Corsendonk Monk's Brown Ale from Belgium in that group.

When a wine-based sauce, like Bordelaise, Poivrade, Marchand de Vin, or Madeira, is employed as an accompaniment to meat, I suggest you reach beyond the standard English ale to the next step up in the complexity ladder, porter. The best from the U.K. and the U.S. to hunt down are:

* Devil Mountain Brewery Porter
* Grant's Perfect Porter
* Red Hook Blackhook Porter
* Sierra Nevada Porter
* Wild Goose Porter
* Samuel Smith's Taddy Porter (England)
* Young's London Porter (England)

Game birds (pheasant, quail, duck), turkey, goose, and chicken each have different needs when it comes to beer pairings. The more complex fowl varieties—namely, game birds and turkey—are often best served with medium-weighted ales, while duck and chicken work better with light- to medium-weighted ales or dark lagers. If a fruit-based sauce (plum, orange, currant) is employed, as it frequently is with duck, a lambic would be a creative and completely complementary beer choice. Look for winners such as:

- Liefmans Kriekbier (Belgium)
- Lindemans Pêche (Belgium)

A superb, hefty lager that goes extremely well with turkey and game birds is Christoffel Robertus Munich Lager (Germany).

Pork, the least complex and the sweetest of meats, goes especially well with bock and alt beers that have a trace of sweetness. Four beers that work particularly well with pork are:

- Dock Street Illuminator
- Celis Pale Bock
- Heineken Tarwebok (Holland)
- Pinkus Home Brew Munster Alt (Germany)

If apples are served on the side or in a sauce for pork chops, tenderloin, or pork roast, porter is a more than fitting suitor.

Seafood and shellfish offer some of the more intriguing challenges to beer and food matching. With grilled red snapper, swordfish steaks, and salmon, I've found that blonde ales make particularly excellent selections, because they have the correct dryness/maltiness quotient to enhance the often delicate flavors of grilled fish. With crab, a crisp pale ale or bitter (ESB) serves as a good companion. The richness and fatty sweetness of lobster demands a bigger ale, like a brown or a nut brown. Seafood dishes go well with:

- St. Feuillien Abbey Blonde Ale (Belgium)
- St. Landelin Blonde Abbey Ale (Belgium)
- Scaldis Special Ale (Belgium)

HAPPY ENDINGS

Before pouring the cognac or single malt at the close of the evening, try a luscious German doppelbock, a high-octane Belgian Trappist ale, or a fruity lambic with the cheese-and-fruit course. The lighter the cheese, the lighter the beer. If you're hauling out the Stilton, English Cheddar, or any other pungent cheeses, go with the heavier styles of beer. In my view no beers from any category are as satisfying in the fruit-and-cheese course as Belgian Trappist ales and German doppelbocks. Track down:

- Chimay Grande Réserve Trappist Ale (Belgium)
- Chimay Red Trappist Ale (Belgium)

- La Trappe Dubbel Trappist Ale (Holland)
- La Trappe Tripel Trappist Ale (Holland)
- Ayinger Celebrator Doppelbock (Germany)
- Paulaner Salvator Doppelbock (Germany)
- Spaten Optimator Doppelbock (Germany)

And now, we've arrived at what many people perceive as the real main course, dessert. If chocolate, especially dark, bittersweet chocolate, is playing the lead in your dessert creation, you'll need either a dark lager with considerable heft and caramelized qualities, or a stout of particularly velvety smoothness to keep pace with the piercing intensity of dark chocolate. That makes it easy. I recommend only three dark beers for bittersweet chocolate. Please note that the Samuel Adams and the Samichlaus are very high in alcohol:

- Brooklyn Brewery Black Chocolate Stout
- Samuel Adams Triple Bock
- Samichlaus Dark Lager (Switzerland)

If heaven exists, it can't be more sublime than enjoying these beers in combination with chocolate. There are writers and chefs who suggest an eye-popping Scottish ale with chocolate, but on trying it, I heartily disagree. The high malt content alone in Scottish ales makes them, at least to my personal taste, too grainy/cereally for chocolate, which needs acid bounce.

When fruit plays a part in desserts, in tarts, soufflés, pies, cakes, or sorbets, serving a raspberry or cherry lambic closes the dinner circle with panache. Once again, like with like wins out:

- De Troch Chapeau Framboise (Belgium)
- De Troch Chapeau Kreik (Belgium)

For the quiet period after the dishes have been cleared and everyone settles into the library for a friendly chat, put the beer away and bring out the cognac, armagnac, and single-malt Scotch. Beer has admirably done its work for the evening.

BEER SERVICE 101

There is nothing for a case of nerves like a case of beer.
—Joan Goldstein

Precious little time is devoted to the topic of how to maximize the experience of drinking beer. Indeed, in comparison to the rituals surrounding the service of wine and spirits, beer enjoyment is a no-frills, straightforward proposition. How many times have you witnessed a restaurant waitperson solemnly presenting a bottle of wine over a gracefully bent arm to a patron and then contorting more wildly than Houdini doing his water tank trick in the act of opening it? Or, when you're visiting with friends, do you ever agonize over which glass to use for a particular wine?

Yet, while beer is far less bound by such service ceremonies and comic trappings, not enough attention is paid to the proper temperature at which it should be served, what type of glassware best accentuates the particular style of beer you like, and even how to properly pour beer into the glass.

As far as serving temperatures are concerned, crisp, American golden lagers, domestic and imported wheats, and the heavier pilseners from Germany and the Czech Republic show their finest virtues when they are served from 44 to 48 degrees Fahrenheit. At any higher temperature they start to taste fat, meaning that they lose some of their inherent razor's edge, or dryness. On the other side of the temperature issue, even lagers should never be served at temperatures that dip below 40 degrees Fahrenheit. Such intense cold mutes aromas and flavors. While I like a cold beer on a hot day as much as anyone else, I often think that beer—even lager—is served too cold in the U.S.

With regard to specialty beers, specifically lambics and barley wines, and medium-to-dark ales, like bitter, pale ale, India pale ale, brown ale, strong ale, Abbey ale, porter, and stout, I like serving them at the temperature of my cellar, where they are kept. (A subterrenean storage situation is preferred for ales not only because of the relatively constant coolness, but likewise because it is dark. Bright light causes injury to beer, be it lager or ale.) This temperature ranges from the high forties in the winter to the middle fifties in the summer. Moderate temperatures allow the natural estery fruitiness of top-fermenting ales to emerge, especially in the aroma, which is easily inhibited by excessive cold.

Glassware is a controversial and frightfully personal topic, and every brewer I've come across has a strong opinion regarding the style of glass in which his or her lager or ale displays its best face. With glass shapes about as infinite as the numbers of beer available, one sound rule of thumb is: the more effervescent the beer, the taller the glass should be in which you serve it. For instance, intensely fizzy pilseners, wheats, and lagers drink much better from tall, slender, conically shaped glasses that flare out at the lip. The compact volume at the bottom and the extended length allow the bubbles to travel upward unimpeded. Since the vast majority of highly effervescent beers are dry and crisp, freedom of movement for the bubbles maintains the desired briskness and snap that one expects from these brews.

For less bubbly beers, like most English-style ales, a simple, straight-up-and-down, thick-gauge, wide-mouthed "pint" glass is perfectly fine. The wide mouth affords the normally thick, creamy head plenty of operating room.

The wine-like, fruity Belgian ales, in particular those from the abbeys, are best suited to stemmed wine glasses, which have a bulbous bowl but flare outward at the lip. This configuration harnesses the innate fruitiness, which intensifies the smell. The concentrated fruitness of lambics is served adequately by tulip-shaped wine glasses, but even better in the traditional sherry glass known as the Spanish *copita,* which resembles a short champagne flute. Champagne flutes are a serviceable substitute to copitas when lambics are on the menu.

Glasses that have gone through dishwashers should be rinsed prior to usage to make certain that all detergent residue is removed. The chemical properties of soap can cause grave injury to the effervescence of a beer as well as to its delicate aroma.

I pour beer the way most brewers have taught me, which is to start right down the center of an upright glass to establish an inch of foam, then tilt the glass at a 45-degree angle and continue pouring down the side of the glass until the glass is two-thirds to three-quarters full. This allows some room for the head to develop at the crown, as well as some space for you to insert your nose to appreciate the bouquet. It's all in the wrist.

The appreciation of beer is more than the sum of all the parts. It's that initial whiff, that first thirst-quenching sip, and the sight of a cloud of foam spilling over the side of the glass. And so it's been for at least five thousand years.

DOMESTIC
BEER REVIEWS

A

ALASKAN Smoked Porter

Opaque, dark brown/black appearance, deep tan foam, less than average head retention; focused, tightly wound nose of bacon fat and wood smoke; the palate feel is moderately thick and very satiny; flavorwise, it sings with smoky, woody, doughy, yeasty, bacon-like flavors that engage the taste buds straight on; the sensuous aftertaste is robust and never awkward or clunky; very small production and, thus, is scarce; one of those word-of-mouth beer legends that gets smuggled around the country via the Samsonite Express.

ALASKAN BREWING COMPANY, JUNEAU, AK

RATING ★★★★   *Highly Recommended*

ALASKAN Amber Beer

Walnut/mahogany color, off-white foam that lasts and lasts; the roasted, toasty, intensely malty nose is semisweet, brown-rice-like and very inviting; smooth as silk in the mouth; flavors of roasted nuts, mild spice, deep-kilned malt; very nice, easy-drinking amber; I can easily understand why this is Alaskan's most popular brew.

RATING ★★★   *Recommended*

ALASKAN Pale Ale

Rich golden/straw hue, off-white to light tan foam, little head retention; the brisk, breezy, crisp nose is tart, bitter, and dry; the taste is hoppy, dry to the point of almost being sharp; finishes cleanly, but in the end a tad too sharp for my taste; pleasant, correct, if uninspiring; a disappointment after greatly admiring the Porter and Amber.

RATING ★★

Almond Brothers Amber Ale

Cloudy bronze/copper color, tan foam, average head retention, no suspended particles that I could see; the bouquet is immediately intriguing as
a sassy, spicy aroma greets the olfactory sense—the almond essence added
by the brewer is inviting, even compelling—the second and third passes see
the concentrated almond continue to rule the aroma roost—my only com-
plaint is that there's very little sense odorwise that this is an ale; in the
mouth, the malt/hops aspects finally make a showing, with a nicely balanced,
if slightly light, mouth presence scoring some points for the home team—
the midpalate point is dominated by the hops as the taste turns pleasingly
bitter and clean; the aftertaste is hoppy and relatively short; I liked this ale
perhaps more than my comments suggest.

BREWED AND BOTTLED BY COLD SPRING BREWING COMPANY, COLD SPRING, MN, FOR PINE

STREET BREWING CO., LOUISVILLE, CO

RATING ★ ★ ★   *Recommended*

Anchor Old Foghorn Barley Wine Style Ale

Very fetching cherry-wood hue, ideal purity, persistent bubbles, excellent head retention; the slightly burnt nose features a top layer aroma of molasses in the first pass, then that vanishes as an intense, dense maltiness takes
the helm for the duration—the malt is supplemented by a black-fruit note
in the final pass; on palate, the roasted-malt component is beautifully balanced by the underlying hoppy bitterness; the aftertaste is complex, long,
and suitably bitter; supposedly, the first mass-marketed barley wine in the
U.S.; it's certainly among the best specialty beers made in the U.S.

ANCHOR BREWING, SAN FRANCISCO, CA

RATING ★ ★ ★ ★   *Highly Recommended*

Anchor Liberty Ale

Pale-amber-color, creamy, white head that has some staying power; I
found the nose to be a bona fide dazzler as perfumy, off-dry hints of violets,
hazelnuts, and fruit came to the forefront in this atypical bouquet; the fruitiness emerges gracefully in the sturdy, firm, sure-footed palate; finished dry
and very grainy; the stabbing bitterness in the tail end of the aftertaste
forced me to knock off a rating star, which would have placed it in the
Highly Recommended category; even with that, however, one of the better
domestic ales to be found.

RATING ★ ★ ★   *Recommended*

Anchor Porter

The molasses, black-coffee color is opaque, and the eye-catching beige
head holds on for a markedly long time; surprisingly, the nose is closed off
and almost totally neutral through four patient nosing passes; traditional,
viscous, thick texture; on palate, it's smooth with a slight coffee-like bitterness that ends up in the back of the throat; this muscle-bound beer, to
my way of thinking, leans more to the stout category than the porter; for
lovers of beefy, pedal-to-the-metal, top-fermenting brews that hold the
promise of curling your teeth, this bruiser should be the ticket, though I
prefer the more flavorful and elegant domestics like Yuengling Porter from

Pennsylvania, Catamount Porter from Vermont, and Samuel Adams's Honey Porter.

RATING ★ ★

ANCHOR Steam Beer

Bright, beguiling honey/amber/orange color, shows off a silvery, but rather docile, head; very pleasant nose of citrus, oatmeal, and hops; bountiful feel in the mouth; intensely grainy, stone-dry on palate, with a mildly steely edge to it; I didn't particularly take a shine to the metallic, minerally aftertaste—in fact, the score dropped off considerably because of the slaty/chalky finish; after hearing rave reviews from my beer-drinking peers about this voguish brew, I found myself confused by their effusive praise; a good, able-bodied beer to be sure, but hardly the Holy Grail of Sudsdom; formally evaluated four times, upgraded to two stars the last two samplings.

RATING ★ ★

ANDERSON VALLEY Boont Amber Ale

Foggy dark-honey/amber hue, tan foam, good head retention; the pleasing bouquet shows traces of red fruit, dark caramel, sour apple, and malt in the first two passes—with aeration, the nose keeps developing in substantial waves of malt, fruit, and hoppy bitterness—very nice; I didn't feel as smitten with the mouth presence as I did with the fragrance, but that's not to say that I found the flavor or texture wanting—it simply didn't fully measure up to the charm promised by the bouquet—the flavor thrust was led by the malt, then at midpalate a solid bitterness born of hops took the wheel, guiding this pleasant amber to the mellow finish; take it for a spin around the block.

ANDERSON VALLEY BREWING COMPANY, BOONVILLE, CA

RATING ★ ★ ★   **Recommended**

ANDERSON VALLEY Belk's Extra Special Bitter Ale

Handsome bronze/golden honey color, creamy tan foam, excellent head retention, some suspended particles noted; the bouquet starts out playing the game very close to the vest, as hardly any aroma is detected right after the pour—things begin to loosen up by the third nosing as a concentrated grain aroma takes the helm—little new in the last pass; this ESB lives on its flavor as a razor-edged hoppy bitterness challenges the palate at entry, then combines nicely with the roasted-malt factor at midpalate, creating a solid, if simple, bitter-ale experience; the stage in which this ESB deepens the most is in the finish, where the hops battle back to dominance; I rode the fence on this one for the simple reason that I thought it got off to a less than rousing beginning in the lackluster bouquet.

RATING ★ ★

AUGSBURGER Golden Lager

Light honey/amber color, ivory-white foam, poor head retention; the properly yeasty/malty aroma starts out with a note of vibrancy, then quickly fades in the second pass—what was there in the first nosing was pleasantly biscuity and malty—by the final nosing, the aroma became rejuvenated; only mildly interesting on the palate as a dry, fabric-like taste holds the taste buds captive through the midpalate and finish, wherein a soapy, almost vinegary aftertaste kills the entire experience; avoid.

STROH BREWING COMPANY, ST. PAUL, MN

RATING ★

B

BADERBRAU **Bock Beer**

Nearly opaque, chestnut-brown color, with a quick tan head; the heady nose reeks with black coffee, road tar, and smoke; the texture is very full and delightfully satiny; on palate, the concentrated smokiness holds court over the lesser flavor attributes of toasted barley, cocoa, and freshly ground French-roast coffee beans; not everyone's cup of beer, to be sure, but a formidable, correct, and tasty example of the Bock style; serve with smoked meats.

PAVICHEVICH BREWING, CHICAGO, IL

RATING ★★★   *Recommended*

BADERBRAU **Pilsener**

Honey color, vigorous, frothy head; bold, malty, heady, faintly floral, tropical fruit (guava-mango), complex nose; medium-weighted, satiny texture; bone-dry on palate, with crisp, curiously tannic (from the choice of hops, I presume), properly bitter flavors that are simultaneously refreshing and impressively full; finishes whistle-clean, with a substantial aftertaste of malt; delicious, well-made Midwestern brew with a future.

RATING ★★★   *Recommended*

BALLANTINE **India Pale Ale**

Beautiful, dark russet, tawny tone, with superb head retention; the nose is elusive, but hoppy, with faint hints of steamed white rice, malt, and black pepper—the bouquet cannot be categorized as effusive or generous, but it's quietly enchanting all the same; it's delicious in the mouth as a mellow, soft, resiny, hoppy bitterness takes charge, leading the taste buds into the dry, acceptably bitter aftertaste, which is clean and very extended; its flavor latitude is rather narrow, which is why it didn't pick up a fourth star, but it's a solid, understated IPA that's worthy of a search.

FALSTAFF BREWING CORPORATION, MILWAUKEE, WI

RATING ★★★   *Recommended*

BELMONT **Marathon Ale**

Tasted on-site; medium gold color, white foam, fair head retention; the bouquet is crisp, yeasty, and clean, almost like a lager—it is, however, a pedestrian aroma with little spark upfront—what I did like was its pleasantly sweet foundation; it's considerably better on palate than in the nose—the flavor is developed, as winsome tastes of light malt and a bit of bread dough keep the taste buds entertained; the aftertaste is clean, simple, but satisfying; an all-purpose beer that's definitely worth a bash.

BELMONT BREWING COMPANY, LONG BEACH, CA

RATING ★ ★ ★ ***Recommended***

BELMONT Strawberry Blonde Ale

Tasted on-site; medium yellow/gold tone, silver-white foam, poor head retention; the nose is unmistakably fruity as a devilishly seductive aroma of fresh-picked strawberries enchants the olfactory sense—purists might fault the lack of beeriness/maltiness, but to hell with them—I admired this grand, summery fragrance; on palate, it's clear immediately that this isn't a serious brew, but that's all right—as an accompaniment to lightly grilled foods, it's acceptable—on the third sampling, the lack of guts and a sound malt core finally got to me, and I finally settled on two stars; the lovely, perfumy nose is the headliner—past the bouquet, it's ordinary.

RATING ★ ★

BELMONT Unfiltered Wheat

Tasted on-site; this wheat looks exactly like iced tea (muddy brown) with lemon and sugar—properly cloudy, ivory foam, no head retention; the alluring bouquet is honeyed and sweet—it's like someone poured honey over Wheat Chex—I responded favorably to this earthy, grainy, and fruity nose; unfortunately, it tripped and fell badly in the mouth as tanky, metallic, and flinty tastes destroyed the hope fueled by the seductive aroma—this beer actually became offensive on palate; too bad after such a sexy beginning.

RATING ★

BELMONT Top Sail Amber Ale

Tasted on-site; deep amber/sorrel/chestnut color with red core highlights, beige foam, decent head retention; the bouquet offers mild toasted-malt charm, even some black fruit, but beyond that there's not much here in terms of depth or dimension; ditto in the mouth—this lame duck doesn't even start running, much less take flight; to finish it off, the aftertaste is harsh and way too astringent; obvious brewing problems; don't drive to Long Beach just for this loser.

RATING ★

BELMONT Long Beach Crude Nut Brown Ale

Tasted on-site; looks like cola—a deep nut-brown color, milky beige foam, excellent head retention; the aroma holds some minor virtues as deep-roasted malt scents mingle with dark-chocolate notes—a ho-hum affair, however, aromatically; once again, the mouth presence has a regrettable trademark flintiness/tankiness that's a significant hindrance—not the kind of thumbprint idiosyncracy that a brewer likes to have; the finish tailspins into oblivion; really lousy.

RATING ★

BERGHOFF Dark Beer / Dortmunder Style

A & W Root Beer appearance, with deep brown tones topped off by a timid, beige-colored head; the aroma is milky, creamy, and opulent, offering succulent, grainy, carob-like scents of honey-wheat muffins, rye bread, and bran cereal; on palate, it's dry to off-dry, tarry, round, firm, mildly chocolatey, and multilayered; the aftertaste is slightly bitter, though not at all unpleasant; a hearty, cereal-like beer, with aspirations of finesse and elegance; I thought that the aroma outshined the flavor and finish.

BERGHOFF BREWERY, CHICAGO, IL

RATING ★ ★ ★   *Recommended*

BEVERLY HILLS Palimony Bitter Ale

Cloudy with thick-as-locusts mists of sediment that are—disturbingly—held suspended in the golden body of the beer—a totally unappealing and unacceptable appearance—it's like a glass globe with snowflakes that you shake to create a wintry scene; the nose is fine, with pleasing aromas of malt and hops making a desperate attempt to redeem the appalling appearance; in the mouth, it's evident that this beer has bitten the bullet, either because of poor storage or poor production practices—I believe this beer suffers from either starch haze or bacterial infection; use caution.

BREWED FOR BEERHOUSE COMPANY, LTD., LOS ANGELES, CA, BY AUGUST SCHELL BREWING, NEW ULM, MN

RATING ★

BLUE MOON Nut Brown Ale

Good, opulent, chestnut/mahogany color, perfect clarity, thin beige foam, unimpressive head retention; right after the pour, the nose offers well-defined and layered aromas of deeply roasted malt, road tar, and pumpernickel—in subsequent passes, the delectable toasty/tarry quality stayed the course; on palate, I favorably responded to the solidly bitter/smoky/oily taste, which proved to be both hearty and clean right through midpalate; the aftertaste is quite long and hoppy; not the stuff of genius, but a very enjoyable dark ale, which is obviously the flagship of the otherwise soft Blue Moon roster.

BLUE MOON BREWING COMPANY, DENVER, CO / BREWED IN UTICA, NY

RATING ★ ★ ★   *Recommended*

BLUE MOON Belgian White

The foggy straw color is topped by a fast-moving, flour-white foam; right after the pour, the comely bouquet is like a basket of ripe yellow fruits, in particular, melon, banana, canteloupe, and apricots—this dramatic aromatic display diminishes by the third pass as a biscuity/vanilla-wafer scent takes charge—the final pass returns to mild estery fruit—an intriguing, alluring nose; in the mouth, the ripeness appreciated in the aroma is nonexistent—what is there is a crisp, but not tart, mouth presence that's moderate in its dry-cereal bounty—the taste turns flat and dumb by the midpalate as though it's disassociated with the bouquet; the finish is timid; if the taste had mirrored the bouquet, it would have gotten recommended; the taste dropped the ball.

RATING ★ ★

BLUE MOON Honey Blonde Lager

Sturdy, sterling, clover-honey/burnished-gold color, superb purity, poor head retention; the wimpy bouquet merely suggests honey and mildly roasted malt without taking the plunge—through all four nosings, no commitment is made by this beer—it remains a lackluster wallflower; on palate, it shows more character as sour tastes of cereal mash and not fully ripened fruit direct the traffic; the finish is clean and crisp, with a dash of mild hoppy bitterness; while not offensive, it's too wayward for my taste.

RATING ★★

Blue Moon Raspberry Cream Ale

Very attractive bronze/amber hue, eggshell foam, short head retention, very pure; the bouquet is very mild, mild to the point of appearing a bit old—meek red-fruit and malt aromas barely make it to the glass's rim—with aeration there's a slight jamminess that I didn't think was appropriate—an ale like this should be giving impressions of lightness and airiness, not syrupiness; the mouth presence is far more enjoyable and animated than the lame bouquet as pleasing flavors of raspberries and sweet malt make a decent showing; the aftertaste is sour/tart and cleansing; okay, but that's about it.

RATING ★★

Blue Ridge ESB Red Ale

Very fetching, brilliant, new-copper-penny tint, off-white foam, excellent head retention, superb purity; the bouquet is so malty in the initial pass that it's almost like cocoa or a chocolate bar—the moderate malty heft in the nose continues through the second nosing and into the third, where it unfortunately begins to take on a "tanky" or metallic aroma—it recovers its poise for the finale as the intense graininess snaps back; on palate, it holds its own as the semirich maltiness dominates the entry, but that quality takes a back seat at midpalate to a bitter hoppiness, which brings this ale home to the astringent completion; a near-buxom ale that shows some serious promise.

FREDERICK BREWING COMPANY, FREDERICK, MD

RATING ★★★ *Recommended*

Blue Ridge Golden Ale

American lager grainy yellow/gold hue, snowy-white foam, very long head retention, good purity; the nose shows ample fruit, malt, and hops right out of the gate—it's not profound, but it is correct and agreeable—much past the second nosing, however, the virtues fade away, victims of aeration and a lack of complexity; in the mouth, there are nice, if simple, tastes of dry grain husk and bitter, mildly floral hops, but that's where it ends, as the tastes vamoose right after midpalate, making for a flat, neutral aftertaste; not bad, not offensive, just middle-of-the-road on its best day.

RATING ★★

Boulder Extra Pale Ale

Pretty bronze/sunset-orange color, fair head retention, ideal clarity; the nose on this brew is round but sculpted, meaning I didn't find it generous—the malt dominates the second and third passes, if reluctantly—the last nosing is guided by a faint mushroom aroma that turned me off; in the mouth, it's clean, mildly hoppy/bitter, and drinkable, but it hardly had me singing the state anthem of Colorado; average, but certainly no match for the likes of Sierra Neveda or Red Feather or Mystic Seaport.

ROCKIES BREWING COMPANY, BOULDER, CO

RATING ★★

BREWER'S CAVE Black Barley Ale

Terrifically pretty mahogany/chestnut-brown color catches the eye, creamy beige foam with good staying power, excellent purity; the nose is seriously anemic in the first two passes—it's muted and stingy—by the third pass the deep-roasted malt comes alive in generous waves that thrill the olfactory sense—I ended up being a huge fan of this toasty, road-tar-like, French-roast-coffee-bean beauty; on palate, there's a mildly pleasant nuttiness at entry that gives way to a nice dance between the dark malt and the hops—I really liked the cocoa quality of the mouth presence; the aftertaste is full, creamy, and rich.

MINNESOTA BREWING COMPANY, ST. PAUL, MN

RATING ★★★   *Recommended*

BREWER'S CAVE Golden Caramel Lager

Harvest-gold/medium-amber hue, eggshell foam, long head retention, pure; the nose offers pleasing notes of cookie batter, vanilla wafer, and sweetish malt in the first two nosings—as it warms and aerates, the tang of hops comes more into play—a very nice bouquet; in the mouth, the caramel malts are keenly evident as the buttery entry taste delights the taste buds— the midpalate is properly bitter and clean—I would have liked more in terms of texture; the aftertaste, to my surprise, is slightly smoky, especially in the last moments.

RATING ★★★   *Recommended*

BREWER'S CAVE Amber Wheat Ale

Bronze/gold/medium-amber appearance, tan foam, excellent head retention, very pure—no turbidity, considering it's a wheat; bouquetwise, this wheat shows little of its base grain in the initial pass, which is closed down except for a cracker-like background aroma—the third pass sees a bit more in the way of aroma as a scent of stale Wheat Thins wafts up from the glass; on palate, it's very refreshing, cleansing the tongue in an efficient manner—the taste is quite neutral, almost like an American lager—the texture is medium-weighted and nice, but the flavor doesn't give away much at all; the finish is medium-long, grainy, and a bit metallic at the end; not in the least offensive, but neither is it more than commonplace.

RATING ★★

BREWERY HILL Cherry Wheat Ale

The appearance is just like unfiltered apple juice—a rosy amber hue that is cloudy, with sparse white foam; I found the bouquet to be amazingly appetizing and inviting—it's juicy without being sappy or sweet, just tart red cherry and the clove-like twang of wheat—the harmonious balance achieved by this ale's fragrance is nothing short of stupendous; on palate, the serious virtues of the aroma become fact in the taste—light, juicy, tart, but not sour, flavors delight the taste buds from entry through to the finish, which is long, tart, and exceedingly pleasant; I'd enjoy this one on a picnic on a hot July day; the best this brewer has to offer to date.

BREWERY HILL BREWING COMPANY, WILKES-BARRE, PA

RATING ★★★★   ***Highly Recommended***

Brewery Hill Honey Amber Ale

Misty, mildly cloudy, honey/amber color, light-tan foam, looks like bits of honey floating about; the nose is simple and one-dimensional, emitting rudimentary aromas of mild honey and malt—there's no sense of depth or complexity in the bouquet in the first three nosings—in the final pass, however, an alluring dark-caramel scent climbs aboard and saves the bouquet from falling into oblivion; in the mouth, it's a study in mediocrity as the caramel maltiness and the honey flavor lie listlessly on the tongue—it's drinkable, to be sure, but neither charming nor deep; the aftertaste is okay as moderately pleasing tastes of malt and caramel extend their stay; wholly average.

RATING ★★

Brewery Hill Pale Ale

Beautiful, harvest-gold/amber/near-bronze hue, pearly foam, average head retention; the subdued nose offers a mild fragrance of malt, but that's about all, in the first three nosings—the final pass unveils a touch of spicy hops, which complements the faint malt element very nicely; on palate, there's a pleasant bitter taste of hops—unfortunately, the hops are not properly supported by an anticipated maltiness, which would be in keeping with the pale-ale-style profile—still, I found this ale drinkable, even if it is average; it's a step up from the outright horrific Black & Tan and the medicinal Raspberry Red Ale.

RATING ★★

Brewery Hill Raspberry Red Ale

Resembles deep-gold apple juice/cider, no foam, good purity; the bouquet, to my surprise, is dead on arrival—in the majority of fruit beers, the aromas are one of the prime characteristics—this nose is so delicate as to be anemic, showing just the mildest trace of red-berry fruit; in the mouth, it reminds me most of fruit-flavored soda pop at entry, then the beery/malty foundation emerges at midpalate, but even then, the overly bitter backnote doesn't mix at all with the meek fruit element; dismal aftertaste; don't waste your time.

RATING ★

Brewery Hill Black & Tan

Really gorgeous appearance—deep, rich, mahogany/chestnut-brown hue, tan foam, perfect purity, average head retention; I was disappointed in the humble bouquet, which offered only modest scents of grape jam, concord grape juice, and other red fruit—nary a hint of cereal grain, hops, or yeast; on palate, this beer is flabby, disinterested, and ill-defined, as soft, mushy tastes of malt and hops can't muster enough character to redeem all the lapses in the aroma; malty, bitter aftertaste; the Brewery Hill people should study the Black & Tans of Micheal Shea and New Amsterdam to see how a black and tan's successfully handled.

RATING ★

BREWSKI Bar Room Ale

Handsome, medium-brown/worn-copper-penny hue, gold core highlights, tan foam, superb head retention; the nose is nutty, sweet, slightly honeyed, estery/fruity, and very compelling—the honey-on-cereal bouquet alone is worth two rating stars; in the mouth, the unabashedly sweet and malty entry is charming—by midpalate, the depth seems to be a trifle eroded, but the grainy flavor keeps it afloat; the finish is quick to fade and ends sweetly; this ale began like a trumpet, but ended like a flute.

BREWSKI BREWING COMPANY, ST. PAUL, MN

RATING ★ ★ ★   *Recommended*

BROOKLYN BREWERY Black Chocolate Stout

Impenetrable, jet-black, opaque appearance, dark tan foam, little head retention; the concentrated, Coco-Puffs nose speaks only about absolutely charred, burnt-to-a-veritable-crisp malt that is translated into aromas of bittersweet chocolate, molasses, oatmeal, road tar, charcoal, and pipe smoke—there's a lot happening here; the wonderfully viscous, thick, and velvety texture is unbelievably dense—this ropy texture is what supports the chocolate-milk-like flavor that expands at midpalate into a multilayered taste banquet that includes brown sugar, burnt toast, molasses, and a resiny bitterness; chunky, full finish; this potent, pungent hunk is the best beer offering yet from Brooklyn Brewery.

BROOKLYN BREWERY, BROOKLYN, NY / BREWED AND BOTTLED BY F. X. MATT, UTICA, NY

RATING ★ ★ ★ ★   *Highly Recommended*

BROOKLYN BREWERY East India Pale Ale

Beautiful sunset-orange/clover-honey/amber hue, off-white foam, average head retention; the intensely fruity nose reminds me very much of ripe apricots and malt in the atypical first nosing—in subsequent passes, the yellow-fruit component gradually ebbs, but not by much—the final pass reveals a hoppy, pear-like flirtation in addition to the apricot and malt—I greatly liked this peculiar but immensely enjoyable bouquet; the yellow fruit continues on the palate—there's more scope in the flavor than there is in the aroma, which was, in reality, a one-pony race; the aftertaste is acceptably bitter, soft, and medium-long; hardly a trendsetter or a touchstone, but a very palatable beer nonetheless.

RATING ★ ★ ★   *Recommended*

BROOKLYN BREWERY Lager

Amber/iced-tea color, wimpy foam; intensely fruity nose of apples, oranges, and even some soft banana qualities, buttressed by a welcome, crisp hoppiness; it's decidedly fruity on palate, though dry and thoroughly refreshing; this nice lager has a smooth delivery and a snappy, lively aftertaste; retasted twice since the initial evaluation and upgraded to three stars.

RATING ★ ★ ★   *Recommended*

Brooklyn Brewery Brown Dark Ale

Medium brown/mahogany color, tan foam, good head retention; the nose displays steely, slightly metallic aromas that elicited concern—there's a backnote of malt that somewhat counters the steeliness; in the mouth, the dry molasses-like, road-tar flavors are fine, if uninspiring; moderate weight; proper brown ale aftertaste that lingers and leans toward tarriness; could use a bigger kick for a dark ale and leans too heavily in the acid direction; given more malty fruitiness, this would be an above-average winner; sampled at least six times, all with similar notes.

RATING ★ ★

Budweiser Lager

White foam, gold color, perfect clarity, storms of enormous bubbles, good head retention; the cardboardy nose is off-dry and very rice-like—a decent and simplistic nose that's been smelled hundreds of times by every American citizen older than five; on palate, it's remarkably clean and grainy—no depth to address, no nuances or layers—this is American lager at its biggest, but not necessarily its best; serviceable, refreshing, and . . . well, wet.

ANHEUSER-BUSCH, ST. LOUIS, MO

RATING ★

Bud Light

Pale yellow/greenish tinge, white, splooshy, then anemic foam; the nose is curiously appealing as roasted-almond and mineral scents tease and prick the nasal cavity; the faint hoppy and malty flavors offer a quiet, dry, nutty fruitiness that, while hardly satisfying, is nevertheless not without a certain basic charm; flat aftertaste with little discernable virtue; on balance, dead meat and uneven in its presentation.

RATING ★

Budweiser Ice Draft

Deep harvest-gold color, with a fast-dying head of limp pearl-white foam; the nose is brazenly steely/metallic/tanky, with faint echoes of hops and even a little cardboard—an absolutely miserable aroma with the personality of a rock; the taste is off-dry and neutral; it's almost like a dessert wine in the texture department—unusually thick and creamy for a domestic lager style; but I ask you, who stole the bouquet and the flavor? The iceman goeth; next huddled-masses gimmick, please; bllechh.

RATING ★

Buffalo Lager

Very attractive, unusual, German-style, honey color, with a weak-kneed, pasty-white head that quickly dissipates; the yeasty bouquet is quite compelling and appetizing as subtle hints of buttermilk biscuits, fino sherry, and raisins take turns showing their aromatic faces—one of the better noses this side of New Amsterdam Amber; on palate, the cake-batter flavor continues on with added accents of lemon peel, woodsy, musty flavors, all finishing in an off-dry, bread-dough taste that I find immensely charming; a substantial, no-nonsense beer of many layers, nuances, and charms.

BUFFALO BREWING, BUFFALO, NY

RATING ★★★

Buffalo Bill's Pumpkin Ale

Beautiful color of orange/amber/dark-honey/tea, beige foam, decent head retention; the beguiling nose has a cinnamon/pumpkin-seed snap to it in the first nosing that's enlivening and delightful—the second and third passes see the zestiness noticeably dissipate, but it's still an enticing pumpkin-pie perfume that exhibits little grain, hops, or fruit; the palate presence indeed shows an astringent pumpkin taste that melds nicely with the biscuity malt foundation; the aftertaste is clean and mildly spicy, allowing once again for the pumpkin influence to come to the fore; as an oddity to try once or twice, I think it's perfectly swell.

CONTRACT-BREWED BY DUBUQUE BREWING, DUBUQUE, IA, FOR BUFFALO BILL'S BREWERY, HAYWARD, CA

RATING ★★★   ***Recommended***

Bunker Hill Lager

Pretty light-amber/honey/apricot-nectar hue, no head retention to speak of; the toasty, roasted-grain nose has a fruity backnote (plums, pears?) quality that rounds out the nosing experience in nice form—a very inviting, off-dry bouquet; on the palate, the taste leans to the acid side of the scale as the suppleness enjoyed so much in the bouquet gets erased by the acute tartness; the finish is very tart and, hence, clean and crisp; though I was disappointed in the directional shift from the aromatic plump fruit and toastiness to the austerity and sharp bitterness of the taste, this is a beer that still earns two stars.

BUNKER HILL BREWING COMPANY, WILKES-BARRE, PA

RATING ★★

Busch Lager

Made by Anheuser-Busch, Busch actually makes Budweiser look like the "King of Beers"—this is one of the most anemic beer experiences I've had; gold/straw hue, pearly white, frothy foam, pure, fair head retention; the nose snaps with effervescence, but there's not much in the way of aroma— I don't want CO_2, I want some recognizable aromas to pick apart; in the mouth, the uncontrollable effervescence almost comes up into my nose— somebody, hose this baby down—the taste takes blandness to new heights; no finish to speak of; it's this sort of loser that makes me grouchy; the A-B ad says, "Head for the mountains"—after tasting this swill, I suggest they change that to "Head for the store to buy something else."

ANHEUSER-BUSCH, ST. LOUIS, MO

RATING ★

C

CARLING BLACK LABEL Light

Yellow/gold color, lively, firm head; the lovely, round, malty (like a whisky distillery mash tun room), sweet nose displays ample character; the entry flavors of almonds and oranges regrettably vanish as rapidly as they appear; no finish to address; the pleasant, fresh nose is worth a star, but that's all it gained for this pallid light; although Carling is a Canadian brewer, this is a domestically produced product; seemed to have some potential, but fell far short in the end; not even close to being an average light.

MOLSON BREWING, CANADA / BREWED IN THE UNITED STATES

RATING ★

CATAMOUNT Bock

Pretty deep-amber/rust color, tan foam, the exceedingly long head retention makes me wonder if I can wash my dishes in the foam; the first nosing made me sneeze as estery aromas flooded my nasal cavity—once over that, I detected enchanting scents of ripe banana, guava, and honey that lingered through the subsequent passes—a highly delectable and ripe bouquet; in the mouth, it's off-dry, slightly buttery, creamy-textured, and capped by an alluring roasted-cereal midpalate that's nicely underlined by a mild hoppy bitterness; the aftertaste is medium-rich, long, and, true to the aroma, engagingly fruity; very solid from top to bottom and well worth a try.

CATAMOUNT BREWING COMPANY, WHITE RIVER JUNCTION, VT

*RATING ★ ★ ★   **Recommended***

CATAMOUNT Porter

Inky, black-coffee brown/black tone, dark beige foam, long head retention; the nose shows ample toastiness, maltiness, and tar—it's not a raging-bull type of bouquet, but its nuanced character is delightfully appealing; on the palate, the roasted-grain quality shines brightly as supporting flavors of molasses, tobacco leaf, and charred malt complement the headlining graininess; nary a whisper of bitterness exists in this gentlemanly porter, and that virtue makes it a pleasant departure from some of the more ferocious dark ales I've evaluated; buy and enjoy.

*RATING ★ ★ ★   **Recommended***

CATAMOUNT Christmas Ale 1995

Possesses the look and bearing of a red ale—rich mahogany/sorrel hue, tan foam, small bubbles, very good head retention; the snappy, tangy, zesty nose is alive with a scintilla of spice, deep-roasted malt, wood resin, and an earthy/woodsy backnote aroma that's delightful all the way through four nosings; in the mouth, the focus is on dry malt and hoppy bitterness, with no residual trace of the spice enjoyed in the delectable bouquet; the midpalate pulses with acceptable bitterness; the finish is all hops/bitterness/dryness; while this ale was very palatable, I would have loved to have experienced more of the zesty spice component in the mouth presence.

*RATING ★ ★ ★   **Recommended***

CATAMOUNT 10th Anniversary Ale Special Edition IPA

Seriously attractive, tawny/bronze tint, beige foam, good head retention, superb purity; while the bouquet could rightfully be categorized as being neither "showy" nor "forward," it does emit an alluring, sweet malt scent that's accented with spicy fruit—to my way of thinking, most consumers wouldn't take notice of this delicate bouquet and would proceed right to the drinking—fine, but they'd be missing out on a truly pleasant noseful; as with all Catamount brews, this mouth presence exhibits a clean crispness that, verily I say unto you, crackles on the tongue as flavors of medium-toasted malt and very bitter hops keep the attention of the taste buds; the highly bitter finish runs the risk of being too astringent, but comes in just under the acceptability wire.

RATING ★ ★ ★   *Recommended*

CATAMOUNT Amber

Medium amber/tortoise-shell hue, tan foam, very extended head retention; the flowery nose emits woodsy, garden-like aromas of jasmine, violets, carnations, and wet turf—while inoffensive, this beany/seedy/earthy bouquet is strangely not compelling at all; it's a mildly diverting lightweight on the palate as brisk, crisp flavors of bittersweet hops, herbs, and chewy malt combine in adequate form and function; the finish is breezily cavalier and doesn't bother to stay too long; it's an okay, middle-of-the-pack amber that's regrettably short on charm and gravitas.

RATING ★ ★

CATAMOUNT American Wheat

Nice yellow/gold tone, pearl-colored foam, long head retention—it's not cloudy at all as you'd normally expect from a well-chilled wheat beer; the nose has a faint, slightly nutty scent very much like Wheat Thin crackers—nothing more of content or import to report on; it has a pleasant, open, friendly manner in the mouth and the texture could almost be characterized as fleshy; the dry flavors of cracked wheat, digestive biscuits, and oatmeal are appealing and correct, but oddly vacant and devoid of much deeper character—there's no pizazz, no giddyap to encourage a drinker's enthusiasm; the aftertaste is benign and short-lived; it doesn't come close to the majesty and panache of the greatest of all domestic wheat beers, Celis White; a passive lamb of a beer.

RATING ★ ★

CATAMOUNT Pale Ale

Lovely color of burnished orange/dark honey, ideal purity, tan foam, good head retention; the fine nose offers controlled, behaved aromas of moderately roasted malt and a pinch of hops—I got the feeling that this nose was held back for some mysterious reason; very bitter at palate entry—the intense bitterness accelerates at midpalate, allowing for too little malt/cereal impact—in other words, this pale ale is off-balance—what it needs is some plump maltiness to counter the acute astringency of the hops—overhopped to a fault; drive right past it.

RATING ★

CELIS White Hefe Weizen

Displays the usual cloudy appearance of a chilled wheat beer, medium straw/gold tone, with a billowy cumulus cloud foam and long head retention; gets dizzyingly high marks immediately for its bountiful, floral, hoppy, orange rind, almost grapey/winey nose that struts its stuff for the olfactory sense through all four nosings—the heady, beguiling, unmalted wheat fragrance leaps from the glass; in the mouth, a startlingly mandarin-orange-like flavor holds court all the way into the mild, whistle-clean finish; doubtless, this beauty is America's most refreshing beer—a nimble, delicious, quaffable, and elegant big-thirst killer that has European skill and tradition written all over it; move over, Lone Star, this must now be considered the new "National Beer of Texas"; outstanding brewing, period; has been retasted five times since the formal review.

CELIS BREWERY, AUSTIN, TX

RATING ★ ★ ★ ★ ★   *Highest Recommendation*

CELIS Pale Bock

Has a superb copper/vermilion/tawny hue that's a knockout, average head retention of the light beige foam; the fine nose is ambrosial and intense in its fresh fruitiness, equaling the splendid bouquet of New Amsterdam Amber, which I hold as a domestic benchmark—this bouquet rockets up from the sampling glass and after a few moments firm, iced-tea-like, road-tar, and hoppy aromas emerge to complement the red-berry-fruit perfume; in the mouth, it's dry to off-dry at entry, going totally desert-dry by mid-palate, aided by a dash of hoppy bitterness thrown in for good measure; this stunning beer finishes quietly and elegantly; top-notch brewing from one of the U.S.'s top five brewers.

RATING ★ ★ ★ ★   *Highly Recommended*

CELIS Ale Grand Cru

Pure, gold/amber/light-honey tone, long head retention; the heady, sweet nose is a delectable cross between dark malted ale and spiced wine—its style reminds me most of the Trappist ales from Belgium, though not nearly as profound; on the palate, the fruity, bubblegum flavor is very charming; the texture is voluptuous and smooth; the aftertaste is medium-long and spicy, pretty much echoing the midpalate; so why do I find myself jotting down three rating stars instead of four?; while I genuinely like this potent beer, the overdeveloped spiciness/herbaceousness prevents me from going further into the "loving it" stage; an interesting, well-crafted, adventurous beer that forces the drinker to ponder it.

RATING ★ ★ ★   *Recommended*

CELIS Golden Ale

Bright golden/yellow color, snowy-white foam, low-to-average head retention; the soft, round bouquet is doughy, hoppy, and biscuity, even slightly nutty—a better than average nose, to be sure; in the mouth, the entry is keenly dry, razor-clean, minerally/slaty, and focused; there's a pleasing bitterness at the tail end of the finish that reminds me of citrus, especially key lime; a well-put-together golden; a later pass on the nose revealed the added scent of unsweetened coconut, making me think of Pilsner Urquell.

RATING ★ ★ ★　　Recommended

Cold Spring Export Lager

Slightly turbid, gold color, white foam, poor head retention; the sweet, malty nose goes nowhere in all the nosings; its full, round, and sweet-sour in the mouth, then it goes completely dry in the appealing, lingering, and yeasty finish; quite a refreshing brew, which I ended up liking more as I evaluated it.

COLD SPRING BREWING COMPANY, COLD SPRING, MN

RATING ★ ★

Cold Spring Honey Almond Lager

Looks just like a traditional American lager—gold/yellow hue, bubbles the size of Boston, pearl-white foam; the pillowy nose highlights the honey most of all, and, as it turns out, I don't have a problem with the one-dimensional aspect of it—in the later passes, a sour-mash/malted-barley aroma joins the honey—an all-right, middle-of-the-pack nose; on palate, it's uncomplicated and honeyed, with bits of corn husk and malt peeping through the veil of honey; texturewise, it's medium-bodied and thinner in the finish than at midpalate; nothing special; if it were mine, I'd turn the volume down on the honey and play up the lager more.

RATING ★ ★

Cold Spring Blackberry Bramble Ale

Good clarity in the pretty harvest-gold color, the off-white foam doesn't show great staying power; the anemic bouquet offers only some distant blackberry notes right after the pour—somebody else might say that they're delicate—the third and fourth passes showed a lot more giddyap in terms of animation as solid, frisky blackberry, and vine-like notes evolved nicely— I ended up thinking that this aroma grew admirably with aeration; where it caved in again was the mouth presence—at entry, the bramble/vine taste was astringent, then that faded away, leaving a meek, unripened blackberry facade; the aftertaste was terribly timid and short; points for the appearance and the latter stages of the bouquet; drinkable, but unexciting.

RATING ★ ★

Coors Winterfest

Seasonal; gorgeous copper/russet color, capped by a frothy beige foam— it's a first-rate appearance; the plummy, fruity nose is very agreeable indeed, as gobs of toasted-honey-wheat-bread fragrance supports the fruit component—I greatly fancied this malty, intensely fruited, and highly stylized bouquet; on palate, it upholds and fulfills all the promise found in the aroma as pleasant, but simple, tastes of malt and hops are accented by red fruit; the finish is off-dry, pruney, and silky to the touch; by a considerable margin, the best beer I've ever had from this mammoth brewer.

ADOLPH COCRS, GOLDEN, CO

RATING ★ ★ ★　　Recommended

Coors Pilsener

Handsome, 14-carat-gold/yellow hue, billowy, white foam, good head retention, no questioning its purity; an invitingly crisp, crackling aroma of rice, light malt, and yeast—a bit citrusy in the third pass; the letdown is in the flavor, which comes off tasting like the pink eraser on your Number 2 lead pencil—for years, Coors was "the" beer to get east of the Mississippi River, where it was scarce—now, of course, it's commonplace; could be that when it was rare and precious, the illusion was that it tasted good—well, it doesn't.

RATING ★

Coors Light

Crystal gold color, fast, weak, widely spaced head; mildly hoppy, steely, metallic nose that drives off the cliff and therefore stimulates little interest; what flavor there is is modestly engaging, but so transparent as to be nondescript; this silver bullet missed the satisfaction bull's-eye by a Colorado mile; when they say "the right beer now," they mustn't mean for drinking; maybe a car wash.

RATING ★

Coors Cutter Non-Alcoholic Brew

Nice, deep gold hue, steady stream of bubbles, silver-white foam, poor head retention; the nose is very sweet, like heavily sugared dry cereal, in the first three passes—by the last nosing, virtually all of the sticky sweetness is gone, leaving behind a stale, cardboard-like aroma—yeccchhh; I was hoping that the flavor would bail out the insipid bouquet, but that simply doesn't happen—Cutter tastes nothing like beer and more like cream soda; pass it by and reach for the far superior N-A from Beck's, Haake Beck.

RATING ★

Coors Red Light

Very attractive, dark amber/copper hue, tan foam, average head retention; the nose takes being ethereal to the extreme, as in, "Lights on, nobody home"—the first three nosings of this limp noodle offered zero, zilch, nil, goose egg in terms of aroma, then in the final pass a meekly cloaked fragrance of tobacco, coffee, and cocoa made itself known; just as I came around to the bouquet, I tasted it—the problems were simple—no flavor to address, and the texture was ridiculously watery—evidently, the Coors brewmaster included key ingredients like yeast and water but forgot to add the grain and hops; one of the most vapid, gutless alcoholic liquids I've ever had in my mouth; Red Light, good night; I was actually tempted to give this dreck a no-star rating; you can tell, I *adored* this one.

RATING ★

Crested Butte White Buffalo Peace Ale

Dullish bronze/medium-amber/honey tint, tan foam, long head retention, very pure; the first whiff following the pour is steely and metallic—the second pass introduces malt to the stage—this is a grudging, stingy nose that doesn't want to give up anything—by the third anemic pass I begin to wonder if it has anything to give—the final nosing reveals slightly more depth to the malt in a sour-mash kind of way—ultimately, this nose goes nowhere; on palate, it's more expressive, as keen flavors of malt and hops come into the mouth nicely at entry, then fall to the background by midpalate, leaving painfully little to grasp onto; the finish is quick, lean, and dry; drinkable, just not enough meat.

CRESTED BUTTE BREWERY AND PUB, CRESTED BUTTE, CO, AND DUBUQUE BREWING COMPANY, DUBUQUE, IA

RATING ★ ★

D

DEVIL MOUNTAIN BREWERY Railroad Ale

Attractive, deep amber/bronze color with mild turbidity, light tan foam, poor-to-fair head retention; the after-pour nose is zesty, round, fruity (red fruits, especially, like plums), and ripe—while the vivacity in the nose does diminish with each succeeding pass, I still responded favorably to the inviting nutty/estery/fruitiness all the way down the line; on palate, there's a firm bitterness that frames the grainy/fruity (orange peel) core flavors, adding an almond thrust in the last tasting; the aftertaste is manageably bitter, but subdued; Bay Brewing is on the right track with this pale ale.

BAY BREWING COMPANY, BENICIA, CA

RATING ★ ★ ★   *Recommended*

DEVIL MOUNTAIN BREWERY Porter

Opaque, black-coffee-tone, beige foam that dissipates too quickly, seems flat; the understated nose has interesting notes of chocolate-covered cherries, malted milk, and burnt toast—I liked the aroma, but you have to work hard to coax it out; the palate entry is very pleasant as fruity/candied flavors of red plum and dark toffee are ejected at midpalate by an intense smokiness, which turns as bitter as French-roast black coffee on the back of the tongue; the finish is properly bitter and medium-long; while hardly brilliant, a good job overall.

RATING ★ ★ ★   *Recommended*

DIXIE BLACKENED VOODOO Lager

Bittersweet-chocolate/molasses color, with a firm beige crown of foam; the gripping, earthy nose is an aromatic banquet, which lays out onto its table delectable scents of hot cocoa, dried flowers, molasses, and dark rum that has been oak-aged—not your ordinary lager nose, thank you very much; on palate, this medium-bodied dark is drier than I thought it would be from the flowery/baked nose, but the briary, almost berry-like flavors are fruity, malty, and altogether delicious; this husky brew is very nice from top to bottoms-up; and I love that name.

DIXIE BREWING COMPANY, NEW ORLEANS, LA

RATING ★ ★ ★   *Recommended*

Dixie Jazz Amber Light

Lustrous russet/burnt-orange hue, little head retention; the nose begins with an opening salvo of high-flying fruit, then goes totally slack after ten seconds, ending up as a slightly sweaty, metallic perfume that confused me, since the start was pleasant, if short-lived—in the fourth and last nosing, I'm pleased to report that the hoppy/fruitiness returned; on the palate, it's as lackluster, listless, and gutless as the overwhelming majority of light beers seem to be; an odd one, though—it started with a flash-in-the-pan pleasant bouquet, went up and down in the aroma department, had an unacceptably thin flavor and texture and a nonexistent aftertaste; nexxxxxt.

RATING ★

Dixie Slow-Brewed Lager

Attractive burnt-amber color, off-white foam, good head retention; the pleasant, malty sweetness/fruitiness in the rather shy nose never fully develops even after fifteen minutes of warming and nosing; the sweetness continues on a medium-bodied palate, then vanishes in a fast, neutral finish; the implied promise of the rich color and nose faded quickly in the uninspiring flavor and aftertaste; mindless drinking.

RATING ★

Dock Street Illuminator Bock

Seriously attractive, copper-penny/rust color, great purity, large, splooshing bubbles, tan foam, little head retention; the nose is closed down right after the pour, then in the second pass, a deep, but elusive, dark malt note is discerned—with aeration, the bouquet gradually unfolds as toasted-dry-cereal, pumpernickel, and mild hops make agreeable appearances in the last two passes—I especially responded to the baked-dark-bread quality; on palate, this properly bitter beauty is endowed with a stylishly viscous texture that forms the foundation for the elemental, sweet flavors of mash, malt, and even a lightning-fast flash of molasses; the finish is rotund; this is the best Dock Street offering in bottle.

DOCK STREET BREWING COMPANY, PHILADELPHIA, PA / BREWED AND BOTTLED BY F. X. MATT, UTICA, NY

RATING ★ ★ ★ ★   *Highly Recommended*

Dock Street Bohemian Pilsener

Though my efforts to visit Dock Street Brewing Company have yet to succeed, this tasting confirms what other people have been whispering to me—that Jeff Ware is one of the top American brewers at the moment; the gorgeous, toasted-oat/amber hue is topped off by a foamy beige head that actually stays around for a while; this splendid bouquet emits fetching fragrances of nut meat and malted barley and is quite dry; on palate, a focused maltiness/hoppiness sails effortlessly from entry to finish; ends on a dry, clean note; an elegant brew; sampled three times.

RATING ★ ★ ★   *Recommended*

Dock Street Philadelphia Amber

Luminous, marginally darker, richer amber/russet color than the Pilsener—sports a long-lasting, beige foam; the nose on this supple amber is slightly sweeter and fruitier than the grainy Pilsener; to the mouth-feel, there's a meatiness and heft that are welcome; the flavor is substantial and fruity, with a decidedly hoppy lean that's very pleasant; the aftertaste is medium-long and very hoppy; purchase this succulent Amber and you'll be hoppy.

RATING ★ ★ ★   Recommended

Dornbusch Alt Ale

Seriously attractive reddish-brown/old-copper-penny/aged-tawny-port hue, beige foam, long head, imperfect purity, with miniscule suspended particles being noted; the nose eloquently tells the story of pumpernickel bread and dark caramel in the first two passes—the third and fourth nosings expand into deep-roasted malt and red-fruit territories, like distant black plums—the overall aromatic impression is very favorable; on palate, this domestic alt offers considerable elegance and poise at entry as a damn-near-opulent sweet maltiness greets the taste buds—the midpalate stage is dominated by the hops, which bring the sweetness of the malt into line; the finish is silky and fruity; very nice brewing.

DORNBUSCH BREWING COMPANY, IPSWICH, MA

RATING ★ ★ ★ ★   Highly Recommended

Downtown Brown Ale

To my considerable ire, this ale erupted like Old Faithful at Yellowstone upon being opened—cascades of frothing brown ale came bubbling out of the spout, covering my tasting table—pretty chestnut-brown color, completely spent effervescence, flat, tan head; the nose is pleasantly fruity and smoky, but there's nothing in the way of complexity or grip to hold the attention of the olfactory sense; in the mouth, bitter flavors of tar and hops aren't counterbalanced enough by malt and/or cereal flavors to render it recommendable; inoffensive and simple, but the exploding entrance indicates problems in production or storage; use caution.

KOBOR WHITE BREWING COMPANY, SCHUYLERVILLE, NY

RATING ★

Drytown Susquehanna Gold Ale

Authentically gorgeous, bronze/copper tone, light tan foam, good head retention; the biscuity nose bursts from the glass in the post-pour nosing like a cat springing at a canary, then by the end of the second pass it settles down into a malty bouquet—the third pass shows a bread-dough face—the final pass is estery/fruity and pleasing; in the mouth, it shows good balance between the malt and hops, but by midpalate the hops take control as the bitterness factor comes to dominate; the aftertaste is dry, but quick and subdued.

DRYTOWN BREWERY, ONEONTA, NY

RATING ★ ★ ★   Recommended

Dubuque Star Big Muddy Red Ale

Very pretty, chestnut/reddish brown/blood color, beige foam, excellent head retention; the nose is bountifully rich in medium-roasted malt that's not quite chocolatey, but more like tea or coffee, even a bit bean-like—I noted an intense grainy/kernel-like backnote that supports the egg cream and nuttiness found in the upfront aroma—it's a superlative nose; the sweet, concentrated maltiness/coffee/honey-wheat flavors in the palate entry are complemented by a keen hoppy bitterness in the midpalate; the aftertaste is clean, crisp, and plump; this is a superdelicious thoroughbred that's ideally toasted, honeyed, bitter, and sublimely harmonious; ya-hoo, Big Muddy Red.

DUBUQUE BREWING AND BOTTLING COMPANY, DUBUQUE, IA

RATING ★★★★   ***Highly Recommended***

E

ED'S CAVE CREEK **Original Chili Beer**

Golden lager appearance, with a blink-and-its-gone head; the chilipepper influence is unmistakable in this zesty, peppery, vegetal nose—any lover of Mexican or spicy Chinese or Tai cuisine would pick out the peppers in the first encounter; on the palate, this beer is too hot, too spicy, too over-the-top even for me, a fanatical maven of spicy foods; the five-alarm chili taste is so overpowering that it obliterates every other taste possibility, making it difficult to accurately gauge the brew as a whole entity; perhaps worst of all though, is that it's blatantly gimmicky; back to the drawing board on this one, and tone down the heat; sampled twice and I've strongly disliked it each time.

CRAZY ED'S BREWING, CAVE CREEK, AZ

RATING ★

ELK MOUNTAIN **Amber Ale**

Could pass for a red, since the color is a very deep umber/copper/cherry-wood brown, light brown foam, remarkably extended head retention; the alluring, come-hither bouquet is rife with toasted cereal, rich sweet barley malt, and even a dash of earthy mushroom—it's a solid, husky, straightforward aroma that's polished and well crafted; at palate entry, the toasted honey-wheat-bread opening salvo promises good times ahead, then the midpalate sweetness suddenly goes completely flat as a bitter hoppiness takes full command of the rudder rather than sharing the directional responsibilities with the comely but overshadowed toasty sweetness; when the out-of-kilter bitterness is toned down and allowed to mesh with the cereal rather than run it out of the room, I'll consider giving it a third rating star and a recommendation, because the foundation is clearly there for a very good beer.

ANHEUSER-BUSCH, MERRIMACK, NH

RATING ★★

ELK MOUNTAIN **Red Lager**

Attractive, copper-penny/orange-pekoe-tea hue, lazy effervescence, off-white foam, poor head retention; the taciturn nose eluded me for fifteen minutes—disgusted, I packed it in and moved on to the taste; on palate, this red makes an early attempt at being plump but only ends up coming off flat and flabby—there are, at most, stray hints of malt and brown rice—the flavor has the depth of a tidal pool; the Elk Mountain Amber at least offered some quaffability—this slender offering is emaciated and unacceptable.

RATING ★

ELM CITY Blackwell Stout

Very deep, but not opaque, nut-brown/chestnut/deep-tawny/black-pekoe-tea tone, excellent clarity, beige foam, good head retention; the toasty nose brims with vibrant scents of pumpernickel, charred malt, roasted chestnuts, and vanilla extract notes—a complex, busy aroma that keeps the accelerator to the floor through all four nosings; on palate, the molasses/sweet-malt foundation flavor is complemented by a smoky bitterness; the texture is only medium-bodied, however, for a stout; the aftertaste features the dark bread, brown sugar, and charred malt sensed earlier; stylistically, more a porter than a stout; I'd change the name, but not the recipe; delicious.

ELM CITY BREWING, NEW HAVEN, CT / BREWED AND BOTTLED BY THE LION INC. BREWING, WILKES-BARRE, PA

RATING ★ ★ ★ ★   *Highly Recommended*

ELM CITY Connecticut Ale

Vermilion/copper color that could be labeled as a red ale, average head retention; the peculiar nose approaches being skunky/stinky in the initial nosing, but is simply intense and malty by the third pass—as the bouquet opens up with aeration, the maltiness is transformed into buttered popcorn and whole wheat bread dough—it's a fascinating nose that keeps you guessing; on the palate, a taste like ripe strawberries is evident and startling, but an appealing departure from the ultragrainy bouquet; the finish is all malt, reverting back to the qualities found in the cereal-like aroma; this handsome brew provides a few intriguing twists and turns while never losing its appeal or sense of direction; nice suds.

RATING ★ ★ ★   *Recommended*

ELM CITY Golden Ale

Picture-perfect appearance of deep yellow/18-carat gold, lazy effervescence, silver-white foam, great purity, poor head retention; the fragrance is very stingy in the first two nosings, giving off very faint scents of rice, soft malt, and wax—the aroma didn't expand much with aeration; in the mouth, it's acceptably clean and crisp, courtesy of the hops, but what's missing is any grain stuffing—it shows very restrained malt character—there's no excuse for that, but sloppy brewing, period; drinkable, yes; recommendable, no.

RATING ★ ★

ERIN'S ROCK Stout & Amber Lager

Owns the appearance of a root beer, that auburn/chestnut/nut-brown color that's quite appealing, light-beige foam, average head retention, proper purity; there's no other word for this nose but "biscuity," since it smells remarkably like a bag of chocolate chip cookies when you first open it—immensely charming through the first three passes, then it settles down into a deep cocoa/milk-chocolate/malty aroma that's very nice; quite sweet in the mouth, this hybrid simultaneously shows the depth of the sweetish stout as ably and clearly as the dry bitterness of the amber lager—I loved the chocolate-malt quality of the midpalate and the plump finish; really enjoyable black-and-tan style that's at once accomplished and a bit wild.

BREWED AT **THE LION, INC.,** WILKES-BARRE, PA, FOR **CHAMPION BEVERAGES,** DARIEN, CT

RATING ★ ★ ★ ★   ***Highly Recommended***

G

GEARY'S London Style Porter

Opaque, brown/black in color, deep beige foam, tiny beads, average head retention; the enchanting, gregarious, and engaging nose is decadently rich, but seamless and elegant—it oozes with creamy, smoky, malty aromas of espresso, charcoal, and absolutely seared toast—this is the best porter bouquet this side of the Atlantic—you can take that assessment to the bank; on the palate, the roasted-malt/bitter-hop alliance is so sublimely balanced and complementary that it's almost sinful; the round, chewy, full-bodied texture perfectly underpins the regal, stately, and potent flavors of wood smoke and chocolate malt; first class in every single sensory department; a true American classic.

D. L. GEARY BREWING COMPANY, PORTLAND, ME

RATING ★ ★ ★ ★ ★   ***Highest Recommendation***

GEARY'S Pale Ale

The cumulo-nimbus-like head explodes out of the bottle and stays riding high in the glass for what seems like an eternity; the cloudy, amber/honey tone forces me to ask, is this ale unfiltered? the concentrated nose emits seductive aromas of chocolate, malted milk, hot cocoa, and is, in short, immensely pleasing; medium-bodied, the flavor harkens back to the chocolate only in meager terms as the taste shifts into a malt/grain gear and remains there through the quick, acceptably steely/bitter aftertaste; the bouquet is a formidable winner that on its own earns two stars; I've never experienced such an eruption of chocolate in a nonstout beer; a best-kept-secret beer.

RATING ★ ★ ★   ***Recommended***

GEARY'S Hampshire Special Ale Winter 1995–1996

Brilliant, luminous, rust/medium-amber/warm-orange color, beige foam, average head retention; the after-pour nose is very delicate, emitting only tiny bits and pieces of hops—with aeration, the bouquet blossoms very slowly into a cake-like, slightly spicy presence that retains its low-key posture; in the mouth, it's acutely bitter and whistle-clean, with a peculiar resiny/piney quality at the front; the finish squeaks, it's so clean; while I liked the austere astringency, it may be too bitter for beer lovers who like their brews on the malty/grainy/fat side of the spectrum; a Bitter freak's delight.

RATING ★ ★ ★   ***Recommended***

Genesee Cream Ale

Gold color, with a rather dull, pancake-flat head; the doughy nose is thick and one-dimensional—fresh bread dough is the name of this particular game; on the palate, it is creamy, by George, and almost viscous, with acceptable, if uninspired, flavors of yeast and anonymous fruit; the finish surprisingly is lightning-quick, considering the firm, square-shouldered taste; there's simply nothing to dissect here—it's bread dough from beginning to end, with not one iota of hops; the lack of crispness leads one to think of it as being flabby; take a pass; while this ale is a staple of the upstate New York and northern Pennsylvania crowd, the reason for its regional popularity eludes me completely.

GENESEE BREWING, ROCHESTER, NY

RATING ★

George Killian's Irish Brown Ale

The nearly opaque brown/black color makes it look more like a porter or even a stout than a brown ale, deep beige foam, very long head retention; the barely perceptible bouquet needs too much coaxing to bother with, so I threw in the towel—there's only an elemental trace of maltiness; on the palate, this broad-shouldered but sinewy beauty comes alive in the form of rich, roasted-grain and Brazil-nut flavors that are nicely complemented by black fruit (plums, especially), road-tar, nicotine, and molasses backnotes; the finish is medium-rich, quite extended, and spotlights the ripe, malty fruitiness rather than the hoppy bitterness; skip the sniffing and proceed directly to the drinking.

ADOLPH COORS BREWING, GOLDEN, CO

RATING ★ ★ ★   **Recommended**

George Killian's Irish Red Lager

It is indeed red, a tawny copper/russet/mahogany hue that's quite the smooth-talking charmer, fast and loose beige head; the nose is uncomplicated, sound, clean, and direct, but not in the least layered or complex—after the third pass, faint echoes of nuts and dried apricots surfaced; in the mouth, I appreciated the sweetish cleanliness of it as overt, ready-to-please tastes of red fruits (berries and red plums) vied for attention; the aftertaste is correct and medium-long; a sound lager that looks better than it really is; has only a fraction of the depth of other domestic lagers, like Pete's Wicked Lager, Samuel Adams Boston Lager, or Dixie Blackened Voodoo Lager.

RATING ★ ★

Georgia Peach Wheat Beer

Properly foggy gold color, eggshell foam, marvelous head retention, pure; I loved the concentrated fruitiness in the opening nosing—it brims with ripe yellow fruit—the second pass saw the fresh fruit perfume drop like a stone, however, to be replaced with a neutral, yeasty aroma that brought the smell part of the program to a halt by the third pass—strangely, the bouquet woke up again in the last nosing; in the mouth, a full redemption of the spotty nose occurred as the zippy, vivaciously fruity flavor took my taste buds on a wild ride all the way through the finish; crazzzzy, man, but likable.

FRIENDS BREWING COMPANY, ATLANTA, GA

RATING ★ ★ ★   **Recommended**

Georgia Wild Raspberry Wheat Ale

Mildly turbid, dull gold (completely in line with the style), bright white foam, short head retention; the ripe bouquet leaves no room for error in the evaluation of its nature: *red raspberry*—top to bottom, stem to stern, raspberry rules the day, with only a minor supporting-role cast for the malted wheat—don't, however, get the impression that I didn't favorably respond to it, because I certainly did; on palate, it's light-weighted, nimble, fresh, moderately fruity, and highly drinkable—by midpalate, the malted-wheat element comes more into the picture; the aftertaste is like a fruit salad, ripe, sweet, and succulent, but not a bit sugary; not profound or cutting-edge, but a nice job.

RATING ★ ★ ★   **Recommended**

Grail Amber Ale

Seriously attractive, nut-brown/mahogany hue, wet-sand-colored foam, very good head retention; the compelling, inviting aroma is all cookie batter, honey, and roasted malt upfront—the second and third nosings are quite toasted—the final pass acts to confirm the findings of the earlier nosings and adds an echo of molasses to the aromatic equation; the taste is bitter at entry, then it expands at midpalate into flavors of chocolate, black coffee, and road tar—not a brilliant amber-ale mouth presence, but more than serviceable; the aftertaste is long, bitter/hoppy, and malty; while the flavor wasn't as solid as the aroma, it's still a sound performer.

MIDDLE AGES BREWING COMPANY, SYRACUSE, NY

RATING ★ ★ ★   **Recommended**

Grant's Scottish Ale

Brilliant, new-copper-penny/sunset-orange color with a dash of red, a marginally longer-lasting head than the India Pale Ale, Celtic Ale, or Weis Beer; the trademark perfume of Grant's is present and accounted for in a rich, sweet, grainy, and malty aroma that's lusty and assertive in the first nosing, then it settles down in the second pass, emitting lovely, candied-red-fruit, and wood-resin notes—a simply dandy nose; svelte, sexy, and satiny on the tongue; the flavors crackle with yeasty freshness, toasty malted barley, and a high-flying Cascade hop bitterness that convincingly won me over; the finish is crisp, almost plump, and very, very extended; superb brewing from the lustrous appearance to the elegant aftertaste; buy by the case.

YAKIMA BREWING AND MALTING COMPANY, YAKIMA, WA

RATING ★ ★ ★ ★   **Highly Recommended**

Grant's Perfect Porter

Opaque, dark chocolate/black coffee brown, tan foam, average head retention; the Dutch-chocolate aroma earns a couple of rating stars on its own—the smoky, chocolatey note in the first three passes is so creamy and milky that you want to scoop it out with a spoon, like cake frosting—a first-rate bouquet, period; in the mouth, this swank beauty is more prone to vanilla extract, molasses, and coffee bean than to chocolate or cocoa, but who's complaining? the midpalate highlights the deep-roasted malt component and carries that theme into the charcoal, road-tar finish; a banquet of charred, toast-like flavors with creamy cocoa; the aroma is fat, compelling, and memorable; bravo, Grant's.

RATING ★ ★ ★ ★   *Highly Recommended*

GRANT'S Imperial Stout

Deep, inky brown/black, opaque, meager head retention; the nose bursts forth from the glass at the first pass, then settles down into a soft, tart, toasted-grain bouquet that shows backnotes of molasses, saddle leather, road tar, and coffee beans; the flavor is intensely smoky, almost creamy, decidedly nutty, and very pleasant overall; the sweet, smoky aftertaste is extended and voluptuous; while not in the same league as Samuel Smith's Imperial Stout from England, this well-crafted domestic is a very nice, palatable ale that deserves the attention of dark-ale fans.

RATING ★ ★ ★   *Recommended*

GRANT'S Weis Beer

The pretty honey, harvest-gold color is topped by a wispy, short-lived, pearl-white foam constructed of enormous bubbles that lazily sploosh on the surface; the appetizing bouquet is charged with luscious honey-wheat, light-clove, and doughy aromas that make for a first pass that's extraordinarily full and untoasted English muffin–like—on the subsequent nosings I discern an acceptable diminishment in the honey-wheat intensity, but it picks up a delicate nuttiness in the third pass—the aroma is outstanding; briskly refreshing on palate as the malted-wheat flavor finds a welcome home in my mouth; the texture is satiny and medium-weighted; the midpalate and finish, however, don't make it a four-star beer, because they fade away too quickly; this beer earns a recommendation mainly on its superlative aroma and palate entry; Celis White is still America's premier wheat beer.

RATING ★ ★ ★   *Recommended*

GRANT'S Celtic Ale

Irresistibly attractive mahogany/chestnut-brown hue, no head to speak of; the nose is round, malty, inviting, and very doughy, to the point of smelling like pumpernickel dough—as with all Grant's beers, the aroma is fetching and seductive; again, an embarrassing deficiency in CO_2 marks it down, but the palate does offer a true maltiness and an engaging smoked-meat quality that is both solidly tasty and supple; a more layered beer of deeper character would have earned a fourth star; as it is, it's a very nice quaff for an American dark ale; the aroma is delightful.

RATING ★ ★ ★   *Recommended*

GRANT'S India Pale Ale

Lovely amber/deep-honey color, the lightning-fast head deflated immediately; the nose is a biscuity, cookie-batter-like triumph of style and panache over substance—while I was charmed by the nose's superficial pizazz, I didn't lose sight of its lack of character; the palate entry is clean and bitter—with a medium body, this IPA would be delicious if it owned more or, for that matter, any effervescence—I responded favorably to the sharp, attention-getting bitterness, but I won't lie and say that I didn't wish for a broader menu of taste; the flabby flatness of it (similar to that of the Weis Beer) took a star away from the final rating; in this case, that demotion made it average and, therefore, unrecommendable.

RATING ★ ★

Gritty McDuff's Best Bitter Ale

Luminous, pure, new-copper-penny color, ivory foam, good head retention; the nose is a stunner, as fully mature, buxom, and off-dry aromas of lightly roasted malt, cereal with honey, and honey-wheat toast dazzle the sense of smell—the tanginess barely diminishes through four nosings—a totally appetizing bouquet that's up there with the finest pale-ale/bitter noses in the U.S.; all the charm, structure, and élan enjoyed in the aroma are found in the taste—the acute hoppy bitterness on palate is beautifully balanced by the cereal richness; the finish is properly bitter and refreshing; one of America's best bitter ales by a long shot.

GRITTY MCDUFF'S BREWING COMPANY, PORTLAND, ME

RATING ★ ★ ★ ★   ***Highly Recommended***

Gritty McDuff's Best Brown Ale

Supremely beautiful, cherry-wood/reddish-brown color, medium-beige foam, average head retention; the warm, inviting nose is luxuriously rich and overflowing with roasted nuts, roasted malt, and mild tobacco smoke scents in the first two nosings—in the third and fourth passes, the roasted malt comes to the forefront; on palate, the feature that impresses me most initially is the plump smoothness of the texture—on this creamy foundation, the tastes of chocolate malt, barley malt, pumpernickel, and burnt honey-wheat toast flourish—it's a thick, viscous ride that's worth every second; the aftertaste is more smoky/bitter than fruity/sweet; delightful—good things are occurring in Portland, Maine.

RATING ★ ★ ★ ★   ***Highly Recommended***

Gritty McDuff's Black Fly Stout

Black as night, opaque, deep-beige foam, very short head retention, pure; the lovely, deep-roasted nose brims right from the first pass with malted milk, bittersweet chocolate, black coffee, and molasses scents—as it warms and aerates, the nose turns more and more bitter, like mocha—by the last pass, there's little further expansion aromatically; in the mouth, the coffee-like bitterness plays top banana at palate entry and continues to lead the flavor charge well into the midpalate phase, leaving little room for anything else; the aftertaste is slightly chalky, extremely bitter and astringent, and not terribly pleasant; my biggest criticism of this stout is that it relies too much on bitterness, not allowing other customary stout characteristics to get involved, such as creaminess, sweet malt, or smokiness; it's not that I didn't like it, because I haltingly did, but I think that this brew was an opportunity lost.

RATING ★ ★

H

HARPOON India Pale Ale

Very pretty amber/honey/copper hue, average head retention; the alluring bouquet is smoky, tarry, molasses-like, even a tad herbal—I very much liked its aromatic marriage of grace and firmness; it's exceedingly smooth, easy, and sweet-sour in the mouth as the velvety and medium-bodied texture supports the flavors admirably—those flavors include wood smoke, red fruit, brown sugar, and toasted barley malt; the finish is clean, but smoky with a trace of welcome bitterness; a sound, well-structured beer that is made in Utica, New York, at the F. X. Matt brewery and that has more than a passing resemblance to both New Amsterdam and Saranac beers.

MASSACHUSETTS BAY BREWING COMPANY, BOSTON, MA / BREWED AND BOTTLED BY F. X. MATT, UTICA, NY

RATING ★ ★ ★   *Recommended*

HARPOON Octoberfest

Really gorgeous orange-pekoe-tea/rich amber color, beige foam, good head retention; the nose is pleasantly yeasty, malty, sweet, and even a bit nutty in a simple, head-on way—no messing around, no frills, just a what-you-smell-is-what-you-get bouquet that I liked more on an instinctive than an analytical level; on the palate, I had the identical reaction—this medium-bodied, no-brainer beer is a good quaff without all the trappings that profundity can bring—the bitter, hoppy, malty, and tarry flavor is cheerful and mellow from start to finish; nice job of keeping it simple and good.

RATING ★ ★ ★   *Recommended*

HARPOON Pilsner

Textbook, golden-hay/orange-blossom/honey color, ivory foam, strong effervescence, good head retention; this first-rate bouquet emits a round, sweet, biscuity aroma that's both inviting and appetizing from the first pass through the last, twenty minutes later; on palate, it shows some genuine depth as the bone-dry bitterness matches up well to the corn-husk/malty fruitiness—it's a nicely balanced combination that works well; the finish is long, though uneventful; good showing.

RATING ★ ★ ★   *Recommended*

HARPOON Alt Ale

Very handsome appearance, deep reddish-amber/ochre, tan foam, average head retention; I found the nose muted through all four nosings, except for very elusive, inconsequential, and distant scents of dry cereal and hops—an alt by virtue of its definition (heavily hopped) should show much more giddyap in the aroma—this beer is not true to the variety posted on the label; in the mouth, it's a mildly pleasant, undemanding ale whose lightish body and understated flavors left me wanting more depth and muscle; the finish is correctly and manageably bitter; a middle-of-the-pack ale that offers little in the way of excitement.

RATING ★ ★

HARPOON Winter Warmer

Similar in appearance to the Octoberfest, just a touch more vivid in the orange tone, beige foam, average head retention; the soft, polite bouquet is seeded with low-key seasonal scents of nutmeg and cinnamon, which overshadow any traces of grain or yeast—I liked this moderately zesty nose because it truly evokes images of the holiday season in graceful fashion; on the palate, however, the cinnamon and nutmeg dominate to the point of exclusion, which removèd the third rating star I had prematurely affixed to it; inoffensive aftertaste of nutmeg at last lets in a bit of malt; too late; could have been much better and on par with the very nice Octoberfest.

RATING ★ ★

HARPOON Golden Lager

Clearly more amber/orange than golden in appearance, but what the heck, what's in a name anyway? average head retention, silvery/light-beige foam; the tutti-frutti, sweet nose has hints of cake batter, cinnamon, and nut meat that do add elements of interest; once on the palate, this lager shows some spice, hops, yellow fruit, dry cereal, and a Muscat-like flavor that comes wrapped in a lean texture; the finish really highlights the Muscat quality, which I find pleasant; it's decent, but for my taste goes over the line in the fruitiness aspect; plus it's woefully misnamed—if this is gold, I'm a gray-haired woman named Maude.

RATING ★ ★

HEARTLAND BREWERY Indiana Pale Ale

Sampled on-site, warm deep-honey/gold hue, pearl-white foam, long head retention; has a very plump, full-bodied ale bouquet with ample hoppy bitterness balanced very nicely by malt and an estery fruitiness; sweet, intensely herbal on the palate with a lemon-lime backnote taste; the finish is richly textured, sweet, and very satisfying, showing solid tastes of citrus and cereal; by a country mile, the pick of the litter, but it would fare better without the cutesy name.

UNION SQUARE, NEW YORK, NY

RATING ★ ★ ★ ★　　*Highly Recommended*

HEARTLAND BREWERY Red Rooster Ale

Sampled on-site; brown/tawny hue, soft beige foam, average head retention; a good, sturdy, malty ale aroma that spotlights a red-fruit bouquet; very toasted on the palate with a backnote of buttered honey-wheat bread; the red fruit reemerges in the clean, mildly bitter-hoppy aftertaste; solid, firm, and very tasty, without being ponderous.

RATING ★ ★ ★　　*Recommended*

HEARTLAND BREWERY Cornhusker Lager

Sampled on-site; gold/harvest tone, white foam, no head retention to speak of; simple, roasted cereal nose, nothing more to address here; dry, crisp at entry, very cereally all throughout the palate; clean finish, which highlights grain and mild yellow fruit; medium-bodied, evident bitterness especially in the hoppy, yeasty aftertaste; okay, not a barn burner.

RATING ★ ★

HEARTLAND BREWERY Harvest Wheat Ale

Sampled on-site; pale, lemon-yellow/hay tone, typically cloudy, egg-white foam, average head retention; the nose was subdued, closed, even miserly on every nosing pass; the cardboard blandness of the wheat wasn't complemented by the malt component until the middle-of-the-road finish, whereupon a mildly charming harmony was achieved; although it was an unsophisticated and inconsistent sensory experience, I gave it two stars for the very nice, in-sync aftertaste, which was impressive.

RATING ★ ★

HEARTLAND BREWERY Farmer Jon's Oatmeal Stout

Sampled on-site; root-beer brown, though not opaque, tan foam, extended head retention; chocolate, black coffee, road tar, and malted milk balls all make an appearance in the aroma; unfortunately, this stout crumbles in the mouth as fiercely bitter, uncontrollably astringent, tarry, and smoky megaflavors make the experience devolve—it's a shame, because the bouquet had oodles of promise; the aftertaste is a mess, as this ale loses all sense of proportion and direction.

RATING ★

HELENBOCH Holiday Ale

Opaque brown hue, deep-beige foam, long head retention, good purity; the nose recalls Angostura bitters in a low-key way—there's spice (primarily nutmeg, secondarily cinnamon), deep-roasted malt, and a keen orange-bitters/orange-peel twang, especially in the later nosings—a decent seasonal bouquet; in the mouth, the taste reflects the fragrance like a mirror in that the spices balance well with the malt and orange—in the last two samplings, the orange peel becomes more pronounced in a positive fashion; well made.

RATING ★ ★ ★   *Recommended*

HEURICH'S Maerzen Lager

Very pretty orange/honey tone, light tan foam, extraordinary head retention; the aroma of this lovely-looking lager is a trifle tanky/metallic/steely just after the pour, then thankfully that problem blows away, leaving behind cardboardy, starched-shirt, even musty scents that dominate the second and third nosings—the last sniff finally shows some succulent grain and clean hops in copious amounts; on palate, it's meek and somewhat hollow at entry, offering only topical flavors of sap and maple—the midpalate supplies tastes of firm grain, butter cream, and candied nuts; the finish is quick and bitter; this beer was all over the map.

HEURICH BREWING COMPANY, WASHINGTON, DC / BREWED AND BOTTLED BY F. X. MATT, UTICA, NY

RATING ★ ★

HEURICH'S Foggy Bottom Ale

Nice bronze/honey color, beige foam, excellent head retention; the nose has the trademark upfront fruitiness of Utica, New York, contract brewer F. X. Matt—beneath the fruit, however, lies a steely, coin-like background odor that's a serious turn-off—by the third pass, the steeliness becomes a sweatiness that is anything but inviting—I wasn't compelled to perform a fourth nosing and, after I did, I was sorry, since the fustiness proceeded to worsen; in the mouth, it's paper-thin, offering no layers of flavor or texture— a dismal performer and atypical for this contract brewer.

RATING ★

Hudson Lager

Pleasant, medium amber/sunset-orange color, pearly foam, very good head retention; the nose displays some minor notes of sour cream, lightly toasted malt, and lemon meringue; on palate, it's so unbelievably sour from entry to finish that I find it undrinkable—there's a terrible flavor of old coins in the pathetic aftertaste; one of the worst domestic microbrew lagers I've tasted; truly dreadful.

WOODSTOCK BREWING COMPANY, KINGSTON, NY

RATING ★

I

Iron City Beer

Deep gold/honey color, frosty-white, solid, long-lasting head; the aroma simply doesn't want to show much of itself—rather lean, austere, and distant scents of gum, rubber, and clove don't endear themselves to me; on the palate, it's medium-bodied, mildly hoppy, but only a trace of malt is there to be found; the aftertaste has a nice balance of fruitiness and tartness, but that positive aspect alone without support from the nose and the midpalate taste is not worth a third star nor, hence, a recommendation.

PITTSBURGH BREWING, PITTSBURGH, PA

RATING ★ ★

J

Jack Daniel's 1866 Classic Amber Lager

Amber/honey/amontillado-sherry color, average head retention; the grainy bouquet charges ahead with generous, easily identifiable aromas of sweet corn, butter, yeast, and barley malt—this slam-dunk nose's finest asset is its upfront welcome; in the mouth, it's creamy and biscuity as gentle, rich flavors of barley malt, corn, and bread delight the palate; the finish highlights the grain and is medium-long; was available in 1995 only in selected markets around the country; it's a supple, opulent, and extremely well-crafted beer that deserves a national audience.

JACK DANIEL'S BREWERY, LYNCHBURG, TN, AND CINCINNATI, OH

RATING ★ ★ ★ ★   ***Highly Recommended***

JACK DANIEL'S 1866 Classic American Ale

Drop-dead-beautiful appearance, stunningly pure, dark-honey/amber/ new-copper-penny tone, beige foam, good head retention; the biscuity/ toasty nose is ripe with roasted malt and behaved hops in the first two passes—the third nosing introduces spice, cream, and caramel elements that are as seductive as they are rich; in the mouth, all the sensuous virtues enjoyed so much in the nose are present and accounted for—overlapping flavors of sweet malt, toffee/caramel, and soft, vegetal hops propel this corpulent ale into four-star territory; the finish is sweet-sour, refreshing, and luxuriously long; I can't decide if I prefer this homespun temptress or the Jack Daniel's Amber Lager—who cares, let's drink.

RATING ★ ★ ★ ★   *Highly Recommended*

JACK DANIEL'S 1866 Classic Pilsner

Textbook, golden-grain hue, silvery-white foam, strong, steady bubbles, extended head retention; the nose is quietly full and firm, emitting immensely pleasing aromas of broth, steamed white rice, cereal mash, and rich malt—it's a dazzling, well-endowed bouquet that's equally elegant and racy; on palate, the fullness acknowledged in the aroma continues as husk-like, cereally flavors disarm the taste buds in friendly waves of malt and reined-in hop tastes; the finish is tart, fleshy, and medium-long; the bouquet is this beer's meal ticket.

RATING ★ ★ ★   *Recommended*

JACK DANIEL'S Oak-Aged Winter Brew

Slow-brewed porter with cinnamon, nutmeg, and raspberry flavorings; gorgeous, mahogany/nut-brown color, extended, pillowy, beige foam, great purity; the nose addresses the red-fruit element immediately while not leaving out the malt—the spices come into play rather inharmoniously in the second and third passes—I just didn't think that the two spices worked well together, at least in the aroma; regrettably, the lack of component integration detected in the bouquet ran over into the flavor, where, even worse, the unripened raspberry plays against the cinnamon and nutmeg while the chocolatey malt gets lost in the brawl altogether—I found it unpleasant on palate, period; the first blank shot by the Jack Daniel's brewery.

RATING ★

JAMAICA BRAND Red Ale

Red it is indeed, with pillows of tan foam atop, infinite head retention; the beguiling nose is actually plummy right after the pour, then other ripe red fruits, strawberries in particular, get into the aromatic act—by the third nosing, traces of malt and caramel make their presence known; on palate, the fruit-salad taste highlights red apple at entry, then a brisk bitterness wipes away the fruit, leaving behind the malt by midpalate; the aftertaste features a tired hoppiness; it's a really intriguing, above-average brew that offers oodles of fun on the surface, but lacks genuine depth of character at the end of the day; a carefree, cavalier domestic—nothing wrong with that.

MAD RIVER BREWING COMPANY, BLUE LAKE, CA

RATING ★ ★ ★   *Recommended*

J.J. Wainwright's Evil Eye Raspberry Wheat

Very pretty, new-copper-penny color with none of the wheat turbidity that one expects to see, eggshell foam, short head retention, immaculate clarity; the nose speaks faintly of raspberry, with an elusive background scent of cracked wheat in the first two passes—the final two nosings reveal nothing new—while not unpleasant, the bouquet is flat, possessing not one iota of depth or dimension; in the mouth, it's refreshingly dry at entry, then it turns slightly metallic/tanky at midpalate, but not enough to be a complete turn-off—I kept looking for a hint of clove in the taste, clove being closely associated with wheat beer, but I never found it; I've had far worse beers that this, but the whispy thinness of it keeps it well below a recommendable rating.

WAINWRIGHT BREWING COMPANY, PITTSBURGH, PA

RATING ★ ★

J.J. Wainwright's Evil Eye Ale

Light bronze color, eggshell foam, superb head retention; the nose is a colossal zero in the first two passes—the third pass tosses out a small aromatic bone in the form of soft malt—the final nosing is a joke because there's nothing to grab onto; on palate, it's about as neutral, bland, and banal as it is in the bouquet—the midpalate offers a timid maltiness that has the backbone of a jellyfish; don't even consider it . . . unless you have a pet jellyfish that drinks beer.

RATING ★

J.J. Wainwright's Evil Eye Honey Brown Ale

Medium bronze/copper/honey hue, tan foam, very good head retention; the stingy nose emits only reticent, soft scents of marshmallow and wort in the first two passes—it's totally without charm and élan—the third nosing introduces a wan honey aroma that barely makes it from the glass; in the mouth, the sour-mash entry is followed by a decrepit maltiness that delivers about as much relief and refreshment as a limp breeze on a scorching July afternoon; gutless, charmless, mundane, and feeble; a waste of a good beer bottle.

RATING ★

J.J. Wainwright's Evil Eye Oktoberfest

Presents an attractive eyeful in the honey/amber hue, light-tan foam, average head retention, admirable purity; the bouquet gives very little of itself in the pass right after the pour—aeration and a bit of swirling reveal touches of soft malt and, regretfully, rubber pencil eraser—the final nosing finally sees a bit of deepening as the malt component takes hold—the question is, how many consumers are as patient as I am when it comes to sniffing a beer?; on palate, the malt flavor makes a game attempt at respectability, but there simply isn't enough depth to make a lasting, positive impression—as it is, the flavor borders on being neutral, which is one of the most insulting things that anyone could say about a beer labeled as "Oktoberfest"; take a pass.

RATING ★

J. J. WAINWRIGHT'S Black Jack Black & Tan

Beautiful, nut-brown/chestnut color, creamy tan foam, excellent head retention; as with the other lame J. J. Wainwright's, there is no bouquet to address, just a dull, humdrum, semisweet maltiness that tries steering a ship that's already run aground—don't these Pittsburgh brewers have senses of smell?; in the mouth, the boring, see-through, skin-and-bones flavor is sickly sweet and grainy—it lacks dimension, texture, and depth; they've got to be kidding—this lemon should be renamed "Slack and Thin."

RATING ★

JUAN PISTOLA'S Acapulco Gold Pale Ale

Tasted on-site; deep honey/gold hue, light tan foam, excellent head retention; the estery nose is an intriguing marriage of sweet malt and yellow fruit—banana and pineapple; on palate, it's clean, full-weighted, and nicely bitter as the hop element dominates, especially at midpalate—a genuinely refreshing ale that's clearly American in its bearing; the finish is long, only slightly malted, and stone-dry; to say I liked the nose is saying little; a delight, particularly with spicy Southwest cuisine.

BAJA BREWING COMPANY, SAN DIEGO, CA

RATING ★ ★ ★ ★   *Highly Recommended*

JUAN PISTOLA'S Baja Tan Brown Ale

Tasted on-site; pretty mahogany/chestnut tone, beige foam, very good head retention; the nose is keenly malty and roasted until the third pass, when some fresh, unroasted nut meat shows up; on palate, the roasted-malt component rose to the occasion in the form of a zesty burnt/charcoal taste that was damn near a molasses-like quality; the aftertaste was bitter/hoppy; I admired the silky texture more than anything.

RATING ★ ★ ★   *Recommended*

JUAN PISTOLA'S Sangria Ale

Tasted on-site; deep amber color, off-white foam, good head retention; served with a wedge of orange—it worked nicely; the nose is an interesting cross between estery ale and tropical fruit—it has a berry-preserve-like quality that's a virtue; I wasn't as impressed with the mouth presence as I was with the bouquet—mostly, it didn't fulfill the promise implied in the nose— even though it has a solid core flavor of malt, I didn't feel that it delivered fully on the sangria part; the finish is dry and a bit like citrus peel.

RATING ★ ★

JUAN PISTOLA'S Amber Ale

Tasted on-site; deep-amber/dark-honey hue, ivory foam, very good head retention; the nose is rich and cereally—the surface aroma is high-flying malt, while the backnotes include a hoppy bitterness that acts as a balance to the malt; where it seriously disappointed me was in the mouth presence, which was almost medicinal in a bitterly astringent way—this brewing problem badly worked against it—the bitter note was too heavily leaned on—this ale lost all sense of cereal/malt in the mouth; it collapsed on itself.

RATING ★

K

KATAHDIN Red Ale

One of America's most dazzling red ales, tawny/medium-amber/black-pekoe-tea color, quick effervescence, fair head retention, light tan foam; the nose showcases the hops more than the malt as a smoky/toasted bitterness sits in the lead car of the aroma parade—the nose doesn't expand much beyond that basic theme, however, as the richness of the malt becomes a major player only in the latter stages of the third nosing; exceedingly clean, keen, and refreshing on palate—the harmonious marriage of malt and hops makes for one terrific and satisfying taste experience; the aftertaste is nutty, smoky, roasted, and long; luscious and buxom.

CASCO BAY BREWING COMPANY, PORTLAND, ME

RATING ★ ★ ★ ★   *Highly Recommended*

KOCH's Golden Anniversary Beer

Medium straw tone, long head retention; the fragrant nose is simple, clean, malty, cereal-like, mainstream, and appreciably vigorous; on the palate, it's a stereotypical domestic golden lager, with but a tad more character than most of the other faceless lagers—it's dry to off-dry, crisp, and refreshing—things could be worse; it finishes with a mildly bitter note; okay, but a snore.

FRED KOCH BREWERY, ROCHESTER, NY

RATING ★ ★

L

LAKEFRONT BREWERY Riverwest Stein Beer Amber Lager

A stunning dark bronze/amber color with fetching core highlights (like honey), firm, light-tan head, very good purity; the bouquet is so voluptuous and rich in deep-roasted malt and cream soda aromas that I want to bathe in it—the second and third passes introduce a host of other wonderful scents, such as honey-wheat toast, nougat, chocolate raisins, and almonds—this is one of the fullest, most satisfying domestic beer aromas I've encountered in the past year—utterly sensational; on palate, everything that's so right about the bouquet becomes manifest for the amusement and decadent gratification of the taste buds—flavors of nuts, malt, and chocolate-flavored cereal are balanced perfectly by the judicious employment of hops; mark this down because you read it here first: This is the best amber lager made in the U.S. and one of the finest beers made in the Western Hemisphere; genius.

LAKEFRONT BREWERY, INC., MILWAUKEE, WI

RATING ★ ★ ★ ★ ★   *Highest Recommendation*

LAKEFRONT BREWERY Klisch Pilsner

Lush hay-like yellow/gold hue, white foam, quick head retention, perfect purity; the supple nose overflows with a comely wet-cereal scent, just like barley that's being steeped in water during the malting process—one of my ten favorite odors—buttered popcorn greets you in the second pass—the malty aromas just get more intense with every nosing; in the mouth, the hops finally come into play as their floral bitterness counters the fruity sweetness of the malt in what must be described as a dazzling midpalate taste experience; the finish is full, long, corn-like, malty, and totally satisfying; a killer of a domestic golden lager.

RATING ★ ★ ★ ★ ★   ***Highest Recommendation***

LAKEFRONT BREWERY Cream City Pale Ale

Radiant, medium bronze/honey color, off-white foam, medium head retention, excellent purity; the nose immediately betrays the trademark biscuity quality of Lakefront—the accent on the malt is so clearly defined that it's like taking a stroll through a malting house—deep, chewy, fully endowed aromas of sweet cereal, cocoa, grain husk, and Butterfinger candy bars; on palate, the hops enter the fray by offering a bitter edge to the plump maltiness that dominates the palate entry—a saltine-cracker quality comes on at midpalate, but the bitter edge continues to frame the taste phase of the experience; the aftertaste is lean, lanky, and properly bitter in the best tradition of the style; one of the premier pale ales in the business.

RATING ★ ★ ★ ★   ***Highly Recommended***

LAKEFRONT BREWERY ESB OCIA Certified Organic Ale

Rich clover-honey/medium-amber tint, white foam, long head retention, superb purity; this bouquet has fetching traces of lightly toasted malt, grain husk, cracked corn, and a vague touch of caramel in the first two passes, then with aeration deeper scents of keenly bitter hops (Pacific Northwest Cascade, maybe?) come alive in the later passes—a well-toned bouquet that's more stylish than the Klisch Pilsner or the Riverwest Stein Beer, even though I liked them both a tad more; the taste offers a whole panorama of flavors, including dry cereal, grainy bitterness, hop bitterness, and a dash of herbs in the background; it closes out the experience in a quiet way, slightly bitter, well-behaved, and delicious.

RATING ★ ★ ★ ★   ***Highly Recommended***

LAKEFRONT BREWERY Eastside Dark Lager

The appearance is of a handcrafted root beer—a deep, almost black, chestnut brown, beige foam, decent head retention, pure; the nose is laden with dark malt, coffee bean, vanilla bean, pumpernickel, malted milk balls, and paraffin—the bouquet, extraordinary in its power and poise (its strength doesn't overshadow the innate elegance) is roasted, toasty, decadent, and luscious; in the mouth, it's less grand than in the bouquet as leaner tastes of roasted malt and cocoa take up the banner at entry and keep it held high to midpalate, when a note of hops jumps in for fun; the finish is leaner still and a touch bitter; a dynamite dark lager.

RATING ★ ★ ★ ★   ***Highly Recommended***

Lakefront Brewery Holiday Spice Lager 1995

Ginger/new-copper-penny hue, white foam, good head retention, excellent purity; the snappy seasonal bouquet is nicely spiced (nutmeg in front) with bits of orange peel and marzipan aromas on top of a malty brew—this nose captures the aromas of the season better than any other holiday brew I've encountered—it's simply irresistibly charming; the fun, however, really shifts into passing gear on the palate as crisp, razor-edged tastes of cinnamon and nutmeg race ahead of the piquant orange peel—at midpalate, the sweet maltiness of the base comes into play without undercutting the spice/orange sideshow; it's only in the aftertaste that a lightening flash of honey makes an appearance; the premier domestic holiday brew, period.

RATING ★ ★ ★ ★   Highly Recommended

Lakefront Brewery Fuel Café Coffee-Flavored Stout

As dark brown as espresso, deep-beige foam, good head retention for the type, pure; the nose is more coffee-like than stout-like, as sharp, bitter aromas of coffee beans and tobacco smoke dominate the first nosing pass—the situation changes little over the next passes as the almost sour coffee element continues to lead the aroma parade—not my favorite bouquet of the Lakefronts; in strikingly similar fashion to the aroma, the flavor spotlight shines just about exclusively on the bitter coffee quality, leaving the stout element in the dust; drinkable, even though I'm not a coffee drinker, but this combination didn't work for me.

RATING ★ ★

Latrobe Bohemian Pilsner

Deep harvest-gold/honey-amber hue, fair head retention, good purity; the nose alone racks up two rating stars as fathomless, biscuity, buttermilk aromas thrill my sense of smell right from the first nosing pass—beneath the buttermilk-biscuit aroma lies a firm, deep-roasted barley malt foundation that supports the entire bouquet—the flowery Saaz hops top off this outstanding, meaty, and complex domestic-beer aroma; the flavor lives up to the aroma as rich, malty, hoppy tastes are complemented beautifully by the round, full texture (influence of the Briess Caramel malt?); the finish is slightly toasted and long; one of the best pilsener-style beers made outside of the Czech Republic.

LATROBE BREWING COMPANY, LATROBE, PA

RATING ★ ★ ★ ★   Highly Recommended

Latrobe Bavarian Black Lager

Black-coffee brown hue, long, tan head, great purity; the bouquet breaks from the gate in a strong scent of black bread, then it subsides in the second pass, emitting only subtle hints of deep-roasted malt—the third pass shows more life, especially in the malt department, as it becomes round, chocolatey, and deep-toasted—a decent dark-lager nose, but not as layered and complex as I'd hoped; shows lots of solid, cocoa, dark-malt flavors from entry through to the finish; not a ponderous, thick, dark lager at all, but a pleasing one nonetheless.

RATING ★ ★ ★   Recommended

Latrobe Pale Ale

Seriously attractive copper/bronze tint, excellent head retention, sand-colored foam, great purity; the nose turns shy after the initial hoppy burst, but with some persistence and aeration it bounces back in the third nosing with aromatic scents of dried plums, dried apricots, and a keen hoppiness (Cascade and Mt. Hood hops from the Pacific Northwest) that is delightfully bitter—it faded a bit too soon in the last pass; on palate, I enjoyed the medium body and crisp, dry-cereal, if slightly candied (hard candy), taste that really came into its own at midpalate; the finish is very clean, mildly hoppy, and a touch sweet, with a properly bitter tail end; a solidly made pale ale that would have garnered a fourth rating star if it had better follow-through in the aroma.

RATING ★ ★ ★   *Recommended*

Leinenkugel's Red Lager

Pretty deep-amber/tawny/dark-rust color, tan foam, very extended head retention; the generous, expansive, sweetish bouquet is all about chocolate malt, egg cream, candied almonds, and shelled nut meat—I found this bold bouquet to be a complete delight, and it reminded me more of a Scotch ale than a red ale primarily because of the heightened degree of roasted malt; on palate, it's not quite as dazzling as it is in the aroma, but, nevertheless, is round, chewy, heavily malted, and dry to off-dry by midpalate as the hop element comes more into focus; crisp, medium-long finish; the aroma promised so much that I think this beer found it difficult to fulfill all the hope.

JACOB LEINENKUGEL BREWING COMPANY, CHIPPEWA FALLS, WI (MILLER)

RATING ★ ★ ★   *Recommended*

Little Kings Cream Ale

Sports a lovely, 14-carat-gold/marigold hue, silver-white foam, quick head retention; the nose is quite malty and off-dry in the first two nosings—the final two passes reveal nothing beyond that; in the mouth, this one-note, simplistic ale is indeed creamy to the touch, but tastewise it offers little other than a rudimentary beer maltiness—there's nothing that stands out on this mouth presence—that's not to say that it isn't drinkable, because it most certainly is—it's just completely commonplace.

SCHOENLING BREWING COMPANY, CINCINNATI, OH

RATING ★ ★

Little Kings Bruin Pale Ale

Pretty bronze/orange color, light-tan foam, no head retention to speak of, pure; the nose shows some buttermilk biscuit, vanilla wafer, light caramel, sweet malt, and even a bit of cocoa—I liked the easy friendliness of this bouquet—uncomplicated and direct; unfortunately, what occurs on palate doesn't fulfill all the promise found in the bouquet as rather wan tastes of malt and hops float on top of a thin body—it's okay, average, but I felt let down by the taste/texture points; the fine appearance and sweet-cereal nose, however, should not go without reward, hence the two stars.

RATING ★ ★

Lone Star Lager

Medium amber color, firm, snowy head with low retention; this hapless nose has no character, personality, or individuality whatsoever—one of the least interesting bouquets in domestic beerdom; what little is found in the nose is mirrored in the feeble, appallingly skimpy, wet-cardboard-like flavor; how could a state as grand, diverse, and colorful as Texas have such a flat-tasting, totally boring, and charmless brew as its so-called National Beer? they should do a serious rethink; Texans like Willie Nelson deserve much better than this anemic no-brainer; this trashy stuff doesn't even deserve a lone star; Celis White, anyone?

G. HEILEMAN BREWING COMPANY, SAN ANTONIO, TX

RATING ★

Lowenbrau Special Pilsener

Big-bubbled, harvest-gold/lemon-yellow color, pure, splooshy, white foam, poor head retention; the off-dry nose features steamed white rice and ripe yellow fruit in the initial two passes, then the bouquet turns painfully meek and ordinary in the third nosing, ending up seriously dumb by the final pass; it's very clean, off-dry, but cardboardy and simplistic at palate entry—not much happening here in the way of profundity or nuance—it's straight-ahead, off-dry, mildly hoppy, and completely commonplace demeanor nominates it for a decent, warm-weather chugalug, but that's where the party ends.

MILLER BREWING COMPANY, MILWAUKEE, WI

RATING ★ ★

M

Magic Hat Irish Style Red Ale

This red owns a pretty cherry-cola/aged-tawny-port-like color, great purity, sand-colored foam, average head retention; the off-dry nose is enchanting as aromas of roasted malt, caramel corn, slightly burnt honey-wheat toast, and a trace of molasses come together beautifully throughout all four nosings—no noticeable diminishment in the last pass; all of the grace, suppleness, and impact enjoyed in the bouquet are present in the taste—there's a touch more of the roasted-grain/smokiness in the taste that deepens the flavor experience; the finish is round, toasty, and properly bitter/hoppy; clearly, the best offering from Magic Hat.

MAGIC HAT BREWING COMPANY, BURLINGTON, VT / BREWED AND BOTTLED BY

KENNEBUNKPORT BREWING COMPANY, PORTLAND, ME

RATING ▲ ▲ ▲ ▲   Highly Recommended

Magic Hat 9 Not Quite Pale Ale

Really gorgeous, copper/rust/medium-amber hue, perfect purity, off-white foam, fair head retention; the estery nose is ambrosial, featuring full-throttle scents of overripe apricots, pears, papaya, cantaloupe, and mango—I was stunned by the pervasive and intense fruit concentration that ruled uncontested from the first through the last nosing—charming, but slightly disconcerting; on palate, the fruit element is nowhere near as vigorous as in the nose—a pleasing balance between mashy fruit and hoppy tartness is struck by midpalate; the nose must be sniffed to be believed.

RATING ★ ★ ★   *Recommended*

MAGIC HAT Blind Faith IPA

Brilliant, deep-copper/sunset-orange hue, silver foam, pure, tired effervescence, fair head retention; the nose is dumb immediately after the pour— the second pass is equally shut down—by the third pass, meager scents of malt, wet cereal, and cocoa peek out from the back recesses of the aroma— the final nosing actually approaches normalcy; thankfully, it's more expressive in the mouth than it is in the bouquet as a keen bitterness reigns at entry and well into midpalate—unfortunately, there's nothing to balance or counter that bitterness—as a result, this IPA is off-kilter and deeply troubled; nexxxxt.

RATING ★

MANHATTAN Gold Lager

Lovely tawny/amber color, decent head retention; the soft maltiness in the restrained, shy aroma is pleasant; in the mouth, it shows razor-edged, straightforward, bone-dry, crisp flavors of malted barley and hops; beautifully balanced; really comes across well in the mouth after the vacant nose; because of its keen dryness, it provides one of the most thirst-quenching domestic-lager experiences around; very good brewing from any standpoint.

RATING ★ ★ ★   *Recommended*

McMAHON'S Irish Style Potato Ale

Good amber hue, off-white foam, very good head retention; there's not much happening in the aroma department other than some very timid waves of malt that barely make their way up out of the glass—all four nosings were identically bland and nondescript; on palate, this limp noodle is so boring and mundane that you want to curl up around the bottle and go to sleep—there's only a pallid taste of malt, backed by a sheepish hoppy bitterness; it's snore-city in the finish; zzzzzzzzzzzzzzzz.

MINNESOTA BREWING COMPANY, ST. PAUL, MN

RATING ★

McSORLEY'S Ale

Very pretty new-copper-penny/burnished-orange/medium-amber color, faint beige foam, little head retention; the nose says hello in expansive waves of sweet, overripe grapes, bubblegum, orange candy, and malt—it's a user-friendly nose that's neither complex nor elegant, but open and straightforward—it remains vivacious and expressive through all four nosing passes; it's pleasantly sweet, estery, and fruity on the palate, with simple backnote tastes of malt and mild hops; the aftertaste is citrusy and only slightly bitter; a more than decent, fundamentally sound pub ale that's unpretentious, likable, and agreeable; if you see it, buy it.

G. HEILEMAN BREWING COMPANY, LA CROSSE, WI

RATING ★ ★ ★   *Recommended*

Meister Brau Light

Golden color, mild, somewhat timid head; at least, this smells like beer, with a hoppy, yeasty, slightly sweet aroma; the painfully limp flavors of nuts and lime, however, don't deliver enough; too bad, it had something good going in the nose, but just couldn't bring it home in the mouth or the finish. 98 calories.

MILLER BREWING, MILWAUKEE, WI

RATING ★

Michael Shea's Black & Tan (Porter and Lager)

Beautiful mahogany/root-beer-brown tone, medium tan foam, good head retention; the nose is lively, fetching, and complex with multiple layers of rich dark chocolate, vanilla extract, maple syrup, orange-blossom honey, malted milk, and charbroiled barley malt—a veritable bouquet banquet; on the palate, it's medium- to full-bodied and intensely chocolatey as the roasted malt comes into full stride by midpalate—there's a good bit of hoppiness in the midpalate, also; the finish is heady, weighted but not awkward; while the taste did not present as much sensory intrigue or pleasure as the dynamite aroma, this is still a smashingly good pint—had the flavor kept up the momentum begun in the nose in terms of complexity and scope, it would have easily garnered a fourth star; it's awfully close.

SHEA'S BREWERY, ROCHESTER, NY

RATING ★★★ *Recommended*

Micheal Shea's Blonde Lager

Pure, corn-yellow/gold color, eggshell foam, very good head retention; this is a compelling, yeasty, doughy, grainy nose that's moderately deep and totally captivating—in the final nosing, there's even a passing whiff of white rice—all in all, it's a good, solid lager bouquet that fulfills every requirement; though it's marginally better in the nose than in the mouth, the mouth presence does provide ample true lager taste to take it over the recommendation hump—the interplay between the malt and hops is nicely pulled off; the aftertaste is full, dry to off-dry, and very estery.

RATING ★★★ *Recommended*

Michael Shea's Irish Amber Lager

Has the look of a pale ale—the bright, bronze/copper hue is really eye-catching and pure, ivory foam, decent head retention; not much happens in the aroma part of the program in the first two nosings, then with warming and aeration, a simple, estery/fruity aroma profile of malt and hops takes form by the last pass; the lightish texture makes it very approachable and quaffable; flavorwise, it's all straightforward hoppy bitterness and roasted grain—nothing profound or thought-provoking; the aftertaste is correct, clean, and almost austere; an amiable chug-a-lug and evening companion.

RATING ★★★ *Recommended*

Michelob Lager

Pale straw color, poor head retention; the nose is quite shy and subdued, but what little is there is devoted solely to fruity hops—beyond that, this lager is devoid of any aromatic complexity whatsoever—I say this in full acknowledgment that this was my beer of choice in the 1970s and early 1980s; on the palate, it's very creamy and velvety—actually the feel of it is very appealing; in the taste arena, though, I detect no layering, scant complexity, and only a mild, innocuous steamed-white-rice flavor that carries you into the off-dry aftertaste; I kept thinking that it would improve and show more character; as it is, it relies on its creaminess for the whole run; a decent chug-a-lug beer, but that's about it.

ANHEUSER-BUSCH, ST. LOUIS, MO

RATING ★ ★

MICHELOB Dry Lager

Pale-to-medium straw color, low head retention; the nose at first is slightly phenolic, meaning that it's medicinal, in this case kind of like Band-Aids, then after that blows off I detect some relatively good, off-dry nuttiness, spice, and an intense yeastiness that reminds me faintly of fino sherry; in the mouth, the steamed-white-rice quality found in Michelob original pops up again but without the malty creaminess—this version is definitely drier and more tart but not one iota more complex or interesting; the finish is fruity and mediocre; I'll concede that the nose here is more intriguing than its sibling, but beyond that, the rest of it is unexciting and nothing more than a moderately palatable slam-it-down beer.

RATING ★ ★

MICHELOB Amber Bock

Very attractive, medium tawny/brown color, tan foam, average head retention; the nose is peculiar in that it smells curiously like chicken soup—if you really inhale deeply three or four times, you pick up notes of carrots, celery, and egg noodles in broth—however, froth and broth don't mix—it's doubtless one of the two or three weirdest beer bouquets I've happened across; obviously, it was difficult for the taste to repair the damage that was already done by the oddball aroma, but this flavor doesn't even try—it's flat, minimalist, damn near neutral; the finish is, well, forget the whole thing; nifty label, though, for all of those superficial beer aficionados who like to look cool while they imbibe.

RATING ★

MICHELOB Light Lager

Pale yellow/gold, moderately firm, frothy head; the lemony nose is a bust, a lifeless mess that goes nowhere; the very smooth and mellow demeanor on palate is something of a shock—the lemon/citrus quality leeches over into the one-note flavor; the gutless aftertaste is not worth talking about; strange that by all rights it should exhibit more character than its supposedly inferior sibling, Bud Light, but such is not the case; it's not exactly that "light" either at a hefty 134 calories; maybe they should call it Michelob Kind O' Light.

RATING ★

MIDDLESEX Brown Ale

Deep, dark chocolate-brown color, little head retention; the nose is soft, mellow, and coy at first, but I get the feeling from it that there's a substantial presence lurking in the background—it's hardly a ripe or gregarious nose, yet it has a raw power; very pleasant on the tongue, this flavor is intensely malty, but stone-dry, with an exceedingly faint pulse of hoppy bitterness found in the farthest reaches of the midpalate taste; it's clean and medium-weighted; the third tasting pass revealed a chocolate-coffee flavor that added some depth and intrigue to the taste experience; sports a quick, quiet finish; nice beer.

MIDDLESEX BREWING COMPANY, BURLINGTON, MA

RATING ★ ★ ★   *Recommended*

MIDDLESEX Raspberry Wheat

Cloudy/milky, as you'd expect from a wheat beer, but amber in tone with a cherry tinge, better than average head retention; the light-footed nose is properly fruity, showing admirable restraint, leaving enough room for the grain element to peek through—I like this balanced bouquet very much even though I generally dislike fruit-infused beers; in the mouth, it's keenly refreshing, squeaky-clean, and only lightly fruited, as the wheat malt foundation is never overshadowed by the raspberry flavoring; the finish is nimble, ethereal, and clean.

RATING ★ ★ ★   *Recommended*

MIDDLESEX Porter

Inky brown/black tone, no head retention to speak of; the shy nose gives away little in the first pass, then the door cracks open in the second nosing, releasing meager scents of gum, molasses, and sugarcane; the entry flavor is surprisingly fruity, then it goes nutty and intensely smoky, mostly wood smoke by the midpalate; the flavor fades in the throat and one is left with loads of smoke in the off-kilter aftertaste; I didn't detect a great deal of depth underneath the sheets of smoke, which by the finish left little room for anything else; okay, but hardly recommendable.

RATING ★ ★

MILL CITY Oatmeal Stout

Jet-black/brown, opaque, deep-beige foam, short head retention, good purity; this hefty, alluring nose is all about black Colombian coffee, mocha, and wood smoke in the opening aromatic salvo—over time, the nose changes deliberately into more of a bittersweet-chocolate bouquet, make that top-quality Swiss or Belgian bittersweet chocolate, not chump-change, supermarket chocolate—a beauty of a bouquet that rivals the best domestic stout noses; in the mouth, the creamy, rich, medium-weighted texture underpins the toasty, smoky flavors of dark chocolate, molasses, brown sugar, and chocolate-covered coffee bean; the finish is thick and ropey; a lovely, well-mannered stout that exhibits as much finesse as power.

LOWELL BREWING COMPANY, LOWELL, MA

RATING ★ ★ ★ ★   *Highly Recommended*

MILLER Reserve 100% Barley Draft

Pleasant harvest-gold color, with billowy clouds of white foam that lasted till the cows came home; the off-dry, biscuity, granola-like aroma is simultaneously grainy, fruity, and sweet—not a powerhouse nose by any means, but solid and pleasing; the very smooth, correct, and satiny texture is the foundation for a highly malted, cereal-with-milk flavor that's one of the better big-volume brewery efforts of late; ripe, sweetish aftertaste; hey, not bad.

MILLER BREWING, MILWAUKEE, WI

RATING ★★★   *Recommended*

MILLER Reserve Velvet Stout

Midnight-black, opaque appearance, excellent head retention; not much in the way of aroma—even after three diligently approached nosings, there wasn't much to address other than a mild tarry, oatmeal scent; not too shabby in the taste department as soft, bitter flavors of black coffee, roasted grain, and tobacco tar come together nicely; the most obvious miscue is in the lightweight texture—one has to expect a stout, no matter domestic or imported, to at least carry some heft in the way of mouth-feel; hence this beer's name is a misnomer, because the texture is anything but velvety; to the good, however, it's a decent attempt by Miller Brewing to expand their heretofore narrow focus, and I see nothing wrong with that.

RATING ★★

MILLER Lite

Very pale straw color, moderately foamy head, no head retention; the embarrassingly bland, salty, tanky, almost nonexistent nose is a total loser; on palate, it's neutral, virtually devoid of taste; the finish is hard, tinny, mere skin and bones; this is a bad, but highly successful joke; just goes to show what clever ad copy can accomplish; no taste—even less filling.

RATING ★

MILLER Genuine Draft Cold-Filtered

Appealing golden/straw color, crowned by an admirably frothy head; the nose is dry and nutty, with just a faint hint of wheat; on palate, it's properly dry and owns a light- to medium-bodied texture; the trouble comes in the almost complete lack of flavor; the taste starts in a nutty way that at first blush is quite pleasant, then any semblance of flavor falls right off the table at mid-palate, finishing neutral; two beer-loving friends suggested I try this popular item from Miller, but I can't say that it impressed me at all after the flavor entry.

RATING ★

MILLER Genuine Draft Light

Golden color, firm, white, big-bubble head; the nose was completely closed off initially, then after ten minutes of aeration, it emitted a putrid, stinky, back-alley stench that was very offensive; slight flavor of grains, but zilch on any other flavors even remotely resembling real beer; they should rename this garbage "genuine daft" because anyone who buys this wounded duck must surely be certifiably crazy.

RATING ★

Miller Icehouse Ice Beer

Golden hay color, brilliant white froth, miserly head retention; the pleasant nose is of sweet grain, especially white corn, and mild hops, but beyond that there's precious little to grab hold of aromatically; in the mouth, it's dry, clean, and totally unremarkable—that's to say that even though there's a good drinkability to it, in terms of aroma–flavor dimension or profundity, it comes up woefully short; might be a decent chug-a-lug on a July scorcher when all you want is something cold and wet, but that's all there is in this beer's otherwise lackluster showing.

RATING ★

Moose Brown Ale

Pretty reddish/brown/chestnut color, off-white foam, average head retention; the nose is fruity, sweet, and malty—quite simple overall; on the palate, a hoppy bitterness takes charge as less impactful flavors of red fruit, malt, and Cheerios scramble for second place in the pecking order; the finish is lean, astringent, and long, reflecting the influence of the bitter hops; not bad, by any means, but it falls short of being recommendable because there's an overabundance of bitterness and a woeful lack of charm.

KENNEBUNKPORT BREWING COMPANY, KENNEBUNKPORT, ME

RATING ★ ★

Mystic Seaport Pale Ale

Alluring, sunset-orange/rust hue, light tan foam, quick head retention; on the first pass the nose is lovely and assertive as deep roasted-malt and sweet caramel notes greet the olfactory sense—after that initial burst, the bouquet settles down, emitting delicate, subtle backnotes of dry cereal, orange-tangerine peel, and orange blossom—it's a seductive, well-crafted bouquet; in the mouth, this balanced, medium-weighted ale is properly bitter and malty right from palate entry, then by midpalate the orange-tangerine nuance makes another appearance; the finish is lean, cleansing, and borders on being too bitter, but it regains its poise at the last moment.

KENNEBUNKPORT BREWING COMPANY, KENNEBUNKPORT, ME

RATING ★ ★ ★   *Recommended*

N

Naked Aspen Raspberry Wheat

Bronze/reddish-gold hue, fat bubbles kill the silver-white head in a hurry, clear no cloudiness, as is traditionally the case with wheat beers; the heavenly nose alone is worth a couple of rating stars—the true-to-the-fruit bouquet is of perfectly ripened raspberries—the light clove accent of the wheat is present, to be sure, but it doesn't impede the motion of the fruitiness—I thought the bouquet was harmonious, inviting, and, in a word, dynamite, when compared with other domestic raspberry wheats; the taste nimbly moves about the palate as the fresh-fruit flavor is balanced beautifully by the clove-wheat bitterness, providing a cleansing sensation that strikes the right chord; the aftertaste is neatly packaged and long, but not juicy or intensely fruity; this fruit-flavored wheat makes a great quaff in warm weather.

NAKED ASPEN BEER COMPANY, COLD SPRING, MN

RATING ★ ★ ★ ★   *Highly Recommended*

NAKED ASPEN Apricot Ale

Lovely, golden, apple-cider-like tint, white foam, good head retention, pure; the bouquet is very fruity (tutti-frutti?) and, to its credit, true-to-the-fruit source, yet I didn't find it as compelling as the Raspberry Wheat, for in this aroma the fruit so clearly dominates the landscape—although I liked it, I didn't find it balanced in any of the nosings; I preferred the flavor more than the bouquet because in the mouth there's the sense that this is really an ale, not a fruit drink—while apricot says "hello" at entry, a pleasing maltiness makes itself known at midpalate; the taste finishes with the apricot and the malt walking into the sunset side-by-side; this ale blossomed in the mouth.

RATING ★ ★ ★   *Recommended*

NAKED ASPEN Pale Ale

Now the question, can these people make a traditional ale?—answer: Not if they're being judged by this ale; the color is good and proper, a solid bronze, white foam, short head retention, seemingly pure; this bouquet has a lemony/sour-mash quality that surprised me, since that's inappropriate for the style—there's actually an out-of-place clove/spice quality that's more akin to wheat beers than to pale ales—but wait, is anybody there?; in the mouth, this ale completely unravels as sour-mash flavors take command of the taste buds and refuse to give them up—I didn't like this taste at all—it's as flat as a pancake and totally mundane and charmless; don't even think of trying it; pale ale, my foot.

RATING ★

NANTUCKET Island Amber

Strikingly pretty amber/copper-penny hue, silvery-white foam, poor head retention; I found myself wishing that the nose was as appealing as the appearance as I patiently waited for something of substance to emerge after the first three nosings—but, zippo—finally after it warmed up, a docile, yeasty, grainy, sugar-coated cereal aroma wafted up from the sampling glass; on the palate, it showed moderate charm as malty/bitter tastes formed the underlying structure of flavor, allowing for more decorative tastes of spice, red fruit, and hops to entertain the taste buds; the finish is quick and clean; middle-of-the-pack, nothing fancy or recommendable.

NANTUCKET BREWING COMPANY, UTICA, NY

RATING ★ ★

NARRANGANSETT Lager

Pretty golden color, with a firm, long-lasting head; the shy nose leans toward minerals and, alas, is slightly tanky and stale; leaving the dubious bouquet far behind, the taste rockets ahead in a full-bodied, nutty, malty, and slightly toasty way—I couldn't believe the difference between the dank, Milquetoast nose and the vivacious, clean, flavorful taste; it finishes smoothly with an appealing richness in the throat; your basic Jekyll and Hyde beer.

FALSTAFF BREWING, WINSTON-SALEM, NC

RATING ★★★ **Recommended**

NEPTUNE **Premium Ale**

Mildly cloudy, medium amber/bronze color, medium beige foam, good head retention; the intriguing aroma is quite fruity (red fruit, especially), and malty at the start, then it becomes even more intense on both accounts by the third pass—I liked the backnote scents of red plums and ripe nectarine—very good job aromatically; on palate, it owns good weight and texture—tastewise, it's keenly estery/fruity and sweetly malted—easy, undemanding drinking; the aftertaste is short-lived, but I didn't really care about that aspect because the midpalate presence was fulfilling enough; good show.

NEPTUNE BREWERY, NEW YORK, NY

RATING ★★★ **Recommended**

NEUWEILER **Stock Ale**

Exceptionally attractive, luminous, bright rust/copper-penny/vermilion color, crowned by a short-lived, off-white head; the intensely estery nose is damn-near ambrosial (though not like a lambic) as aromas of ripe red cherries, raspberries, and strawberries leap from the glass—there's hardly any evidence of malt or hops to speak of, just red fruit—I liked this upfront nose; finally, in the mouth, the first traces of beer components come into play as roasted malt and highly fruited hops dance gracefully together, especially at midpalate; the finish is pleasingly malty and hoppy; the bounteously fruity nose is supported well by the foundational malt and hops found in the taste and finish.

NEUWEILER BREWING, ALLENTOWN, PA

RATING ★★★ **Recommended**

NEUWEILER **Traditional Lager**

Handsome harvest-gold/amber-grain hue, pearl-white foam, quick head retention; the nose is seriously yeasty, malty, and uncomplicated, with a sweet-corn-like backnote—the initial burst of aroma settles down by the second pass, becoming softly estery—in the final two nosings I detect little except for a barely discernable malt foundation; this northeastern Pennsylvania lager has a velvety texture that I liked, but beyond a rudimentary maltiness in the palate entry and midpalate and a miserly trace of hops in the finish, this lager is destined only to be a fast-and-loose guzzle on a steamy, hazy-hot-humid July afternoon in Allentown; could be that that's all it was designed for.

RATING ★★

NEUWEILER **Porter**

Opaque, midnight-brown tone, beige foam, good head retention for a dark ale; the atypical nose is a peculiar mix of ripe red fruit, rubber pencil eraser, and bubblegum—for a dark ale it's unusual to emit virtually no evidence of deep roasted malt or dark bread in the bouquet—that's not to say I didn't like the bouquet, because I did—it just took me by surprise; in the mouth, it's semisweet, fruity (black fruit), and, at long last, malty—the mid-palate turns bizarrely sweet, yet neither fruity nor creamy; too far outside the customary porter standards to be recommended; while I somewhat liked the aroma, the flavor and aftertaste I thought to be ill-conceived.

RATING ★ ★

NEUWEILER Black & Tan

Absolutely beautiful chestnut-brown/tawny hue, with feeble head retention; the nose is meek, at best, and finally after several minutes of aeration begrudgingly gives up a faint wave of fruit-nut fragrance—gee, thanks so much; on the palate, it's clean but without much character or depth of flavor as the barely perceptible red-fruit/nut taste combination struggles to be noticed; no aftertaste to address; it's not unpleasant, just lackluster; in fact, after it warms, the flavor becomes significantly more pronounced, forcing me to raise the rating to two stars.

RATING ★ ★

NEW AMSTERDAM New York Amber

Tea/tawny/warm-amber color; the incredibly individualistic floral, garden, fresh-herbs nose is one of domestic beerdom's greatest pleasures; in the mouth, the satiny, feline, creamy texture glides down the throat while ultrasensuous flavors of vanilla, cream, and dried flowers gently wrap around the taste buds; it finishes like a champ—sure and effortless; stands head and shoulders above most other domestic ambers; one of the U.S.'s finest beers and a superb beer to have with a substantial meal.

NEW AMSTERDAM BREWING, NEW YORK, NY / BREWED AND BOTTLED BY F. X. MATT, UTICA, NY

RATING ★ ★ ★ ★   *Highly Recommended*

NEW AMSTERDAM New York Ale

Gorgeous, luminous tea-like color, standard cream-colored, moderately vigorous head; the fruity, evolved, malty, downright ambrosial nose grabbed my attention immediately and stayed concentrated through four nosings; the delicious tropical-fruit flavors mingle perfectly with the barley-malt underpinning; the sublime aftertaste is off-dry, fruity, and very satiny; a most satisfying, alluring, and refreshing homegrown beer; the well-defined, gentle fruit component sold me right from the start; yet another gem from this outstanding brewer; the heady, biscuity aroma alone is worth three stars.

RATING ★ ★ ★ ★   *Highly Recommended*

NEW AMSTERDAM Black & Tan

Dark amber tone, medium head retention; the savory, off-dry nose highlights the floral/estery presence of the New Amsterdam Amber, which is one of my favorite domestic beers, rather than the dark beer, resulting in a bouquet that is more delicate than pronounced, more violin than trumpet—only after the fourth nosing does some hint of maltiness come into the picture; in the mouth, the taste of smoke (from the dark element) and red fruit (from the amber component) merge harmoniously, lasting long into the mellow, slightly sour aftertaste; nice combination taken from an old theme of English brewers; New Amsterdam continues to offer interesting and tasty beers.

RATING ★ ★ ★   *Recommended*

New Amsterdam Winter Anniversary Dark Ale 1995–1996

Deep, opaque, black-coffee brown tone, deep beige foam, good head retention; I rated the 1994–1995 version three stars; the buxom, heavily roasted aromas of French-roast coffee beans, chickory, dark toffee, molasses, and charred malt leave a deep impression with the sense of smell—what comes to mind most is the similarity to black coffee, as the bitter aroma of burnt toast dominates the bouquet; on palate, the intense bitterness found in the nose is more contained, allowing for a dry, malty midpalate that's very savory; the aftertaste shows a touch of grainy sweetness beneath the concentrated coffee-like taste in the tail end; this hearty, porter-like ale satisfies in fine form.

RATING ★ ★ ★   *Recommended*

New Amsterdam Blonde Lager

Opulent, honey hue and beige foam, average head retention; this generous bouquet leaps from the glass as inviting aromas of yellow fruit (lemon and banana) and brewer's yeast are balanced by an atypical woodsy-earthy quality that I liked—most of all, I appreciated the upfront manner in which the bouquet approaches the drinker—there's no razzle-dazzle, no coyness; once in the mouth, however, I was less impressed, as the flavor turns steely and metallic by midpalate; the finish briefly returned to the fruitiness, but by then I felt disappointed; neither bad nor unpleasant, just an uneven, disjointed effort by one of my favorite brewers; sampled five times.

RATING ★ ★

New Amsterdam Light Amber

Pretty honey color, with a moderately firm, white head; carries the trademark New Amsterdam aroma of honey wheat, hops, and dried fruit that I've come to instantly recognize; feels firm, solid in the mouth, but what it excels in, in terms of texture (especially for a light beer), it lacks in flavor; while I just didn't respond to the lackluster flavor, I scored heavily in favor of the biscuity/cake-batter bouquet and the round, almost endowed texture; give it more oomph in the taste and it'd be one of the best lights around, until then, it's pleasant but average.

RATING ★ ★

New England Oatmeal Stout

Opaque, jet-black color, deep beige foam, surprisingly good head retention for a stout; I liked this off-dry nose quite a lot—the aromatic highlights are hot Quaker oats (sans Wilfred Brimley), deep roasted malt, black coffee, charred wheat toast, and molasses; in the mouth, the seared grain flavor was true to the style, but the ale lacked the textural depth and flavor dimension that would place it in the classic category—actually, at this stage, it's got a way to go before reaching that classification, but for a domestic attempt it's a very good effort; the finish is heady, intensely smoky, and malty; I look forward to sampling future bottlings to see if the brewer has revved up the character.

NEW ENGLAND BREWING COMPANY, NORWALK, CT

RATING ★ ★ ★   *Recommended*

NEW ENGLAND Atlantic Amber

Superb appearance, gorgeous, light-catching, tawny/medium-amber/ burnt-orange hue, limp effervescence, eggshell-colored foam, poor head retention; the lovely nose is deep into bread dough, rye, yeast, caramel, and a touch of ripe red plum—I adored this cookie-batter/doughy aroma from the pour to the final nosing; while I preferred the estery nose to the flavor, the taste does have its allure, as roasted/toasty grain and hoppy elements mingle with an odd green-vegetable/earthy quality; the aftertaste is correctly bitter, a bit smoky, and medium-long; solid brewing from coastal Connecticut.

RATING ★ ★ ★   *Recommended*

NEW ENGLAND Gold Stock Ale

Cloudy, orange/amber hue, good head retention; the lovely nose says oranges and tangerines by the bushel, even if this bouquet is short on overall depth and scope; on the tongue, a mild bitterness kicks off the taste part of the program at entry, then it gains some softness by midpalate, but it still exhibits far too little character; by its refreshing and clean demeanor, my guess is that the brewmaster tossed in more hops than were really necessary, thereby gutting the fruit element; it's an honest, quaffable ale with some charm—however, the bitterness rides this horse too far past the finish line to be considered recommendable.

RATING ★ ★

NEW YORK HARBOR Amber Ale

Very attractive copper/russet color, fast-dealing head; the coy nose needs too much coaxing, showing painfully faint hints of malt and earth; the intense toasty flavor is bone-dry, bitter, burnt, seed-like, and quite substantial—I liked the taste enormously but could discern no traces of fruit, sweetness, or hops; the aftertaste is like biting into a slice of burnt rye-bread toast; atypical, but utterly charming and intriguing nevertheless.

OLD WORLD BREWING, STATEN ISLAND, NY

RATING ★ ★ ★   *Recommended*

NEW YORK HARBOR Dark Ale

Opaque, black-coffee brown, dark tan foam, fair head retention; I had hoped for more octane in the nose—the initial two passes were more shut down than a steel trap—only after ten minutes did this ale begin to exhibit some aromatic stuffing as comely scents of dark rye bread, pumpernickel, and chocolate malt showed up for work; this ale is more impressive in the mouth than it is in the nasal cavity, as meaty, bread-dough-like, roasted-nut, and grain flavors entertain the palate through every pass; the finish finally displays a hop element; able brewing.

RATING ★ ★ ★   *Recommended*

NORTH COAST Ruedrick's Red Seal Ale

Pretty new-copper-penny/sunset-bronze color, eggshell foam, long head retention, perfect purity; the nose comes off being a tad too soapy in the first pass right out of the bottle, but then that blows off and what's left behind in the second and third nosings is a concentrated fruitiness that's pleasant in an uncomplicated way—very little in the depth department, but the care-free style is appealing; in the mouth, it's keenly bitter and dry at entry, then a sweet maltiness/fruitiness takes charge at midpalate; the refreshing after-taste highlights the hops, making for a sound, clean last impression; not pro-found, but a highly drinkable ale that would be a great companion for salsa and corn chips.

NORTH COAST BREWING COMPANY, MENDOCINO, CA

RATING ★ ★ ★   *Recommended*

NORTH COAST Blue Star Great American Wheat Beer

Harvest-gold/honey amber hue, not the least bit cloudy considering that it's a wheat; white foam, short head retention, very pure; the bouquet is spicy, sweet, and grainy in the pass right after the pour—beyond the initial aromatic rush, such as it is, there's little expansion or development in sub-sequent nosings; in the mouth, there's way too little in the way of flavor to grab onto—even though there's ample effervescence, it comes off as being flat—cardboard, grainy flavors is all that this wimpy brew can muster in terms of taste; weak-in-the-knees aftertaste; skip it.

RATING ★

NORTH COUNTRY Fat Bear Stout

Opaque bittersweet-chocolate brown color, massive, wet-sand-colored foam, very extended head retention, great purity; I kept detecting different aromatic nuances through my four nosing excursions, everything from burnt rubber to burnt matches to coffee with cream to walnut meat to chocolate raisins to cigar smoke—I was more intrigued by this chameleon of a bouquet than by the aromas of this brewery's other beers; in the mouth at entry, there's a creaminess that's born of the deep-roasted malt, then the taste turns bitter, like coffee, and markedly smoky at midpalate—I admired this changeover because it wasn't abrupt—it evolved and developed; the fin-ish is smoky, but not to the point of distraction; clearly, the pick of this litter.

NORTH COUNTRY BREWERY, SARATOGA SPRINGS, NY

RATING ★ ★ ★ ★   *Highly Recommended*

NORTH COUNTRY Whiteface Pale Ale

Luminous bronze/copper-penny color, blonde foam, good head reten-tion, very pure; the nose is toasty, malty, and fully endowed right from the first pass—the second run-through shows a bit of ripe yellow fruit, which I found enchanting, and unbaked bread dough—while I didn't necessarily feel that this aroma was deep, I liked it anyway, especially for its full, malty fruitiness; in the mouth, it's as clean as a whistle, with the hoppy bitterness leading the charge and the malt bringing up the rear; good, supple texture; the finish is satisfyingly bitter and refreshing; good brewing.

RATING ★ ★ ★   *Recommended*

NORTH COUNTRY Maple Amber Ale

Gorgeous harvest-gold/medium-amber hue, tan foam, good head retention, great purity; the bouquet smells like corrugated cardboard in the first pass—the subsequent two nosings can't shake the cardboard—I failed to pick up the maple component at all until the fourth nosing, when it, at last, blossomed—my final impression was brighter than my initial one on this bouquet, but I still wasn't nuts about it; in the mouth, the maple syrup gets in the way of the malt from entry through to the finish at least to my taste buds' way of thinking—I didn't dislike it as much as I wished for the maple to go away so that I could see what the ale was like on its own.

RATING ★★

NOR'WESTER Blacksmith Porter

Opaque, brown/black color, deep beige foam, extended head retention; out of the bottle, the nose is roasted to the point of being nearly as smoky as a rauchbier—the second and third passes only enhance the first impression by offering a very defined, cigarette-smoke aroma—in the final nosing, a distant, bitter cocoa/coffee-bean note is discerned and greatly liked—this bouquet is no syrupy-sweet, chocolatey fat man—it's twangily bitter and focused; in the mouth, the intensity of the deeply charred malt takes the flavor form of seared, dark bread toast and looseleaf tobacco—the complexity and bitterness continue on into the midpalate, where they take a welcome excursion into bittersweetness, like the best dark chocolate from Belgium or Switzerland; the finish is a shockingly harmonious event, as the bittersweet chocolate and tobacco join forces; a stunning achievement in domestic beer making.

WILLAMETTE VALLEY BREWING COMPANY, PORTLAND, OR

RATING ★★★★★   *Highest Recommendation*

NOR'WESTER Hefe Weizen

Nice and cloudy, damn near opaque, foggy yellow hue, pearly white foam, very extended head retention; the bouquet, right out of the bottle, is mashy sweet and very desirable—the second nosing introduces the assertive clove/lemon element, which is tucked inside a top layer aroma of sour cream—the third pass focuses more on the sour cream, while the last nosing merely confirms the previous highly favorable impressions; in the mouth, the absolutely sensational creaminess of texture makes it voluptuous to the sense of touch—tastewise, malty, citrusy, and spicy flavors are tightly woven together at entry—at midpalate, there's a bit of a slip when a steely backnote flavor almost undermines the otherwise splendid mouth presence; the finish is grainy, dry, and medium-short; gives Celis White, long America's greatest wheat beer, a serious run for the biscuit.

RATING ★★★★   *Highly Recommended*

NOR'WESTER Raspberry Weizen

Properly turbid, woolly orange/honey tone, eggshell foam, quick head retention; the delicious, appetizing bouquet starts out a little shaky and tanky in the first momentary stages right after the pour, but then it explodes into an ambrosial aroma that concentrates fully on raspberries and malted wheat—the last three passes serve only to bolster the initial pass sans the minor tankiness—a truly lovely, authentic bouquet; on palate, the raspberry component acts as the ideal complement to the malty wheat foundational flavor from entry through midpalate—a yin/yang relationship is struck between the two primary flavor elements; the aftertaste is compact, sweet-sour, and medium-long; a purposeful, well-crafted, fruit-flavored beer that deserves plenty of attention.

RATING ★★★★　*Highly Recommended*

NOR'WESTER Best Bitter Ale

Really pretty bronze/honey-gold color, light tan foam, fair head retention; the nose is a trifle mute in the first go-round, then it picks up the pace in the second nosing as the substantial hops measure becomes quite impactful—the third and fourth nosings feature delectable notes of bacon fat, malt, and crisp, dry hops; on palate, it's keenly bitter, but neither sharp-edged nor harsh, as there's more than ample malt/grain influence to balance the hops— the midpalate leans even to an off-dry stance because of the fullness of the sweet malt; the finish is stone-dry and admirably long.

RATING ★★★　*Recommended*

O

O'DOUL'S Premium Non-Alcoholic Brew

Has all the visual earmarkings of an American lager beer—sturdy golden hue topped off by a snowy head; toasty, aromatic, decent bouquet, really; clean on the palate, with wispy tastes of mild nut meat and dry cereal; as expected, light in body but hardly timid or frail; overall in view of the genre, I'd say that this citrusy, tart entry is at the upper end of the pack's middle segment; while still quite a distance behind Haake Beck, the prototypical N-A brew from Becks, far worse N-A brews have passed my lips; for you beer snobs that swear you'll never drink anything from Anheuser-Busch, this one may surprise you.

ANHEUSER-BUSCH, ST. LOUIS, MO

RATING ★★

OLD COLUMBIA Strauss Stout

Tasted on-site; opaque, midnight-black/nut-brown tone, beige foam, good head retention; the nose is lovely, as deep-roasted malt teams with black fruit, molasses, brown sugar, and spice in a glorious dark-ale extravaganza—I liked this bouquet right from the first whiff—a substantial, pumpernickel-like aroma that's a textbook example of the style; on palate, it exhibits genuine presence even though it's not viscous or soupy—the nimble texture is a huge plus—the tastes of smoked meat, cigar box, molasses, and heavily roasted malt are compelling and lovely.

KARL STRAUSS' OLD COLUMBIA BREWERY, SAN DIEGO, CA

RATING ★★★★　*Highly Recommended*

Old Columbia America's Finest Pilsener

Tasted on-site; pretty hay/straw-yellow/light-gold, pearly white foam, long head retention; the nose is mannered and lovely in a biscuity, grainy, vanilla-wafer, sweet way—it's persistent, strong, perfumy, and estery, with that fine vanilla accent; sweet to the taste, the flavor of ripe yellow fruit makes a splash with my taste buds—musclebound but sinewy, this pilsener is a gorgeous, understated lager that is one of a handful of domestic pilseners that approaches being profound.

RATING ★ ★ ★ ★   *Highly Recommended*

Old Columbia Karl Strauss' Amber Lager

Tasted on-site; honey tone, eggshell foam, decent head retention; displays a seriously attractive, bread dough, zesty, fruity bouquet that I liked immediately—the malt is evident and mildly sweet from the first to the last nosing; off-dry to sweet at entry, then it goes very malty at midpalate; good character, medium depth, and a dazzler of a bouquet.

RATING ★ ★ ★   *Recommended*

Old Columbia ESB Ale

Tasted on-site; medium amber/rust tone, off-white foam, decent head retention; the aroma is round, fruited, and atypical for the style in that I find an awful lot of sweet malt where I believe I should be finding intense hoppy bitterness and even some flowers; on palate, it's savory and fine-tasting, but I'm confused because it's the sweetest, plumpest Extra Special Bitter I've ever sampled—it doesn't fit my definition of the type, but I liked it regardless; a nice, biscuity ale that's more an amber than an ESB.

RATING ★ ★ ★   *Recommended*

Old Columbia First National Bock

Tasted on-site; really gorgeous, deep copper/rust/burnished-orange color, tan foam, very good head retention; either my sense of smell has stopped working, or this bouquet is as docile as a lamb—the sole echo that I pick up is an elusive roasted-malt aroma way in the background; in the mouth, I like the texture and feel, but I don't favorably respond to the overly toasted-bread taste that leans far more to the bitter than to the sweet; okay, but totally lackluster and middle-of-the-road.

RATING ★ ★

Old Columbia Ed's Hoppy Birthday Pilsener

Tasted on-site; the appearance is much paler than the splendid America's Finest Pilsener (AFP)—steely/white-corn hue, white foam, fair head retention; the nose is more bitter than the AFP but far less attractive—I really preferred the seductive, sweet, doughy bouquet of the AFP; on palate, this has marked snap and hoppy bitterness—the vegetal/hop element makes this pilsener more complex than the AFP, but oddly nowhere near as enjoyable; the hollowness in the flavor makes it average, at best.

RATING ★ ★

OLD COLUMBIA Karl's Cream Ale

Tasted on-site; straw-yellow/light-honey/gold color, off-white foam, good head retention; the nose is doughy and hoppy, but I missed the cream completely; I found the mouth presence dull and unexciting, no profundity, no charm whatsoever; the thin, watery texture makes me wonder where they get off calling this flyweight a cream ale.

RATING ★

OLD COLUMBIA Karl Strauss' Light Lager

Tasted on-site; very pale gold hue, silvery-white foam, good head retention; the nose offers a touch of dry cereal, especially Wheaties, in all four nosings—it's not a bad lager aroma; where it crumbles is in the taste, which is cardboardy and fabric-like, almost synthetic; in the mouth it went down the tubes faster than a greased Eskimo Pie on an iceberg.

RATING ★

OLD PECONIC Hampton Ale

Gorgeous tawny/amber color, topped by a billowy head of foam; aromawise, it speaks of malted barley, Hershey's milk chocolate, tea, and a touch of sweetened coconut; light- to medium-bodied; on the palate, it's bitter, resiny, and moderately toasty; the finish is bitter and long; I would have given it a fourth star had it been more generous to the touch and taste; the promising bouquet was let down slightly by the taste; overall, I enjoyed the experience; clearly, these intrepid Long Islanders are on the right track; worth keeping an eye on. (Available only on Long Island, New York.)

OLD PECONIC BREWING, SHELTER ISLAND, NY

RATING ★ ★ ★ **Recommended**

OLD SMUGGLER Pale Ale

Lovely, bronze tone, beige foam, long head retention; the nose is inviting, warm, and biscuity as mildly bitter waves of hops complement the underlying maltiness—a very sound, confident aroma from the first nosing through the last; on palate, the hoppy bitterness eclipses the malt right from entry—the midpalate is nicely bitter, even a tad nutty; the aftertaste leans to the hops more than to the malt, but that's fine; this well-crafted ale fits the pale-ale style profile very competently.

COOPERSTOWN BREWING COMPANY, MILFORD, NY

RATING ★ ★ ★ **Recommended**

OLD THUMPER Extra Special Ale

Gorgeous, luminous copper color quite like an amontillado sherry, below-average head retention; the sensationally voluptuous, atypical, woodsy, and generous bouquet emits seductive fragrances of sauteed Portobella mushrooms, key lime, nut meat, and paraffin, with nary a hint of grain, yeast, or hops—I admired the nose right from the first nosing pass; on the palate, it's whistle-clean, crisp, medium-weighted, brisk, and jammed with flavors from wood smoke at the entry to cedar/pine and malt at midpalate; the aftertaste is moderately bitter, hoppy, ultraclean, long, and absolutely a winner; deserves every rating star it received; a smashing beer.

KENNEBUNKPORT BREWING COMPANY, KENNEBUNKPORT, ME

RATING ★ ★ ★ ★   **Highly Recommended**

OREGON Nut Brown Ale

Eye-popping lovely, deep garnet/rich earthy brown/Pedro Ximenez sherry hue, little foam, thus no head retention; the shyness of the aroma somewhat irritated me during the first three arduous nosing passes—by the fourth pass I decided to pack it in because this ale was simply not going to crack aromatically; what it lacked in aroma it more than made up for in taste, as deep, heavily roasted malt and bittersweet-chocolate flavors spearheaded the taste effort with grace and aplomb—this is no burly, sock-in-the-chops ale, but a quietly potent beer that doesn't need to hammer you in order to get its point across; after twenty minutes out of the bottle the nose at last blossomed, offering succulent scents of licorice, molasses, and honey wheat; bravo and a fourth star.

OREGON ALE AND BREWING COMPANY, PORTLAND, OR

RATING ★ ★ ★ ★   **Highly Recommended**

OREGON Honey Red

Really attractive red/brown color, pink/tan foam, very good head retention; in keeping with the dubious house style, the aroma is deaf and dumb on the first and second passes, then it blossoms in the third pass in the form of comely aromas of honey-wheat bread, red cherries, deep-roasted malt, and a trace of hops—not a staggeringly good bouquet, but serviceable; the sweet, cereally richness of the roasted malt comes keenly into play in the toasty, supple flavor, which is robed in a medium-bodied texture; the finish is properly bitter and clean; hardly America's flagship red ale, but a better than average effort all the same.

RATING ★ ★ ★   **Recommended**

OREGON ESB

Lovely, burnished/bay-brown color, tan foam, excellent head retention; the coy nose offers itty-bitty scents of medium-roasted malt, walnuts, and hops—like the other beers of this Portland brewery, the aroma is timid and distant even after ten minutes of aeration and three thorough nosings—at last, in the final nosing a very charming, deep-roasted maltiness emerges—thank you, thank you, thank you so much for sharing; on the palate, the nutty, hoppy taste offers only moderate depth, especially at midpalate, when you want something to grip onto; the finish is crisp, acceptably bitter, and troublingly steely; a mediocre bitter-style ale that hugs the center stripe of the road the whole way; somebody should cut this ale loose from the restraints.

RATING ★ ★

OREGON Hefeweizen

Shows the expected and proper turbidity in the Sunday-dinner-biscuit gold/medium-amber color, the silvery foam has below-average staying power; the aroma is closed off completely in the first two passes—I re-poured, only to have the identical vapid experience—finally, in the third pass, faint hints of dry cereal grain peek through—it's difficult to evaluate a vacuum; the taste is mildly pleasing, but gives away little in the way of depth or scope—I found the sore lack of sensory character to be perplexing and off-putting; one of the more vague, shallow, and insipid domestic beers I've encountered.

RATING ★

OREGON IPA

Textbook deep-amber/tea/clover-honey tone, putty-white foam, quick head; the intensely fruity/estery nose is ripe and even ambrosial as high-flying scents of plums, tea leaves, hops, and minerals intrigue the olfactory sense; the almost neutral palate entry is immediately followed by an unpleasant astringency that made the inner walls of my mouth feel like they had been painted with lead—the horribly acidic/tannic/metallic flavor is diametrically opposed to the message sent out by the aroma; this frightful beer is so out of sync that it squeaks; a disaster once it goes into the mouth; maybe Bigfoot has been tampering with the malt and hops at Oregon Ale and Brewing.

RATING ★

OREGON Raspberry Wheat

Cloudy, medium amber/orange/honey hue, white foam, decent head retention; the nose is alive with the semi-inviting aroma of raspberries, not freshly picked, mind you, more like frozen—the aroma has a "manufactured" bearing; on the palate, I found the taste to have an underpinning flavor of metal and seeds—a barely ripe raspberry surface layer of flavor mingled with a kernel-like, astringent graininess that left a tanky/steely aftertaste that busted this crummy beer from a mediocre two stars down to a dismal score of one star; this is simply a lousy beer that resembles a wheat about as much as I resemble Barbra Streisand.

RATING ★

OXFORD Raspberry Wheat Ale

Extraordinarily pretty, brilliant, luminous, copper/rust color, silvery-white foam, average head retention; the nose is a major-league blockbuster that thrusts red raspberry in your face in the first pass and hardly relents in the second and third nosings—the final pass allows an astringent wheat aroma to come through that complements the ripe fruitiness of the raspberry; in the mouth, it's far more tart than sweet, more acidic than fat—in fact, a coin-like, metal flavor rears its head at midpalate, which temporarily undercuts the gains made in the dazzling bouquet—third and fourth samplings see the metal disappear, returning this wheat to its previous splendor; very nice, but uneven.

OXFORD BREWING COMPANY, LINTHICUM, MD / DUBUQUE, IA

RATING ★★★ **Recommended**

OXFORD Class Amber Ale

A lovely, garnet/tawny-port hue, medium beige foam, good head retention; there's little to deal with aromatically in the first two passes, then in the third nosing a dash of roasted malt peeks out, but that's about it—the last nosing is a waste of time; in the mouth, just like the bouquet, you have to fight, scrape, scratch, and cajole any flavor loose—Oxford Amber seems okay on the tongue, but it's so reticent, it's difficult to discern any definable flavors; the finish is, well, dull and featureless; a phantom ale.

RATING ★

P

PERRY'S Majestic Lager

Brilliantly luminous new-copper-penny color, off-white foam, extended head retention, less than impeccable purity, as heaps of sizeable sediment are spotted; the nose is completely shut down in the first two passes—by that, I mean zero aroma—at last in the third pass, a meager hint of malt emerges; I can't say that I wanted to take a sip with all the goop floating around, but I did—the taste is barely more expressive than the bouquet—a muted, one-dimensional, meek, bordering-on-neutral flavor of malt is all that's detectable; the finish is nonexistent; a waste of good brown bottle glass.

FRANKENMUTH BREWERY, INC., FRANKENMUTH, MI

RATING ★

PETE'S Gold Coast Lager

Beautiful walnut/amontillado-sherry/amber color, with an off-white crown of foam; owns a perfumy, floral, peach, apricot, fresh-garden nose that's endlessly charming—one of the best domestic-beer bouquets; the succulent, ripe, fruited flavors on the tongue provide one of the more satisfying domestic beer experiences around—there's absolutely no trace of bitterness amid the luscious layers of malty fruit; silky, sexy finish that's full, nutty, and fruity; well done, mates.

PETE'S BREWING COMPANY, ST. PAUL, MN

RATING ★★★★   *Highly Recommended*

PETE'S Wicked Lager

Very attractive light-amber/honey color, topped by a cream-colored foam; the nose is sedate, even shy; but in the mouth, this roasted, toasty lager is medium- to full-bodied and satiny in texture and exhibits a round, fruity middle that develops into a long, off-dry to semisweet, mellow, and hoppy aftertaste that's simply smashing; this stylish, classy, well-crafted beer holds its own with America's best lagers.

RATING ★★★   *Recommended*

PETE'S Wicked Winter Brew

Flavored with raspberry and nutmeg; copper/orange/rust color, average head retention; the pleasing bouquet deftly exposes the raspberry flavoring in the first nosing—thankfully, a subtle hand was exercised in the flavoring, as the hint of raspberry in the nose is quite charming; in the mouth, the graininess of the beer mingles comfortably with the nutmeg and rasp-berry flavor enhancements; disappointingly, it finishes meekly on a fruit/berry note; a nicely made but ultimately unexciting beer that in the hands of a less skillful brewer could have lost the delicate balance between the fruit, spice, and grain.

RATING ★ ★

PETE'S Wicked Honey Wheat

Lovely, cloudy (the expected and typical appearance for a chilled wheat beer), vermilion/rust color, extralong head retention; the fruity, dry to off-dry nose has an exciting rush of assertive aroma at the front end, then rapidly goes tame by the second nosing, virtually neutral by the third pass, then mysteriously returns to a dried-fruit posture after five minutes—I can't help but wonder, why the up-and-down routine in the nose?; it's got a pleasant, velvety mouth presence, with very clean, tart flavors of lime, Wheaties, and white corn dominating—I must have missed something, be-cause neither of the two bottles that I sampled exhibited any honey element whatsoever—wheat, yes, honey, no; I was expecting something else . . . like a beer resembling what the label states; that aside, it's decent, nothing more.

RATING ★ ★

PETE'S Wicked Red Amber Ale

One of the reddest beers I've ever evaluated—a brilliant deep-orange/burnished-red/russet color, low head retention; the nose is restrained and rather stingy as red fruit and mild spice scents barely make it out of the sam-pling glass—I resent coy bouquets like this one; in the mouth, I find this amber to be pleasant but one-dimensional in flavor, as a monotone bit-ter/steely/minerally taste stands alone, with no traces of grain or fruit; it fin-ishes cleanly, but in that slaty, astringent manner; it's all right, but lacks the definition and depth required to be recommended; this beer plays it too safe.

RATING ★ ★

PIG'S EYE Pilsener

Attractive, harvest-gold hue, scant head retention; the soft, nuanced bou-quet is properly hoppy, minty, and malty, but uninspiring overall; in the mouth, this zesty beer comes alive in a biscuity, malty, rich flavor that has accents of lemon/citrus; the finish is opulent, long, and very creamy; it's a sturdy, well-made pilsener that goes a long way to please.

MINNESOTA BREWING COMPANY, ST. PAUL, MN

RATING ★ ★ ★   *Recommended*

PIG'S EYE Red Amber Ale

Terrific appearance—sunset-bronze hue, off-white foam, short head re-tention, perfect purity; the nose offers a round, biscuity opening right after the pour, which remains solid through the third pass—the cookie batter/bis-cuitiness is the result of the roasted malt—mild dashes of light caramel, tof-fee, and cocoa make themselves known in the last two nosings—I liked this supple, malty bouquet quite a lot; the taste shows moderate depth as the malt drives the flavor engine from entry to finish—the bouquet is better than the taste, but the taste certainly scores some points on its own, especially at the toasty midpalate; firm, bitter aftertaste; simply a good amber ale.

RATING ★★★   *Recommended*

Pike Place Pale Ale

Light-to-medium amber/bronze hue, eggshell-white foam, excellent head retention; the nose is a bit too tanky, metallic, and old-coin-like for me, but a good number of people, including some of my peers, swear by it—even after at least six separate samplings both in my office and on the road, I find this bouquet unappetizing; the flinty, steely taste is a mirror image of the annoying coin-like aroma—in more recent samplings, I've grown somewhat accustomed to the metallic quality and have found it more approachable; the hoppy aftertaste is properly bitter and my favorite aspect; upgraded to average on the two most recent blind tastings.

PIKE PLACE BREWERY, SEATTLE, WA

RATING ★★

Pink Triangle Light Beer

Very pretty harvest-gold/yellow color, medium-long head retention; the mildly interesting bouquet is more malty than hoppy and offers a mild, dry-cereal aroma that's quite pleasant; tastewise, the flavors are of malt and a touch of nuttiness and even saltiness; the finish is clean, lean, and one-dimensional, but not in the least offensive; while not a bad light beer when compared to most others in the marketplace, it still owns that familiar metallic light-beer taste.

PINK TRIANGLE BREWING, DUBUQUE, IA

RATING ★★

Pyramid Best Brown Ale

Pleasant appearance of tawny port/sunset orange, with a firm, beige head that's medium-long; the soft, plump bouquet offers compelling aromas of honey, sweet malt, cola, and a low-key, distant note of vanilla; in the mouth, there's a touch of bitterness at entry, then the taste/texture combination goes pillowy and clean; the vanilla factor reappears in the medium-length aftertaste; even though this beer's presence on the palate wasn't up to what was promised in the nose, the aromatics of it alone are worth the recommendation; give this ale more stuffing in the flavor and it's a potential four-star ale.

HART BREWING COMPANY, KALAMA, WA

RATING ★★★   *Recommended*

R

Rattlesnake Lager

Very pale hay/straw color; the nose is correct, nicely balanced, beery, yeasty, and citrusy; the dry, nutty flavors give way to an oddly sour finish that disappoints and adversely affects what would otherwise be considered a finely brewed, crisp, and tasty, if banal, beer; too bad; tasted twice with the same result.

KERSHENSTINE'S DIAMOND BEER, LA

RATING ★

RED BARON Cherry-Flavored Beer

Lambent rose color, quick head; the pleasant, malty, maraschino-cherry nose offers a moderate amount of depth, though I wouldn't consider it layered; in the mouth, the medium-sweet, ambrosial, red-cherry-juice flavor dominates the malt, hops, and yeast elements to a point at which I wish it would tone it down a bit to let some of the other components express themselves; it finishes too tutti-frutti, too cherry cola for my taste; I didn't find it offensive as much as it seemed overbearing in the fruit addition.

RED BARON BEER COMPANY, WILKES-BARRE, PA

RATING ★ ★

RED BONE Red Lager

More a teak brown than a red to my eye, but pure—off-white foam, good head retention; the nose doesn't give any indication of anything other than the neutral type of blandness brought about by mass brewing—there's nothing to grip, no sense of aromatic direction or depth; in the mouth, it's off-dry, mildly hopped, and moderately malty—the midpalate isn't bad, as the grain offers some substance in a semisweet fashion; quaffable, but banal, rudimentary, and middle-of-the-pack, but better than the other woeful red bow-wows, like Red Dog and Red Wolf.

RATING ★ ★

RED DOG

Golden hay/yellow color, white foam, scant head retention (they call this stuff red? uh-huh, how many fingers?); the tanky bouquet offers marginal, insipid, grainy/yeasty/doughy aromas, but the nose as a whole entity and experience brings new meaning to the term "simplistic"; ditto with the facile, sweetish, almost plump flavor and texture, each of which does nothing to undo the massive damage caused by the misnamed appearance and dead-on-arrival bouquet; this beer's unintentionally hilarious motto is, "There's only one Red Dog"—all I can say is, Thank you for not reproducing.

MILLER BREWING COMPANY, MILWAUKEE, WI

RATING ★

RED FEATHER Pale Ale

Turbid but appealing dusty-red/copper hue, little head retention; the nose is a fruity/malty feast that's assertive and generous without being aggressive or tutti-frutti; on the palate, a hoppy bitterness is introduced to perfectly balance the red-fruit component; after enjoying the rollicking bouquet and taste, the aftertaste disappointingly falls a bit flat; but I still found enough virtue in the appearance, nose, and flavor to recommend it.

ARROWHEAD BREWING COMPANY, CHAMBERSBURG, PA

RATING ★ ★ ★   **Recommended**

Red Hook ESB Bitter Ale

Prototypical, bronze/copper/orange bitter hue, ideal clarity, persistent effervescence/small bubbles, good head retention; the nose, to my surprise, is mute and unimpressive in the initial two passes, then in the third nosing distant images of off-dry malt and hops start emerging—with aeration and time, the final pass proved to be the best, as a genuinely lovely sweet-malt/toffee bouquet develops—be patient, the bouquet is worth the wait; it's predictably bitter and cleansing on palate, especially at entry, showing an intriguing nutty element that complements the dense layers of hops; the aftertaste is whistle-clean and mouth-puckering, with wholly appropriate flinty/slate-like bitterness; a top domestic ESB, this beauty delivers the goods.

RED HOOK ALE BREWING, SEATTLE, WA

RATING ★ ★ ★ ★   *Highly Recommended*

Red Hook Blackhook Porter

Almost opaque, nut-brown/black-coffee color, tan foam, poor to fair head retention; the nose is intensely smoky right after the pour—the second pass adds captivating aromatic twists of brine, wood chips, resin, and oak—the third and fourth passes highlight off-dry, deeply charred malt and coffee-bean scents; in the mouth, the creaminess lends weight and texture to the smoky, roasted-malt flavor that peaks at midpalate, then subsides in the off-dry, moderately bitter aftertaste; a finely tuned domestic porter that relies more on balance and finesse than potency and grit; truly luscious and deserving of four stars.

RATING ★ ★ ★ ★   *Highly Recommended*

Red Hook Ballard Bitter India Pale Ale

Good, coppery, traditional bitter appearance, tan foam, good head retention; the nose emits pleasant, nuanced aromas of dry cereal, sweet, ripe, yellow fruit (pineapple, banana), and even a faint trace of raisins—I fancied this understated bouquet; in the mouth, this savory, sweetish IPA does its best work when the correctly bitter, but nicely textured, flavors of malt, hops, and yellow fruit converge at midpalate in an impressive display of harmony; the aftertaste is fast, austere, and hoppy; a good, thirst-busting brew for a hot day or a spicy meal.

RATING ★ ★ ★   *Recommended*

Red Hook Rye Ale

Unfiltered; solid, harvest-gold/honey color, mildly foggy, white foam, short head retention, good purity; the nose distantly resembles rye bread, while upfront it emits soft odors of cracked cereal grain and dried herbs—in later passes, the rye influence emerges with more gusto as the ale aerates—what I particularly admired was the doughy dryness of the bouquet; on palate, the dryness continues not as bitterness brought on by hops, but as lack of sweetness in the grain—I found it round and firm on the tongue; another case of the aroma out-pointing the taste, but the overall package shines brightly enough for a hearty recommendation; these people simply know what it takes to produce highly palatable beers, period.

RATING ★ ★ ★   *Recommended*

Red Hook Wheat Hook Ale

Solid, harvest-gold/marigold color, robust effervescence, absolutely no turbidity, as you'd expect from a wheat beer, silver-white foam, average head retention; the tart nose is alive with the millhouse scent of dry cereal and banana—by the third pass, the barley-malt element comes on the scene—for a wheat beer, the malt is atypically pronounced in the aroma; the palate entry is whistle-clean and bone-dry—the dry-cereal flavor headlines the midpalate, along with acceptably steely/metallic/cornhusk tastes in the background; the finish is clean, fast, and uneventful; good and very drinkable, but a wheat beer that bears very little resemblance to the wheat-beer profile in appearance, aroma, and taste.

RATING ★ ★ ★　　*Recommended*

Red Tail Ale

The attractive rust-colored appearance is littered with the worst case of unsightly sediment I've ever seen in any beer, imported or domestic—the grayish-tan particles of various sizes (some are chunks) resemble an asteroid belt floating through space—this is the filthiest beer I've ever come across; the smell is of old, shriveled fruit (apricots, mainly) and sheet metal; I refused to put this garbage into my mouth; while it certainly could have been a bad bottle (at least I hope it was), be alert and closely examine any bottled beer from this brewer—from what I could make out about the dating, it was within the bounds of freshness.

MENDOCINO BREWING COMPANY, HOPLAND, CA

RATING ★

Red Wolf Lager

Brown/rust tone, beige foam, long head retention; the bouquet is intensely grainy, malty, and mashy in the initial nosing, then it turns down the volume by the second nosing, where corn husk and honey aim to please—I've smelled far worse lagers than this puppy; the Montana-sized letdown comes in the sweetish, run-of-the-American-Lager-mill, cereal flavor and texture that each exhibit as much character and distinction as Kato Kaelin; it limps across the finish line virtually devoid of any flavor or aftertaste; what started out fairly respectable crumbled at palate entry; don't waste your time or your greenbacks on this bow-wow; should be renamed Red Mouse.

ANHEUSER-BUSCH, ST. LOUIS, MO

RATING ★

Rheingold Light

Pale golden hue, wimpy head that vanished in an instant; pleasant, sweetish, heavily malted fragrance, which has more guts than many other Light beers in the marketplace—the uptown nose is a huge plus; on the palate, it's simple, decent, with a pronounced hoppy/floral flavor; as Lights go, quite good; the downside is that at 110 calories this baby ain't so light.

G. HEILEMAN BREWING, LACROSSE, WI

RATING ★ ★

Rhino Chasers Dark Lager

Another drop-dead looker from the Rhino brewmaster—the deep chestnut/tawny/reddish brown color is crowned by a bounteous foam for an extended period—truly gorgeous; the toasty, roasted-grain, dark-cereal bouquet needs a wee bit of coaxing, but once loose and on the prowl it's hearty, full, and malty-sweet—a granite-solid aroma that reeks of dark bread dough; on palate, its full-weighted, velvety, indeed creamy texture is a sure-fire winner; flavorwise, scrumptious tastes of smoke, hoppy bitterness, pumpernickel, roasted malt, and oily resin make for an engaging taste experience that's the most satisfying of all from this contract brewer; the aftertaste mirrors the zesty, comely midpalate; a genuinely luscious dark that's near the top of its type.

WILLIAMS & SCOTT COMPANY / BREWED AND BOTTLED BY F. X. MATT BREWING COMPANY, UTICA, NY

RATING ★ ★ ★ ★   *Highly Recommended*

Rhino Chasers American Ale

Spectacular, new-copper-penny/burnt-orange/deep-amber color, off-white foam, minute bubbles, excellent head retention; the nose highlights a fine marriage of fruit, malt, and hops in the first two nosings, then the bouquet retreats somewhat in the third and final passes, leaving behind the decidedly sweet impression of roasted malt and hard candy; on palate, it shows good balance between the mashy malt taste and the easy, low-key bitterness of the hops; what it lacks in depth it more than makes up for in poised, harmonious drinkability; a beer that's more a hot-day thirst-cruncher than one you ponder; dazzling to the eye.

RATING ★ ★ ★   *Recommended*

Rhino Chasers Amber Ale

Fetching dark-amber/copper color, little head retention; the seductive, fascinating nose features estery traces of red fruit (especially ripe plums and raspberries), honey, and unsweetened coconut—a lovely, atypical bouquet that fleetingly reminded me of a chilled Beaujolais; in the mouth, it's subtle, very clean, lemony, and slightly smoky; the finish is sweet-sour and lengthy, with a honey-wheat tang at the very end; a handsome, wine-like amber that with a tad more character in the flavor would definitely merit a fourth star; outstanding aroma and appearance.

RATING ★ ★ ★   *Recommended*

Rhino Chasers Peach Honey Wheat

Moderately foggy appearance, hay/harvest-gold/honey tint, pearly white, short-lived foam, excellent purity; there's no denying that the peach-wheat aromatic tag team is completely captivating, refreshing, and fun—the honey takes a back seat while the fruit plays footsie with the grain in all four passes—the peach element, in particular, proves irresistible—a fabulous nose, no other word for it; there's a slight shortfall on palate in terms of flavor impact, but I responded well to the lithe body and the whistle-clean entry taste that featured the wheat—the peach, which was so prominent in the bouquet, faded into the background in the mouth, leaving the door open for the wheat and honey parts of the equation; it finishes nicely, with the honey emerging in a big way; oh, that peachy perfume.

RATING ★ ★ ★   *Recommended*

Rhino Chasers Winterful

I'm a long-standing fan of the tasty RC Amber Ale, and this handsome copper/crimson/tawny-colored seasonal is its equal; the nose is subdued in the first and second go-rounds, but then it opens up as it warms up, emitting gentlemanly aromas of moderately toasted malt and fruity hops, accented by fetching but barely discernable backnotes of red fruit and spices; it's on the palate that this ale earns its stars, as crisp but bountiful flavors of malt, orange peel, and hops are underpinned by a subtle fruitiness that definitely worked for me; the finish is round and supple and provides a stylish closure for this well-made ale.

RATING ★ ★ ★   *Recommended*

Riverside Brewing Golden Spike Pilsner

I found myself dismayed at the outrageous amount of sediment that was spotted floating about in this golden amber; brilliant white foam, short head retention, highly questionable purity—use caution; the nose is very biscuity and dough-like upfront, with supporting aromas of lychee nuts, malt, and yellow fruit—it's a sound, correct bouquet; on palate, this pilsner has very serious problems, which, I would guess, coincide with the snowfall of sediment—the taste, such as it is, has turned slatey, chalk-like, and metallic; "dismal" doesn't even begin to tell the story; if you see it at your local beer merchants, get out of the store.

RIVERSIDE BREWING COMPANY, RIVERSIDE, CA

RATING ★

Riverside Brewing Pullman Pale Ale

Owns a very appealing reddish/copper color, but then when you look real close, you see a blizzard of dark sediment, tan foam, short head retention, purity problems; the nose right out of the bottle is as flat as a table, emitting only a perfunctory, weak-kneed maltiness that holds little depth or charm—the second and third nosings begin to pick up spotty aromas that seem off—there isn't a clear problem with this bouquet, just the hint of something gone wrong, and, maybe, that's what's so disconcerting about the nose; in the mouth, the limp, insipid flavor and lanky texture tells me one sure thing—this ale died some time ago and should not be available for sale; use extreme caution.

RATING ★

Riverside Brewing Victoria Avenue Amber Ale

This brew from Riverside Brewing likewise shows some sediment, though not nearly as much as the terrible Pullman Pale Ale and Golden Spike Pilsner; beige foam, short head retention, questionable purity; the bouquet is simply god-awful, offering genuinely horrible scents that more resemble my Michelins than any beer I'm aware of—the rubber-a-rama continues in the second and third nosings—by the fourth pass (at which point I'm gleeful that this is nearly over) I realize that the smell is exactly like the inner tubes we used to use for floating on a fresh-water lake when I was a child; in the mouth, it fails as miserably as it did in the nasal cavity—unsavory, putrid, and disgusting; if this is for sale in your home town, think of relocating.

RATING ★

RIVERSIDE BREWING **Raincross Cream Ale**

The medium amber/honey hue is occupied by a cloud of infinitesimal black and transparent particles, wimpy beige head, one of the most impure-looking beers I've ever come across; the nose reminds me the locker room at my health club—so malodorous and gamey that I don't even want to take this stuff into my mouth—so you know what, I won't—this is perhaps the worst-smelling, rankest beer I've ever evaluated—it's shocking to me that this garbage is available for sale—I purchased this bottle, as well as the other Riverside beers, at a highly reputable retailer, whom I regularly buy beer from; give this fetid mess a wide berth; it doesn't even deserve one star.

RATING ★

RJ's RIPTIDE **Oatmeal Stout**

Tasted on-site; opaque, dark brown, tan foam, very good head retention; the nose reminds me strikingly of espresso—backnotes of tobacco smoke and bittersweet chocolate round out the fine bouquet—the last nosing introduces burnt pumpernickel—totally within the boundaries of the style, this handsome aroma is more dry than sweet, and captivating; fully textured and creamy; on palate, flavors of cigar box, black coffee, and charcoal malt lean to the bitter end of the taste spectrum—I like the mouth presence very much because of the exceptionally elegant notes of soot and smoke; a black beauty.

RJ'S RIPTIDE BREWERY, SAN DIEGO, CA

RATING ★ ★ ★ ★   *Highly Recommended*

RJ's RIPTIDE **Original Honey Ale**

Tasted on-site; pale yellow/straw color, snow-white foam, excellent head retention; the sound, yeasty, flowery nose is quite subdued, but solid all the way through the final nosing—the honey is a distant background vaguery; in the mouth, it's easy-drinking and surprisingly dry, at most, off-dry—the honey exposed itself at palate entry, then faded to an echo—the real thrust flavors are hops and malt; not the stuff of genius, but a full-weighted, exceedingly pleasant ale just the same.

RATING ★ ★ ★   *Recommended*

RJ's RIPTIDE **Two-Berry Ale**

Tasted on-site; stunning copper/vermilion hue, pearly white foam, poor head retention; the nose is ambrosial and intensely berry-like (the two berries are raspberry and blackberry), but, to the brewer's credit, the malt and yeast elements aren't lost in the berry patch; on palate, I found it irresistible, as the balance between the fruit and malt is gracefully achieved—my sole criticism is a detectable metallic/flinty presence in the flavor background; other than that, the positives outweight the negatives; a good warm-weather quaff before a meal.

RATING ★★★ **Recommended**

RJ's RIPTIDE Charger Gold Ale

Tasted on-site; honey/gold tone, silver-white foam, excellent head retention; the nose owns a friendly citrus quality that backs up the malty richness—I liked the bouquet a lot, mostly because of the cleanness encouraged by that elusive citrus-peel character; the bitter entry runs the danger of going flinty, but it skirts that peril by developing a round maltiness by mid palate; the finish is very bitter but good; almost an ESB style.

RATING ★★★ **Recommended**

RJ's RIPTIDE Dunkel Weizen

Tasted on-site; turbid, muddy-water brown color (as it should be), tan foam, exceptional head retention; I found this nose closed down in the first two passes—the third pass introduces a roasted-wheat quality that's both clean and pure—unfortunately, the bouquet stays a one-dimensional entity for the duration; in the mouth, I appreciated the purity, but I wasn't bowled over by the flavor, which seemed strangely flattened out—no zip, no vivacity here—I wonder if it's old—but it's been drawn off the tap, so how could it be advanced in age? all right, but I wouldn't ask for it again.

RATING ★★

RJ's RIPTIDE Red Ale

Tasted on-site; beautiful, henna/dark-copper hue, beige foam, superb head retention; the nose possesses a very charming, deep-roasted maltiness that fades in the third and fourth passes, but it shows enough character and depth right off the bat to amply enchant the olfactory sense; on palate, the emphasis is on the hops and the heavily roasted malt—I was disappointed in the flavor because it didn't fulfill the promise of the aroma; even so, it's an okay ale; would show its best side with grilled foods.

RATING ★★

ROCK ICE Amber Lager

Pretty, medium amber/orange-blossom-honey color, off-white foam, good head retention, perfect purity; it's very stingy in the bouquet department, giving off scant, unconvincing aromas of bubble gum, mild malt, faint spice, and juniper blossoms—through all four passes, I really had to work hard to coax out any fragrance whatsoever; on palate, there's a little more to analyze as the sweet-sour flavors of citrus, sour malt, and light toffee dash around in confusion—there's little cohesion among the various flavor elements; drinkable as it is, there's no sense of layering or depth, just a slam-it-back lager without a sense of identity.

LATROBE BREWING COMPANY, LATROBE, PA

RATING ★★

ROGUE American Amber Ale

Gorgeous, chestnut-brown/mahogany color that resembles a cream-sherry tone, extralong head retention; the nose is irresistibly fetching, endowed, roasted, and moderately sweet, with highlights of tropical fruit (guava and banana, especially), molasses, cocoa, and intense malt—a dynamite, compelling Amber bouquet that runs with the best in America and alone earns this beer two stars; it's so smooth on the palate that you have only one thought—more, please; the multilayered flavor shows hints of nut meat, toasted malt, honey wheat, and hops; the finish is balanced, clean, and supple; easily one of this country's top ten Ambers.

OREGON BREWING COMPANY, NEWPORT, OR

RATING ★ ★ ★ ★　　*Highly Recommended*

ROGUE Mogul Ale

Looks like root beer, a medium brown tone, meager head retention; the fact that six types of hops are added to this zesty ale is evident right from the first nosing as a floral, almost fruity aroma grabs on and won't let go— also there are creamy scents of dark chocolate and roasted nuts, even some honey in the background; on the palate, a sweetish, chocolatey entry dazzles the taste buds, then by midpalate the interplay between the four kinds of malts and a half-dozen hops becomes a harmonious and luscious taste treat; the aftertaste shows a distinctive, mildly bitter quality that's balanced by a cocoa creaminess; great job.

RATING ★ ★ ★ ★　　*Highly Recommended*

ROGUE Smoke Rauch Style Ale

Very attractive, brilliant copper/tawny-port hue, little head retention; the first nosing reveals a major-league aroma of smoked sausage, smoked trout, smoldering charcoal, and roasted chestnuts—get the picture here? name and form are truly one with this beer; the taste takes on more of a wood-smoke quality on the tongue and by midpalate is saturated with top-notch maltiness; the aftertaste is silky and only moderately smoky; the body is medium-weighted; an ideal domestic choice for meals that headline smoked meats, turkey, fish, or cheeses; dynamite and different.

RATING ★ ★ ★ ★　　*Highly Recommended*

ROGUE Shakespeare Stout

Opaque brown/black hue, average head retention; this nose is delightfully animated and chockful of intense, savory scents of coffee, molasses, bittersweet chocolate, malt, chickory, and tobacco smoke; in the mouth, the flavor soars with malty, deeply toasted tastes of dark chocolate, black coffee, mocha, and cocoa cream; the texture is firm, but hardly chunky or overly viscous, as some stouts tend to be; more a fortifying food than a libation; the aftertaste is toasty, clean, and muscular; one of the few domestic stouts that can seriously compete with the great stouts of the U.K. . . . and that, I believe, says all that you need to know about this exquisite beer.

RATING ★ ★ ★ ★　　*Highly Recommended*

ROGUE Old Crustacean Barley Wine Style Ale

Turbid, rather dull medium brown, almost like cherry-wood, no head retention; the compelling, multilayered nose offers an astounding array of aromas, from cherry Jell-O to fresh-cut roses to malt to raspberries to melon to honey wheat—it's one of the most complex beer bouquets I've come across, a nose that alone is worth the purchase of a bottle; in the mouth, the quality menu narrows a bit to focus on the hoppy bitterness, red-plum fruit, lightly toasted malt, and red grapefruit; the finish shows more of a bitter than a fruity face, but that's fine, because it's so clean and complementary to the first-class nose and flavor; a must-have domestic beer.

RATING ★ ★ ★ ★   *Highly Recommended*

ROGUE-N-BERRY Ale

Beautiful tawny/cranberry/oloroso-sherry color, weak head retention; the inviting bouquet beckons with toasty, malty foundational aromas that are laced and supplemented with an appetizingly tart red-berry balance— a clean nose that is so well balanced you never lose sight of the beer/malt component; in the mouth, this is a briskly clean rather than carefree wheat beer, in which the taste of tart, even sour, berries is far more evident than in the aroma; the aftertaste is quiet, quick, and very lean; a pleasant quaff for a picnic or before a meal; the stellar appearance and fragrant nose are the real highlights.

RATING ★ ★ ★   *Recommended*

ROGUE Dead Guy Ale

As is usual for Rogue, the appearance is immensely appealing—it displays a totally fetching and pretty auburn/henna/copper hue, tan foam, average head retention, perfect purity; lots of roasted malt and toasted cereal grain, with teasing dashes of molasses, light honey, red fruit, and hops in the lovely, substantial bouquet—to this ale's credit, the potency of the fragrance never diminishes even after ten minutes of aeration; on palate, the hoppy bitterness takes the cat-bird seat as the other supporting flavors of dark malt and dried fruit acquiesce to the will of the hops; bitter in the finish; at the end of the day, I thought the nose was superior to the taste and finish.

RATING ★ ★ ★   *Recommended*

ROGUE Mexicali Ale

Firm, harvest-gold color, brief head retention; the shy bouquet needs some coaxing—by the third nosing, I, at last, detected some chili bite, which at first took me by surprise, actually making me sneeze—with five minutes of aeration, the nose dramatically opened up, offering zesty waves of chili pepper and malt; on the palate, Mexicali is quite nimble and not in the least unruly or objectionable, as the controlled, tangy flavor of chipolte peppers makes a complementary component to the malt; it finishes well, leaving other chili beers in the desert dust; initially, I wasn't going to recommend it, but I kept returning to it, and it won me over.

RATING ★ ★ ★   *Recommended*

ROGUE Ale

Pretty russet/burnt-orange hue, average head retention; the nose is some-what shy at first, then a keen maltiness emerges by the second nosing—by the third pass, a mildly sweet cereal perfume appears, quite like Cheerios and sugar—I enjoyed experiencing the development of this svelte bouquet;

on the palate, it's user-friendly, uncomplicated, and adequately hopped, with an appealing flavor base of malt; the aftertaste is direct, clean, and has a hoppy bitterness that's delightful.

RATING ★ ★ ★   *Recommended*

ROGUE ST. ROGUE Red Ale

Handsome, burnished-red/dark-copper color, little head retention; the amiable bouquet speaks volumes about the virtues of toasty malt, as a back-note fragrance of dried red fruit makes it an interesting nose; in the mouth, it's musclebound, but not chewy in texture; the taste reflects the fourth-gear malty bouquet as an intense, roasted, but not quite smoky malt flavor drives this ale with the accelerator slammed to the floor; the finish is focused, clean, and concentrated; add more flavor dimension and it picks up another star; St. Rogue is a workmanlike, recommendable ale.

RATING ★ ★ ★   *Recommended*

ROGUE Maierbock Ale

Smashing copper-penny hue, meager head retention; the splendid nose brims with roasted, toasty, malty aromas, with just the merest hint of nut meat lodged way in the back—by the third nosing the roasted quality gives way to a hoppy bitterness; in the mouth, the toastiness balances well with the maltiness; the texture is round, even supple, but not in the least fat, awkward, or overbearing; if this fine ale offered more flavor impact or dimension, it would be a four-star beer—as it stands, three will have to do.

RATING ★ ★ ★   *Recommended*

ROGUE Golden Ale

Lovely, medium amber/golden-wheat tone, with long, tightly knit head retention; the nose emits a nicely balanced fragrance of roasted malt and light hops—while I liked it, the nose didn't bowl me over; Golden Ale owns the correct crispness, as the hops wrestle away the flavor spotlight from the malt and keep hold of it through the mildly bitter/metallic/slaty finish; decent, but to my taste it leans a bit too heavily on the side of hoppy bitterness; perhaps most of all, though, I didn't favorably respond to the taste of metal or slate in the aftertaste, which is surely a stylistic choice of the brewmaster, not an indictment of quality.

RATING ★ ★

ROGUE Mo Ale Belgian Style

Cloudy, blonde/iced-tea/warm-brown hue, virtually no head retention at all; the intriguing nose offers tantalizing aromas of Indian curry, fresh ginger, and herbs, with hardly any reference to wheat, other grains, or hops— by the third pass the bouquet had run its course, and all that was left was a trace of coriander; the taste mirrored the general mildness found in the nose, as pleasant, but ultimately bland flavors of Wheat Thins and ginger took center stage, if briefly; the finish is timid, but inoffensive; I didn't think that the taste and finish fulfilled the promise implied in the unique, tempting nose.

RATING ★ ★

Rogue Mocha Porter

Opaque, dark chocolate-brown color, average head retention; I searched for a bouquet through the first two nosings, but came up empty—the best it could do in the third and fourth passes was a miserly malt scent—I found the nose to be a serious disappointment; in the mouth, this porter goes nowhere in terms of flavor at palate entry, then at midpalate it gets magnanimous and tosses out a spindly bone of bittersweet chocolate; this beer lacks the two basic qualities you look for in beer, aroma and flavor; back to the drawing board; and, hey, where's the mocha that I was promised?

RATING ★

Rolling Rock Extra Pale Lager

Pale gold color, eggshell foam; good head retention; on the nose, feather-light scents of hops and yeast present a proper beer bouquet; light- to medium-bodied and somewhat creamy-, silky-textured; exceedingly pleasant, middle-of-the-road, nicely balanced beer with the barest hint of sweetness; ideal ice-cold July-heat-wave antidote accompanied by a salami sandwich or barbecued beef; currently enjoying a cult status in the East's caverns of steel; sampled three times for review; upgraded in the last two.

LATROBE BREWING COMPANY, LATROBE, PA

RATING ★ ★

Rolling Rock Bock

A stunningly rich copper/bronze color, good head retention; one of the more eye-appealing domestics I've come across; the nose is mildly sweet, honeyed, biscuity, and vanilla-bean-like, but at the end of the day not very layered or complex, considering it's labeled as a "bock"; in the mouth, it's light- to medium-bodied, off-dry to sweet, pleasant but hardly inspiring—the entry is rather meek, then a smoky, fruity flavor gets going at midpalate; unfortunately, the finish succumbs to blandness; I wanted very much to recommend this domestic because I was so taken by the smashing appearance, but there's simply not enough character in the nose, taste, and aftertaste to warrant another star.

RATING ★ ★

Rolling Rock Light Lager

Pale yellow tone, very firm, billowy, frothy, long-lasting head; the walnut/hazelnut nose goes nowhere in a hurry; the moderately alluring, dry lager flavors of hops and mild malt are refreshing and simple; it finishes clean, dry, and fast; a featherweight with modest ambitions and talent; take a pass.

RATING ★

Ruffian Extra Special Bitter Ale

Tasted on-site; pretty bronze/honey hue, eggshell foam, good head retention; the nose is huge, biscuity, and intensely hoppy with background scents of citrus and juniper—has the trademark Mountain Valley Brew Pub touch of underlying sweetness; on palate, it sails right down the throat with lovely, warm, inviting flavors of lightly roasted malt, yellow fruit, and hops making this the most harmonious and satisfying beer yet from this red-hot micro; lingering, moderately bitter aftertaste.

MOUNTAIN VALLEY BREW PUB, SUFFERN, NY

RATING ★ ★ ★ ★   *Highly Recommended*

RUFFIAN Copper Ale

Tasted on-site; medium amber/iced-tea color, low head retention; the compelling, sweet nose is all about honeyed cereal, malt, and vanilla bean, with barely perceptible traces of molasses, brown sugar, and sweet pipe smoke; on palate, it's medium-bodied, slightly tarry, off-dry to sweet, and moderately complex—an excellent food accompaniment; it finishes sweetly, with a roasted-almond quality that's pleasant; the zesty nose is its strong suit, but flavorwise I fear that it runs the risk of being too sweet for some people.

RATING ★ ★ ★   *Recommended*

RUFFIAN Porter

Chocolate-brown/cola tone, no head retention; the nose is elusive, then gets friendlier as toasty scents of sweet wood smoke, road tar, and malted milk waft from the sampling glass; in the mouth, it's pleasantly fruity/sweet at entry, then goes mildly bitter and roasted by midpalate, finally ending in a red-fruit/charred/tar flavor burst that's typical for the style and, in this particular case, quite alluring; give it more layered flavor in the midpalate and it's a four-star candidate.

RATING ★ ★ ★   *Recommended*

RUFFIAN Blonde Bock (seasonal)

Dark straw/light amber tone, no head retention; the assertive, but playful bouquet comes at you with a strawberry/grape-juice perfume that's as unusual and surprising as it is ambrosial—it's the most intensely fruity beer nose I've encountered other than that of fruit-infused beers; the remarkable fruitiness continues in the headstrong flavor as a cream element is introduced in the midpalate; the finish is off-dry to sweet and clearly the weakest part of this unique beer experience.

RATING ★ ★ ★   *Recommended*

RUFFIAN Irish Red Ale

Tasted on-site; really pretty, garnet-red/deep-amber hue, beige foam, fair head retention; the nose has decent malt content, mild hops, but little else; the flavor has the trademark taste of all Mountain Valley Brew Pub beers, a honeyed/malty sweetness—the entry is almost sticky-sweet, then that bold sweetness dies down at midpalate, leaving behind a roasted-malt element that seems limp to me; the finish is nicely bitter and clean, showing more malty punch than the midpalate; an up-and-down ale from this normally reliable brewer.

RATING ★ ★

S

St. James Ale

Standard-issue, golden color, stark-white foam, average head retention; the common, malty, hoppy, and tart bouquet doesn't change at all from first nosing through the fourth—it's all right, but simple and lackluster; in the mouth, it's acceptably citrusy and sour at entry, then at midpalate it veers off course completely as the sourness goes unchecked—the midpalate seems almost like it's been doused with lemon peel; ditto the aftertaste; do yourself a favor and avoid this . . . lemon.

RATING ★

Samuel Adams Double Bock Dark Lager

Simply stunning mahogany color, with a moderately firm beige head; the shy nose is finely layered with cherries, molasses, oatmeal, and malt, and it grows more intense as it warms—the layering of aroma is state-of-the-art; on the palate, a satiny, unctuous cloak gently wraps around the tongue like an ermine stole; deep, power-packed flavors of earth, cocoa, coffee, and pipe smoke are perfectly balanced from palate entry to finish; the aftertaste is silky, sound, and fruity; a scrumptious, jammy bock that I can't get enough of; superb brewing; my favorite domestic beer, period.

BOSTON BEER COMPANY, BOSTON, MA / SAMUEL ADAMS BEERS ARE CONTRACT-BREWED IN VARIOUS BREWERIES IN PENNSYLVANIA, CALIFORNIA, AND OREGON, AS WELL AS AT THEIR HEADQUARTERS IN BOSTON.

RATING ★ ★ ★ ★ ★   *Highest Recommendation*

Samuel Adams Honey Porter

Dark amber/cola color, little head retention; the friendly, compelling nose is all about roasted cereal grains, wood smoke, malt, brown sugar, roasted almonds, and black coffee—I could barely detect the honey, which is added at fermentation, in the nose—what it reminds me of most is honey-wheat toast; it's buxom on the palate as smoky, toasted flavors of malt delight the taste buds; I pick up more of the honey in the highly satisfying finish, which is off-dry, extended, and elegant—the aftertaste is the star of this show; a dandy addition to the ever-expanding and remarkably innovative portfolio of brewer Jim Koch; tasted three times for review and upgraded the last time.

RATING ★ ★ ★ ★ ★   *Highest Recommendation*

Samuel Adams Dark Wheat

Fetching chestnut/dark-amber/clover-honey color, with a firm, beige head; the grainy, dry-cereal nose is all wheat and nothing but the wheat so help me, God; on the palate, the toasty, yeasty, honey-wheat flavor becomes so intense that it goes tar-like, charcoal-like in the smoky, brawny, and expansive aftertaste; a splendid, round, chewy, well-endowed, creamy-textured beer that's trailblazing new ground for domestics in a style that will be hard to beat; a simply fabulous brew of the first rank.

RATING ★ ★ ★ ★   *Highly Recommended*

Samuel Adams Triple Bock 1994 Brew Reserve

At a head-snapping 17.5 percent alcohol, this is the biggest, most auda-cious beer currently available in the U.S.; it's so viscous, it resembles a chocolate liqueur or a cream sherry; no head whatsoever; the unctuous nose speaks of raisins, madeira, overripe fruit (prunes especially), and even yeast and sour dough—the nose is so atypical and unique that it's hard to clas-sify it strictly as a beer; flavorwise, it's a cross between bock beer, cream sherry (in particular a Pedro Ximenez), malmsey madeira, and a chocolate liqueur; there exist two distinct levels of flavor—the ambrosial top layer, which reminds me of sweet madeira most of all, then the drier, underpin-ning level, which is all about the beer basics of grain and yeast; I like it very much as an oddity, but I wouldn't choose to make it a regular libation (nor could I afford to), since at the end of the day I'd still gravitate in the direc-tion of either the Samuel Adams Double Bock or Honey Porter.

RATING ★ ★ ★ ★   ***Highly Recommended***

Samuel Adams Scotch Ale Triple Malt

Handsome, sturdy appearance of reddish/dark-honey/deep-amber/ brown, beige foam, little head retention; the nose overflows with opulent barley malt and smoky aromas that remind me of single-malt-Scotch dis-tilleries, especially in the mash tun rooms, where the pungent odor of bar-ley often has my socks rolling up and down—this is a robust, sweet, and virile bouquet that's as rowdy as it is luscious; the presence of passing-gear malt is wall-to-wall in the mouth; medium- to full-weighted texture; at mid-palate a fine, roasted, moderately smoky, slightly iodine bitter flavor ushers the taste buds into the surprisingly mannered aftertaste; not for everyone, but if you relish Scotch whisky (like yours truly), give this earthy, ram-bunctious ale a try.

RATING ★ ★ ★ ★   ***Highly Recommended***

Samuel Adams Boston Lager

Golden/light amber color, pearly white froth, good head retention; the malty, yeasty, almost coconut-like nose has top quality written all over it; slightly sweet on entry, but dry, tart, and nicely balanced on palate; medium weight; faint citrusy fruit component in the finish; when I first tried this beer some years back, it failed to win me over, but as I've gone back to it over time, I've come to admire its regal bearing and sound, rock-solid character.

RATING ★ ★ ★   ***Recommended***

Samuel Adams Boston Ale

Solid dark-amber/medium-brown tone with copper highlights and beige head, better than average head retention; the perfumy nose is toasty, malty, and off-dry, with subtle background elements of road tar, burnt wheat toast, and tobacco—it's a firm, no-nonsense aroma that's as sound as it is supple; on the palate, this dry-cereally ale is whistle-clean, very refreshing, and un-complicated—the flavor range spans from biscuity, dry cereal at palate entry to smoky, burnt, bitter, and hoppy tastes in the very long finish.

RATING ★ ★ ★   ***Recommended***

Samuel Adams Boston Lightship Light

Good gold/straw color; wimpy foam; noticeably sweet, fruity, cherry-like, freshly cut flowers are found in the beguiling aroma; quite firm, substantial body for a light beer with less than 100 calories; delicious fruity quality follows through nicely on palate; medium-length finish; delightfully handsome light that doesn't seem like a light at all; bravo, Boston Beer Company and Jim Koch.

RATING ★★★ *Recommended*

Samuel Adams Cream Stout

Opaque, chocolate, espresso brown, with an endless, foamy beige head; the nutty bouquet itself is worth the price—it's brimming with cocoa, brown sugar, butter cream, dark chocolate, and espresso coffee; the coffee-like flavor is elegant in a brooding way—I also pick up the taste of caraway seeds in abundance; a good, if one-dimensional, stout that shows well in the immediate sense, but when you back away and ponder it you realize that no matter how nice this stout is, it's still no match for the peerless stouts of the U.K.

RATING ★★★ *Recommended*

Samuel Adams Golden Pilsner

Radiant, resplendent, 18-carat-gold color, eggshell foam, very good head retention; the pleasing aroma starts off on a biscuity note, then in the second pass develops a lemony/citrus backnote that's unusual for the style, but totally fetching nonetheless—as the beer warms and aerates, flowery, yellow-fruit perfumes take charge—it concludes on a biscuity, grainy note; delightfully tart and clean in the mouth, it's medium-weighted—neither complex nor profound, but a fundamentally sound pilsner that's a great performer in warm weather.

RATING ★★★ *Recommended*

Samuel Adams Winter Lager 1995–1996

Attractive, deep amber/orange-pekoe-tea/bronze tone, tan foam, fair head retention, superb clarity; the off-dry nose is very toasty, densely malted, and hearty in all four nosings—a compelling, grainy brew that's ideal for cold-weather quaffing; on palate, the roasted malt and hops combine in a taste that's bittersweet and acceptably burnt; the aftertaste puts the spotlight squarely on the hops; as expected from Jim Koch, a well-crafted contract beer.

RATING ★★★ *Recommended*

Samuel Adams Cherry Wheat Ale

A noncloudy, harvest-gold tone, snow-white foam, poor head retention; the comely nose is brimming with black-cherry perfume in the opening aromatic salvo, then the cherry quality dies out in the second pass, leaving behind a grainy, cherry-pit (kernel-like) bouquet that's nowhere near as gripping as the first nosing—the last two nosings are subdued and inconsequential; crisp and clean at palate entry as the stony, pit-like cherry flavor mingles but doesn't marry with the malted-wheat taste—the midpalate is tart, seed-like, and desert-dry; the finish is muted and distant and fails to bring a sense of closure to the experience; the cherry and the malted wheat never seemed to find the right rhythm.

RATING ★★

SAMUEL ADAMS Wheat Brew

Vivid, harvest-gold color, with a firm white chapeau; the atypical, pungent nose smells like cooked brown rice, a full laundry basket prior to washing, and Nabisco wheat thins; the sour, brown-rice quality follows through onto the palate and aftertaste; all in all, it tastes to me like cardboard; I simply find nothing positive to say about it; I appreciate Jim Koch's adventurous spirit as much as anyone, but this experiment falls disastrously short of the mark compared to the other Samuel Adams beers.

RATING ★

SARANAC Adirondack Amber Lager

Keenly handsome, medium amber/orange/russet color, white foam, average head retention; the comely, seductive bouquet possesses the thumbprint of Utica, New York, contract brewer F. X. Matt, in that it offers more hoppy fruit than malty grain—the third pass adds a faint dash of spice—all in all, it's lovely, but so subtle that I fear the majority of beer drinkers, except for the most fastidious, would never expend the patience required to appreciate its aromatic nuances; silky, smooth, medium- to full-bodied; the mildly bitter taste leans more to the hops (American Cascade and German Hallertau) than to the malt—elegant, but firm in the mouth; the aftertaste is long, malty, and ideally bitter; one of my favorite two Saranacs.

F. X. MATT BREWING COMPANY, UTICA, NY

RATING ★★★★   *Highly Recommended*

SARANAC Chocolate Amber

Porter-like appearance, chestnut/mahogany color, beige foam, very good head retention, pure; the off-dry nose is delightfully rich, creamy, milky, and chocolatey in the first two nosings, then the deep-roasted malt signature kicks in and brings it home—it's a luscious, decadent bouquet of the first rank; on palate, all systems are go as the toasty mainline chocolate-malt core stays firm—around this core orbits lesser flavors of hops, pumpernickel, and black fruit; the finish is very extended, deeply toasted, and malty; a malt-a-thon that elevates the Saranac label.

RATING ★★★★   *Highly Recommended*

SARANAC Season's Best Nut Brown Lager

Truly gorgeous, reddish brown/blood/sorrel hue, firm, long-lasting beige foam; the coffee-bean, chunky-chocolate nose is a total winner right from the first nosing through the last—the chocolate-malt blast in the first and second passes knocked me out—I detected some subtle anise/licorice fragrance in the final nosing; in the mouth, the malt presence is finely, not overly, roasted, nutty, a tad smoky, and top-flight, particularly at midpalate; the aftertaste has a good balance of hoppy bitterness, road tar, roasted grain, and dryness; gets better with every sampling.

RATING ★★★★   *Highly Recommended*

SARANAC Golden Pilsener

Harvest-gold/honey color, weak head retention; like all the beers that come out of this superb upstate New York contract brewer, the nose liberally emits a semisweet, concentrated fruit perfume (especially red berries) that's immediately likable and identifiable—clearly the F. X. Matt brewmaster loves the hops that encourage fruitier notes in the nose, but a mild concern arises in how the aromas of the majority of Matt-generated beers seem to be shaped by the same cookie cutter; in the mouth, this light- to medium-weighted pilsener is basic and minerally, yet extremely pleasing to the taste buds; let's face it, sensory pleasure needn't always be profound.

RATING ★★★   **Recommended**

SARANAC Pale Ale

Pretty copper/russet/orange tone, with better than average head retention; true to the F. X. Matt house style, the bouquet is open for business immediately on pouring, showing amiable and fruity scents in the first nosing, then by the second and third passes the aroma advances into a grainy smell that's passable, but lackluster; in the mouth, tart, hoppy bitterness rules the roost, leaving absolutely no room for fruit or grain flavors; the finish is lean and crisp; there's a razor-edged cleanness that I liked very much in this hoppy ale, but I admittedly missed the expected fruit component in the flavor and aftertaste that I've come to look for from this brewer; after first being concerned with uniformity, I must reverse course and admit that I prefer the high-flying fruity style over this stone-dry, bitter direction; all the same, the brewing is very solid.

RATING ★★★   **Recommended**

SAXER Three Finger Jack Stout

A rare domestic lagered stout; midnight-black, opaque, black coffee appearance, tan foam, decent head retention; the aroma is dry and bitter in the first nosing, then it accelerates with deep-roasted malt, cocoa, molasses, brown sugar, and dry-toasted-cereal scents in the second and third passes; on palate, it shows considerable depth and very little sweetness as the desert-dry bitterness gives this stout its signature feature—admirably clean and quaffable, this unusual stout exhibits remarkable agility and never comes off heavy or cloying; the finish is tidy and quick.

SAXER BREWING COMPANY, LAKE OSWEGO, OR

RATING ★★★★   **Highly Recommended**

SAXER Three Finger Jack Hefedunkel Dark Lager

Really beautiful, medium amber/russet/brown tone, light-tan foam, good head retention; the nose displays oodles of toasted malt, but not much else in the first two passes—the third nosing introduces a fruity dimension, which is reined in, but pleasant; in the mouth, it's round, supple, sinewy, and medium-weighted—flavors of light toffee, dry cereal (especially Rice Chex), and roasted malt are backed up by a firm hoppy bitterness that supports the entire mouth presence; savory finish.

RATING ★★★   **Recommended**

SAXER Three Finger Jack Amber Lager

Owns an attractive copper/medium-amber/iced-tea tone, off-white foam, very good head retention; the aroma is a bit sharp after the pour but settles down into a biscuity mode that highlights the malt and hops in a showcase of harmony; on palate, I found the vanilla-wafer sweetness very nice at palate entry, then it turns too bitter on the way to midpalate—at midpalate, a rich, toasty sweetness reemerges and lasts through the suddenly flat-as-a-pancake aftertaste; what began with promise, ended up being average and middle-of-the-road.

RATING ★★

SAXER Lemon Lager

Pretty golden/honey hue, firm white foam, good head retention; the snappy nose is vivaciously alive with crisp citrus-peel zest, which overlays the background malt notes—I was fascinated, but not necessarily smitten, with this unique bouquet; in the mouth, I was mildly disappointed with its crackling effervescence, which distracted me from the taste—when I did get around to the flavor I found it pleasantly serviceable, but uninspired—I wanted more malt for my money and ended up settling for too much lemon; interesting concept, almost pulled off.

RATING ★★

SCHAEFER Pilsener

Medium straw color, moderately long head retention; the nose initially is like fabric, new cotton to be precise, then it changes with aeration into a pleasantly hoppy, bread-dough fragrance that's more than acceptable; the texture is creamy; tastewise, it's slightly steely/tanky/metallic, but also shows some yeasty/doughy flavors that while totally mainstream and ordinary, aren't bad either; the aftertaste is off-dry and quick, but at least it shows up; a decent chug-a-lug.

F. & M. SCHAEFER BREWING COMPANY, DETROIT, MI

RATING ★★

SCHMIDT's Light

Pale straw hue, excellent head retention; the nose is hoppy, lemony, and, most curiously, like wet sand, though not in the least unpleasant—it's just strange; typically lame domestic light-beer/golden-lager feel and taste, which plays up the hops in a floral/fruity/estery flavor that drops right off the table by midpalate; the finish is cardboard-like; not even worth beating up.

G. HEILEMAN BREWING COMPANY, LACROSSE, WI

RATING ★

SCRIMSHAW Pilsner

Standard-issue, golden-hay/light-honey color, but mildly foggy, fried-egg-white foam, poor head retention; I really fancied the generous, vanilla-wafer, cookie-batter aroma, which is in-your-face right after the pour—with aeration, however, the freshness dissipated quickly and the bouquet devolved into a sweaty, footlocker stench that was both unfortunate and unacceptable; on palate, the metallic/flinty taste does nothing to rescue the

experience—in the third in-mouth sampling, this flimsy pilsner gives up the ghost; don't bother going to the funeral; let this lemon rest in peace.

NORTH COAST BREWING COMPANY, FORT BRAGG, CA

RATING ★

SEA DOG Riverdriver Hazelnut Porter

Outstanding appearance of chestnut/nut-brown hue, with red/mahogany core highlights, sand-colored foam, very long head retention, excellent purity; the concentrated, hazelnut, nougat nose dazzled the daylights out of my sense of smell—the employment of the hazelnut, it should be pointed out, doesn't in any way detract from the opulent, malty foundation of this sterling porter—rather, the hazelnut brings out the malt richness in a manner that one rarely sees in domestic porter/stout brewing—this is an instant classic aroma; if that's not enough, the taste breaks new ground in the multilayered flavors of nut meat, tobacco smoke, mocha, cocoa, and deep-roasted malt—top-drawer from palate entry through the smoke-filled, lush aftertaste; a big-league porter from one of my favorite eastern brewers.

SEA DOG BREWING COMPANY, BANGOR, ME

RATING ★ ★ ★ ★ ★   *Highest Recommendation*

SEA DOG Old Gollywobbler Brown Ale

Deep amber/tawny/umber/russet hue, pure, sandy foam, good head retention; the yeasty/doughy/honeyed aroma jumps from the glass in fat waves that delight the olfactory sense right from the pour—in the third pass, a round, deep-roasted-malt quality eclipses the dough aroma—the final pass introduces chestnuts—a completely fetching bouquet; the mouth presence mirrors the aroma as succulent flavors of wood smoke, roasted malt, dark bread, and nuts are balanced by a mild, hoppy bitterness; this Sea Dog ale shows remarkable joie de vivre and quality; find and buy by the six pack.

RATING ★ ★ ★ ★   *Highly Recommended*

SEA DOG Windjammer Blonde Ale

Splendid, burnished-gold/medium-amber tone, perfect purity, dirty-white foam, very good head retention; the smashing bouquet launches itself from the glass in opulent, biscuity, inviting waves of light caramel, vanilla, sweet malt, honey, and toast—the vivacity and roundness of this charmer remain sound through all four nosings—the vanilla-wafer quality is voluptuous and compelling—the nose alone is worth two stars; the crisp, malt/hop tandem steers the flavor from entry to finish—the taste is drier and more bitter than the bouquet, but that's quite all right, since they complement each other nicely; the aftertaste is acutely bitter and cleansing; really nice job.

RATING ★ ★ ★ ★   *Highly Recommended*

SEA DOG Old East India IPA

Exceptionally lovely, burnished-copper hue, tan foam, short head retention, a tad foggy, but pure; the assertive but friendly bouquet swept me off my feet with genuinely appealing just-out-of-the-bottle aromas of red fruit, sweet malt, flowery hops, and even a distant note of spice—then in the second pass, I noticed that the forcefulness found in the opening gush had significantly diminished—the third pass introduced a curious odor that, while not offensive, reminded me of tin—the final pass ended up being really perplexing as the odd odor changed from metal to sweet malt, then back to metal—quizzical, strange; my palate really responded to the flavor entry, which tried to redeem the meandering and changeable bouquet—the mid-palate proved soft, almost chewy, and very malty; the finish was sweet and long; the erratic nature of the bouquet was unsettling enough to garner this otherwise savory IPA no more than three rating stars.

RATING ★ ★ ★   *Recommended*

SHARP'S Non-Alcoholic Brew

Has the golden appearance of genuine beer, except that the bubbles cease rising from the glass bottom almost immediately and the head bids adieu within thirty seconds; has a sweet, almost floral, steamed-rice nose; lightweight body; dry on palate but is predictably, no, make that pathetically, short on any semblance of beer flavor . . . or any flavor, for that matter; no finish to speak of; a complete waste of water; 68 laborious calories.

MILLER BREWING, MILWAUKEE, WI

RATING ★

SIERRA NEVADA Stout

Midnight-brown, opaque appearance, sturdy, firm, long-lasting foam of tightly beaded bubbles; the superb, bewitching nose opens with a volley of bubblegum, pineapple, and nectarine in the first pass, then adds fortified wine, chocolate malt, and fabric in the second and third, and egg cream and coffee in the final pass—this complex, assertive, multilayered bouquet keeps building—remarkable; on palate, it's creamy, opulent, and full-bodied texturewise and layered and decadent flavorwise as the chocolate-malt component runs with the ball to the ten-yard line—the coffee-bean element crosses the goal line for the score; the lovely, roasted, burnt-honey-wheat-toast finish kicks the extra point; this dark ale has it all . . . finesse, depth of character, balance, and potency; say hello to America's very finest stout.

SIERRA NEVADA BREWING COMPANY, CHICO, CA

RATING ★ ★ ★ ★ ★   *Highest Recommendation*

SIERRA NEVADA Porter

Dark brown/cola color, very extended head retention; lovely scents of roasted nuts, cracked grain, molasses, caramel, cocoa, and dark roasted malt thrive in the bouquet, which is deep, concentrated, and genuinely appealing; on the palate, the hefty flavor delights the senses as sweet, toasted layers of cream, brown sugar, nuts, and chocolate-covered cherries hold court—what's so fascinating about this flavor is that not one of these strong tastes overshadows the others—it's an extremely harmonious presence in the mouth; the balance is keenly evident in the long, toasty finish; lovers of brawny, musclebound dark beers need apply; a luscious meal in itself.

RATING ★ ★ ★ ★   *Highly Recommended*

Sierra Nevada Pale Ale

Pale amber tone, with good to very good head retention; the nose is delightfully hoppy/floral/spring-garden fresh, with ethereal hints of spice and yeast; on the palate, it's keenly fresh, crisp, squeaky-clean, and mildly sweet, with a pleasant, easy bitterness that lands squarely on the tongue; it finishes well in the mannered, subdued fashion of the aroma; this is a solidly made, but polite, beer—a beer that doesn't take chances but, nevertheless, is very drinkable and likable.

RATING ★★★   **Recommended**

Simpatico Amber Lager

Absolutely smashing color of deep rust/tawny, pure, tan foam, fair head retention; the nose is biscuity, doughy, wonderfully fruity, nutty, and toasty in the first two passes—in the third pass a maple/burnt-wood/smoky scent makes things interesting—the last pass highlights the fruit, maple, and toasted nuts; in the mouth, this peculiar amber offers a charred, almost caramelized flavor that seems awkward at first, then after the second sampling I became accustomed to it, though I didn't like the taste as much as I did the aroma; it sits on the ratings fence with me, but the overly burnt, candied flavor makes me lean toward a thumbs-down.

DUBUQUE BREWING & BOTTLING, DUBUQUE, IA

RATING ★★

Simpatico Golden Lager

Good, solid gold/honey color, billowy white foam, very good head retention; the underwhelming bouquet doesn't go out of its way to court you, as it offers meager, mundane, and pedestrian aromas of cardboard (always a great sign), wheat, oatmeal, and mild malt—it's a lazy, snooze-o-rama nose that goes nowhere because it never gets started; the lackluster mouth presence does nothing to improve the situation, as tame, flabby tastes of grain (mostly rice) bore the taste buds to distraction; ditto the banal finish; don't waste your time and money; no simpatico to be found here.

RATING ★

Slo Brewing Co. Cole Porter

Jet-brown, opaque, looks like a draft root beer, pretty sand-colored foam, extralong head retention, good purity; the nose shows up well and totally in-line with the style—compellingly dry, heavily toasted, almost seared aromas of Colombian coffee beans, bittersweet Belgian chocolate, pumpernickel bread, and tobacco smoke set my olfactory sense spinning—there's lots to grab onto here and several layers to browse through—a solid aromatic performer from first to last nosing; on palate, the smoke greets the taste buds, then a lovely, well-behaved, and nicely conceived mocha/black-coffee taste takes charge at midpalate; in the finish, there're expansive waves of bittersweet chocolate and dark bread to take the experience home; very nice job, indeed, and worthy of the name of America's quintessential songwriter.

SLO BREWING COMPANY, NEW ULM, MN

RATING ★★★★   **Highly Recommended**

SLO BREWING CO. Blueberry Ale

Sound, honey/amber color, off-white foam, superb head retention, excellent clarity; this nose bursts from the bottle with the succulent aroma of perfectly ripe blueberries—first-pass splendor—regrettably, by the third nosing the ripe blueberry has turned slightly spicy and herbal, almost forest-like—once again, here's a beer that has had fruit juice added to it in which the beer aspect in the bouquet is all but lost in the ambrosia—by the final pass, this bouquet has become neutral; on palate, a steely/metallic taste can't be eluded through the whole taste exercise; this ale lost its way in the final stages of the bouquet and never recovered; avoid.

RATING ★

SLO BREWING CO. Brickhouse Extra Pale Ale

The golden amber appearance confused me because it was slightly cloudy, exhibiting a mild fogginess that, to me, was totally inappropriate for the style; eggshell foam, very good head retention, questionable purity; the nose seems right on the money for the type of beer—it's pleasantly malty and hoppy simultaneously—beyond the pedestrian, rather commonplace malt-hops interplay there's nothing to crow about in this bouquet; in the mouth, the hoppy bitterness overshadows the malt factor as though the hops want the malt out of town—we're talking total domination here, no sense of balance, no sense of working together to create something better than the individual aspects; drinkable, less than average, too out of sync, say good-night, Gracie.

RATING ★

SPANISH PEAKS Black Dog Pale Ale

Seriously attractive tawny/deep-amber/iced-tea brown color, billowy beige foam, endless head retention; the nose is deep in ripe red fruit, tangy hops, and racy malt in the compelling first nosing, then it becomes much more subdued in the second and third passes—all the positive notes of the first pass are reprised in the final nosing; the nut-like bitterness of the palate entry rules through the midpalate and the aftertaste; warning: Since there's little flavor impact from the malt, this ale is for Bitter aficionados only; this one-sided ale rides the rating fence in terms of recommendation, but I'm going with three stars largely because of the sterling appearance and better than average bouquet.

SPANISH PEAKS BREWING COMPANY, BOZEMAN, MT

RATING ★ ★ ★   *Recommended*

SPANISH PEAKS Peaches & Cream Ale

Attractive honey-brown tint, medium-beige foam, short head retention, impeccable purity; in the opening aromatic salvo, the nose is right on the mark as far as the peach factor goes, but less so with regard to the cream ale aspect of the equation—subsequent nosings see the ripe-peach aroma calm down to the point of it being a secondary scent by the fourth and last pass—it's at this juncture that the cream ale element breaks through; on palate, this is one of the infrequent instances in my beer evaluations when I decidedly prefer the flavor to the aroma—the velvety nature of the texture is a pleasure to behold, as is the high quotient of malt at midpalate; supple, mildly fruity aftertaste; the top-quality mouth presence pushed this into recommended territory.

SPANISH PEAKS BREWING COMPANY, NEW ULM, MN

RATING ★★★   ***Recommended***

Spanish Peaks Black Dog Ale

Pale-to-medium amber, hardly any head retention; the nose is very coy at the first nosing, then it reluctantly emerges in manageable waves of dry cereal, mild esters, and apples; in the mouth, it's crisp, rather lean, even a bit salty and tannic, but refreshing all the same—the flavor is bitter and tart, but not unpleasant; the finish is somewhat meek; while mildly tasty, it's minimalist beer making taken too far; I feel that it lacks definition and sufficient complexity in the bouquet, flavor, and finish to make it a three-star and, therefore, recommendable beer.

RATING ★★

Spanish Peaks Honey Raspberry Ale

Sports a fine reddish/deep-amber/honey color, off-white foam, average head retention; the nose is delightfully fruity and berry-like right from the start, though there's scant evidence of malt/grain/hops, but that's all right considering that it's a knock-off of the lambic style of beer from Belgium; in the mouth, the flavor is disturbingly weak-kneed, because neither the raspberry nor the honey elements take command—they don't seem to blend all that well either—the only fleeting hint of honey is as a meek backnote flavor; give me the character and essence of ripe, vibrant raspberry if you're advertising it on the label, none of this deferential, docile stuff that comes off like the artificial flavoring in sugar-free Jell-O; this is a bad joke and simply lazy brewing by someone that hasn't done their homework.

RATING ★

Spanish Peaks Black Dog Wheat Ale

A rare uncloudy wheat, harvest-gold color, eggshell-white foam, poor head retention; the lackluster nose is so closed off that hardly any aroma breaks through the barrier in the first three passes, except for a coin-like, metallic scent that's remarkably unappetizing—by the final nosing, a damp fabric aroma is all that's discernable—this nose must have been developed by Black Dog; the disemboweled mouth presence doesn't improve the situation one iota; okay, *you* rate a beer that smells like a T-shirt coming out of the dryer too soon, tastes like a stale cracker, and ends in a tasteless, characterless finish; one star? hey, you're catching on.

RATING ★

Sports Light

Golden tone, white foam, no head retention; the dry, yeasty, grainy nose is too coy for me—I really hate waiting around for a nose to show up—this pathetic bouquet never bothered; rather bland, neutral flavors on palate; unexciting overall, scant character, cardboard-like taste; not being a chemist, it's my guess that this beer has been gutted by the process of making it lighter; what's the point of serving it up if it hasn't any taste? where's the beer?

MANHATTAN BREWING COMPANY, NEW YORK, NY

RATING ★

STAR **Raspberry Wheat Ale**

Murkily turbid reddish gold, which is consistent with the style, white/pink foam, short head retention; this bouquet offers the cardboardy malted wheat as the headliner rather than the raspberry fruit—the second and third passes merely maintained what had been established in the opening pass, namely, wheat over raspberry; I liked the sour-mash lean to the flavor, which was accented further by unripened raspberry—some beer drinkers might shrink from the tartness offered by this ale, but I really liked it as a refreshing quaff on a warm day; very European in its bearing.

STAR BREWING COMPANY, PORTLAND, OR

RATING ★ ★ ★   *Recommended*

STEGMAIER **1857 Lager**

Pretty and pure harvest-gold color, vigorous beige foam, extralong head retention; the nose is zestily hoppy and malty, even creamy—the second pass reveals a white-rice component that works well, especially with the keen hops; in the mouth, this beer's finest virtue is its admirable balance—the hoppy bitterness is underpinned by a firm malt/rice base, which seems unshakable; the finish is acceptably bitter, medium-long, and very refreshing; a blocky, chunky, sturdy domestic lager that delivers the goods with honesty and unpretentiousness; go for it.

THE LION INC. BREWERY, WILKES-BARRE, PA

RATING ★ ★ ★ ★   *Highly Recommended*

STEGMAIER **Porter**

Superpretty, cherry-cola/deep-mahogany tone, beige foam, better than average head retention; the chocolatey/cocoa/malty nose is pleasingly sweet, but only moderately complex—the nose surprisingly turns timid by the third pass as it loses the chocolate and cocoa and goes solo with the roasted malt—it lacks the creaminess that a porter should possess; it's pleasant, simple, and direct in the mouth as, again, the maltiness seems to hold the fort on its own, with no supporting flavors evident—there's nothing in the way of layering or dimension; malty, off-dry aftertaste; drinkable, but disappointing; surely not as good as the other eastern Pennsylvania porter, Yuengling of Pottsville.

RATING ★ ★

STEELHEAD **Extra Stout**

Opaque, black/brown color, brown foam, quick head retention; the tarry nose speaks of little but deep-roasted malt and charcoal—there's no sense of creaminess or opulence, just malt and smoke—the stout profile demands more than what this lame aroma delivers; the mouth presence is better than the underwhelming nose, but the texture is nowhere near as thick and viscous as the style demands—on the plus side, flavors of roasted malt, toasted almonds, and tobacco smoke do make an honest attempt at respectability; the finish is disappointingly restrained; this dark ale needs some work.

MAD RIVER BREWING COMPANY, BLUE LAKE, CA

RATING ★★

Stoudt's Golden Lager

The harvest-gold/honey color is truly lovely, lacy off-white foam, fair head retention; the sweet, doughy, cake-batter nose captures the attention of the olfactory sense immediately—with aeration and warming, the nose expands to include scents of glue, pencil eraser, and white rice; on palate, it firmly showcases tart, properly bitter tastes of hops and lightly toasted malt; the snappy, crackling finish brings an ideal sense of closure to the experience; the balance and the solid structure of this beer make it an outstanding lager by any measure; bravo.

STOUDT BREWING COMPANY, ADAMSTOWN, PA

RATING ★★★★   *Highly Recommended*

Stoudt's Fest Marzen Style Lager

Smashing color of burnished gold/bronze, light-tan foam, pure, quick head; the nose is surprisingly vegetal (asparagus) in the first pass after the pour, then it regains its composure and offers an intensely bitter core aroma, which is framed by scents of moderately roasted malt and brown rice—I wasn't doing handstands over this mediocre and slow-to-develop bouquet; it definitely comes on strong in the mouth as potent, laser-beam flavors of burnt toast and hops challenge the taste buds—I enjoyed the workout; the finish is sound and very bitter; not everyone's cup of suds, to be sure, but a structurally sound, keenly bitter lager that goes a long, circuitous route to please; be patient and enjoy it.

RATING ★★★   *Recommended*

Stoudt's Honey Double Mai Bock

Golden/apple-juice/orange color, white foam, good head retention; not much happening here on the aromatic front—even after extended aeration, only faint hints of malt and a shadow aroma of honey make themselves known . . . barely—it's a stingy aroma; on palate, the honey influence is obvious, but slack and lifeless—then, out of the blue, the honey taste completely covers the malt component in a blanket of dull, off-dry, almost woody, paraffin-like flavor—this bock is a dismal failure and a real disappointment in light of the other Stoudt winners.

RATING ★

T

Telluride Lager

Light-to-medium amber hue, with good head retention; the nose is uninteresting not because its bad but because it's as profound as a Chuck Norris movie—there's not much there to describe other than some rudimentary yeastiness and hoppy bitterness—the magnificent beauty of Telluride, Colorado, is worthy of a better beer namesake than this feeble cup of nothing; in the mouth, it's no more characterful than the snooze-o-rama bouquet; this should be filed as contract brew gimmick number 13B59—I can hear it now, "Hey, let's name our beer after a trendy Rocky Mountain ski playground and people will certainly buy it by the case" (note: this beer is made in the high alpine country of Wisconsin).

TELLURIDE BEER COMPANY, MONROE, WI

RATING ★

THE SHIPYARD Longfellow Winter Ale

Opaque, jet-black/brown color, saddle-leather-tinted foam, good head retention; the heavily toasted nose offers equal parts wood smoke, Colombia coffee beans, charcoal briquettes, soy sauce, and hops—it's an upfront style, but not an especially layered or profound one; not everyone's cup of ale on palate, as it highlights highly bitter tastes of burnt whole-wheat toast, espresso, and smoke without the slightest whisper of cream, molasses, sweetness, or fruit; the finish is long and painted with bitter black coffee; a medium-weighted porter-stout style that is lacking in texture but that is nonetheless a better than average quaff for those of mean or disorderly constitutions.

KENNEBUNKPORT BREWING COMPANY, KENNEBUNKPORT, ME

RATING ★ ★ ★   ***Recommended***

THE SHIPYARD Export Ale

Handsome, brilliant pekoe-tea/medium-amber/orange hue, off-white foam, average head retention; the nose is sweaty, skunky, and as appealing as damp clothes after one comes in from the rain—the strange, fusty aroma evolves from an irritating dankness into a full-blown mushroomy, old-footlocker stench that's enormously offensive; in the mouth, there's no evidence of the malodorous cloud that poisoned the bouquet—in fact, the mannered, structured flavor of roasted malt and hoppy bitterness is clean and engaging from palate entry through to the long finish; the bad news is that the industrial-strength mustiness never blew off and, therefore, proved to be unacceptable enough to ruin everything, despite the perfectly fine appearance, taste, and finish.

RATING ★

THE SHIPYARD Goat Island Light Ale

Sturdy, harvest-gold tone, pearl-white foam, average head retention; the flat, hopeless, eviscerated, kernel-like nose smells most like the sticky, pasty white rice you get from a storefront Chinese take-out joint with a name like Woks Up, Doc; if you think the aroma is cooked, lame, and defective, wait until you expose your taste buds to the cardboard-like taste—better yet, don't even put yourself through that trauma—leave that to poor saps like me who do this sort of thing for a living; really deserves a zero-star rating and is a beer that even a goat couldn't love. 110 calories.

RATING ★

THE SHIPYARD Bluefin Stout

Chocolate brown/black, opaque appearance, good head retention; the nose could never be accused of being either effusive or generous—what I did detect was a toasted/charred-grain, almost fruit quality that did little for me; on the palate, it's smoky and tarry, with a sour-fruit finish; it owns none of the heft and dimension you expect and should have from a stout; I purchased two bottles, and both suffered from the identical malady—absence of style and character—and both were fresh bottles; no excuses; take a pass.

RATING ★

W

WEINHARD'S Red Lager

Lovely, eye-appealing, copper/tawny/burnished color, tan foam, average head retention; the round nose is biscuity, malty, and fruity, with subtle notes of hops and cream—there's a definite sense of scope and layering here; in the mouth, the medium-bodied texture is velvety-smooth while the bittersweet flavor of hops and fruity esters pleases the palate in graceful, yet potent, fashion; the finish is clean, long, hoppy, sound, and malty; easily one of the leading domestic reds currently available.

BLITZ-WEINHARD BREWING COMPANY, PORTLAND, OR

RATING ★ ★ ★   **Recommended**

WEINHARD'S Blue Boar Pale Ale

Pale golden color, white foam, poor head retention; the nose refused to come out and play through the first three passes, even with different pourings, swirling, and other assorted aeration tricks—nothing worked—in the final pass, miserly scents of corn husk and flat malt emerged, but failed to please—a stingy, tightfisted aroma; on palate, this flabby ale showed more verve than the anemic nose as plump tastes of malt and adjunct grains dominated the midpalate; the texture is fleshy and unappealing; the aftertaste is fruity and malty sweet; this one disappointingly goes nowhere compared to the sibling, the red lager; what turned me off the most was the fat feel of the texture—this beer owns no crispness, no bite, no snap, and clearly too little acid.

RATING ★

WHITE KNIGHT Light Ale

Very attractive, gold/honey color, flat-white foam, poor head retention; right after the pour, the aroma is generous, open, and friendly, exuding succulent scents of barley malt, yellow fruit, and sugar biscuits—subsequent passes are all positive, even as the aromatic powers diminish; in the mouth, it's simple, clean, and nicely proportioned as the primary taste elements of yeast, malt, and hops convene at midpalate—it's not complex or layered, but it is very quaffable just the same; the aftertaste is mildly bitter as the hops become King of the Hill.

MIDDLE AGES BREWING COMPANY, SYRACUSE, NY

RATING ★★★   **Recommended**

WILD BOAR Special Amber Lager

Medium amber color, crowned by a long-lasting off-white head; fresh, herbal, garden-like nose that hints of hops, malt, leather, and buttered almonds; on palate, it's unabashedly sweet compared to many other domestics—what I respond to most favorably is its sensual buttermilk-like texture; the flavor reminds me of ripe peaches or, even better, nectarines; it finishes as fruitily as it begins; a superb beer effort, but a word of caution: If you're not too keen on sweetness in your beer, stay away.

WILD BOAR BREWING, DUBUQUE, IA

RATING ★★★★   **Highly Recommended**

WILD BOAR Classic Pilsner

Medium amber/honey hue, with extralong head retention and miniscule bubbles; this nose is chockful of interesting nuances as at one moment a sweet-sour hard-apple-candy aroma dominates, while in the next nosing sweet, dry cereal takes the helm—an evident product of noble Saaz hops, it's easy to discern that this is a two-tiered bouquet with the apple element on top; on the palate, the entry is very malty and dry—this evolves into a mouth-puckering hoppy bitterness by midpalate; the finish, while acceptable, didn't impress me as much as the aftertaste of the Wild Boar Amber; overall, a very nice beer.

RATING ★★★   **Recommended**

WILD BOAR Wild Winter Spiced Brown Ale

Stunning, wildly effervescent, rich copper/rust color, beige foam, very extended head retention, great purity; the nose, to me, is more steely/metallic than spicy—I didn't like the aroma at all; in the mouth, a cinnamon/ nutmeg backnote does add sexy zip to the heavily malted taste and texture; the aftertaste is thick, mildly spiced, and very sensuous; the only weak spot is the overly flinty nose—other than that, this is a finely made dark ale that keeps the spice under control.

RATING ★★★   **Recommended**

WILD GOOSE Porter

Nearly opaque, black-coffee brown color, beige foam, very good head retention; the fusty nose smells of rubber in the first pass, then, thankfully, this blows off, allowing an intense milk chocolate aroma to establish itself by the third pass—the final nosing is like double cream, malted additive (especially Ovaltine), wood smoke, and charred grain—what began rather dubiously ended up being opulent, roasted/toasty, and by and large on the money; heavily smoked on the palate, this porter is moderately creamy texturewise and jam-packed with road tar, wood char, and smoked-meat flavors both in the midpalate and the aftertaste; not for the faint-hearted and, while tasty and correct for the style, not really profound.

WILD GOOSE BREWING, CAMBRIDGE, MD

RATING ★★★   *Recommended*

WILD GOOSE Amber Ale

Dusty, amber/honey color, with a voluminous beige-tan head; divinely sweet in the nose—positively enchanting, berry, prune, biscuity, fruity aroma; in the mouth, it goes dry, almost like tart sour apple candy, then it hints coyly of malted barley, steamed white rice, and soy sauce; fascinatingly different; idiosyncratic; strangely, it's as though the bouquet and the flavor are so diametrically opposed they don't belong in the same beer together, yet I found this brew very alluring even in its state of chaos; worth the search.

RATING ★★★   *Recommended*

WILD GOOSE India Pale Ale

This is the "head that devoured Manhattan"—ridiculously thick pillows of tightly packed tan bubbles create mountains of foam atop a deep amber/tawny/honey-colored beer—the fizz is unbelievably volatile—have a whip and a chair handy before you pop open this feral beast; funnily, for all the tumultuous effervescence, the nose couldn't be characterized as being effusive—in fact, it's difficult to pick up any aroma through the shaving-cream, insulation-like layer of foam—all I do detect is way too much CO_2 even after four nosings, two pourings, and too much wasted time; in the mouth, it's drinkable, moderately bitter, but that's about all; just bitterness in the aftertaste; the CO_2 level is prohibitive and totally out of control; stick with the amber or the porter from this brewer.

RATING ★

WILD GOOSE Spring Wheat Ale '96

Dazzling, copper/bronze hue, no cloudiness, eggshell foam, good head retention; the nose is fresh, estery, and even a trifle nutty, which is atypical for a wheat-based ale; in the mouth, the bitter entry is quite keen—it fails to develop any complexity at midpalate as the lightweight texture doesn't provide any stuffing; the metallic bitterness nearly becomes acute in the finish; what started out as generally inviting in the nose turned overly astringent and wholly unappetizing in the mouth.

RATING ★

WIT Amber

Rich bronze/copper hue, beige foam, very extended head retention; the odd, spicy nose offers up a curry-powder-like bouquet that threw me way off in the opening pass—the second and third nosings add caraway seed, rye bread, unbuttered popcorn, corn tortilla, and ginger—it's one of the most singular beer aromas I've encountered—I keep going back to it because it's so different and exotic—with every return, I find yet another intriguing side to it; it tastes very much like it smells—spicy and seed-like—cumin, tumeric, caraway—plus it also tastes like steamed corn tortillas—finally, after all the exotica, I note some lovely malt; not everyone's cup, I'm certain—if given time to develop, it grows on you in leaps and bounds.

SPRING STREET BREWING, ST PAUL, MN

RATING ★ ★ ★ ★   ***Highly Recommended***

WIT Black

Deep blood-red/mahogany/nut-brown color, beige foam, short head retention, good purity; the roasted nose is chockful of interesting notes, including molasses, coffee beans, dark caramel, and milk chocolate—all four passes show amazing resilience and poise as the aromas sustain their potency and charm—the malt intensity really picked up in the fourth pass—good show; on palate, the semisweet chocolate entry flavor is balanced by a sound hoppiness—by midpalate, the menu of tastes includes mocha, caramel, toffee, and malted milk; the finish is deep and long, highlighting the malt.

RATING ★ ★ ★   ***Recommended***

WIT White

Purposely cloudy, foggy-gold, white foam, poor head retention; the ambrosial nose is doughy, perfumed, and nothing short of delightful—an herbal explosion that's especially keen on sage, clove, and basil, even some pine needles; in the mouth, the herbal potency melds gracefully (but less impressively than the beguiling nose) with the yeasty doughiness; the finish is very piney, vegetal, and herbal; after starting off with a blast, this oddity settles down into an intriguing, somewhat idiosyncratic beer experience.

RATING ★ ★ ★   ***Recommended***

WOODSTOCK Arnold's Amber Lager

Seriously attractive, deep amber/rust tone, tan foam, long head retention; the heady bouquet bolts out of the sampling glass in amber waves of grain, heavy-duty barley malt, dark chocolate, bread dough, and pencil eraser and stays that powerful from the first to the final nosing—an opulent, potent, million-dollar perfume; the mouth presence is moderately rich—the flavors of malt, egg cream, and roasted nuts aren't as animated and overt as the aroma, but are tasty nonetheless; it finishes slightly bitter as the hop influence finally kicks in; a solidly made amber that should please both beer veterans and neophytes.

WOODSTOCK BREWING AND BOTTLING, STEVENS POINT, WI

RATING ★ ★ ★   ***Recommended***

Y

YUENGLING Porter

Firm, beige, long-lasting head, molasses/cola-brown color, with a crimson core, nearly opaque from top to bottom; on the nose, it's multidimensional, with toasty aromas of roasted nuts, cocoa, and bittersweet chocolate;

substantial, muscular texture; in the mouth, deep, burnt-toast, intensely malty, road-tar, dry flavors are nicely underscored by a wonderful satiny feel that generously coats the palate; long finish, in which the tar, burnt wheat toast, and hazelnuts dominate and harmoniously come together; a well-done dark beer that pleases every time I taste it.

YUENGLING BREWING, POTTSVILLE, PA

RATING ★ ★ ★   ***Recommended***

YUENGLING Lord Chesterfield Ale

Gorgeous, billowy, cumulus cloud head that shows astounding staying power even after ten minutes in the glass, pretty, harvest-gold color; the inviting, subtle, slightly floral, and sweet bouquet shows a noticeable yeast component; the dry, correct entry gives way to a lovely, if monotone, malty flavor; has an extended, dry aftertaste of dry roasted nuts and licorice; plumply textured; a good brew that overall is very attractive and enjoyable; recently upgraded—tasted six times.

RATING ★ ★ ★   ***Recommended***

YUENGLING TRADITIONAL Amber Lager

Short-lived, silvery head; appealing honey/amber color, with orange/copper highlights; the gravelly, flinty, wet-slate nose has an intriguing fruit element that underlies the stone-like top-level aroma; the fruit peeks out on the palate with barely discernable flavors of berries and malt; light- to medium-bodied; the finish is medium-long and rather neutral; what it lacks in body and finish, it picks up in freshness and agility; a nimble, one-note beer that is an amiable, but hardly great, quaff.

RATING ★ ★

YUENGLING PREMIUM Light Lager

Moderately firm head; gold/hay/straw color; grainy, hoppy nose, tinged with a doughy yeastiness; very crisp, bone-dry, very lean, flinty flavors wrapped in a medium-weighted body; while it shows more textural presence than many other domestic light beers I've sampled, it still lacks the flavor structure and sensual satisfaction of full-strength lagers; a decent, honest effort nonetheless for its type, but is no match for the likes of Boston Lightship; gets points for a decidedly malty finish, pleasant nose, mouth-feel, and good color; gets demerits for flavor deficiency.

RATING ★

Z

ZIMA Clearmalt

Colorless, no head, it pours like tonic water; the nose has elements of peach, nectarine, mandarin orange, and a remote resemblance to Cherry 7-Up; the taste is sweet-sour, soda-pop-like, and clearly manufactured to be a bridge from the likes of Coke, Dr. Pepper, et cetera, into the world of beverage alcohol; it's a kiddie brew that I found way too sweet in the mouth, as the flavor of mandarin orange neatly conceals the taste of alcohol; it sits in the funny position of tasting like Kool-Aid but kicking like a mainstream beer; may be all right for the uninitiated palates of juveniles, but for anyone over twenty-three years of age it'z something ztupid.

ZIMA BEVERAGE COMPANY, MEMPHIS, TN

RATING ★

ZIP CITY Vienna Amber Lager

A dense, amber, turbid, intensely malty/cereally brewpub beer; the reason for the cloudy appearance is that it's not filtered, a quality that makes this lager lusciously chewy, voluptuous, and even bold; of the batches I've tasted of this beer from early 1994 through early 1996, the quality has improved substantially enough to merit a recommendation.

ZIP CITY BREWPUB, NEW YORK, NY

RATING ★ ★ ★   *Recommended*

ZIP CITY Oktoberfest Amber Lager

This beer's appearance is mildly turbid and sports a foggy amber hue—shows scant head retention; the nose shows a smoky, musty presence that has little or no hop influence, but owns a subtle yeastiness at the backdoor—overall, it's a limp-noodle kind of bouquet that could use more assertiveness; in the mouth, this beer picks up the tempo as lean flavors of nut meat and citrus refresh the palate; the finish is clean, but slim, highlighting the smokiness; unexciting and pedestrian, but drinkable just the same.

RATING ★ ★

IMPORTED
BEER REVIEWS

A

ADNAMS Nut Brown Ale (England)

Seriously handsome chestnut-brown/blood-red color, rich beige foam, average head retention; the malty nose doesn't leap out at you, you have to work at it and be patient—as the ale warms, traces of spice, dark toffee, caramel, and dark bread make themselves known—it's a well-mannered bouquet that requires some patience; on the palate, it's medium- to full-bodied, satiny-textured, and jam-packed with roasted malt, toasted bread, dark chocolate, and coffee flavors that coexist in near-perfect harmony; the aftertaste is medium-long and highlights the charred malt; superb dark-ale drinking.

RATING ★ ★ ★ ★   *Highly Recommended*

ADNAMS Broadside Ale (England)

Attractive russet/dark-copper hue, khaki-colored foam, poor head retention; this shy nose leans more to the hops element than to the malt as astringent, nutty aromas barely waft out of the sampling glass—even by the final nosing, there wasn't much aromatically to sift through; the strong suit of this ale clearly is in the flavor, where a sweet-sour, Brazil-nut taste welcomes the taste buds at entry, then the hoppy bitterness and semisweet maltiness collide in the wake-up-call aftertaste; solid, honest, working-class ale.

RATING ★ ★ ★   *Recommended*

ADNAMS Suffolk Extra Ale (England)

Consider it an ESB—Extra Special Bitter class; foxy appearance of brilliant, translucent copper-penny/burnt-orange/reddish-amber tone, quick head of eggshell-white foam; the nose is luscious, compelling, and rich as aromas of fabric, rich toasted malt, and fruity hops combine to create a highly perfumed bouquet that has a spicy, zesty snap in the fourth pass; the texture seems a bit thin on the tongue, but the fine hoppy flavor cleanses the palate completely; the finish is long, mildly bitter, and austere; to be sure, it's not in the class of Brakspear's Henley Ale, but it's good just the same.

RATING ★ ★ ★   **Recommended**

AECHT SCHLENKERLA Rauchbier (Germany)

Lovely, copper/rust/deep-amber color, pure, ivory foam, good head retention; the stunning aroma immediately makes me think of sausages on the barbecue—the bouquet is sweetly smoky, woody (from the beechwood that's used to kiln-dry the malt), and intense—the similarity to fine smoked breakfast sausages and smoked meats is astounding—I loved the full-throttle, take-no-prisoners bouquet, in part, because it's unique and defining; in the mouth, the smokiness is less dense, allowing for peeks of malt, meat, wood, cigar tobacco, and even hops way in the background; the finish is gentlemanly, malty, and off-dry; the world's prime smoked-beer superstar.

RATING ★ ★ ★ ★ ★   **Highest Recommendation**

AFFLIGEM Dobbel Abbey Ale (Belgium)

This abbey was founded in 1074; the red/brown/mahogany color is breathtaking, beige foam, infinite head retention; the bouquet is all red apples, comice pears, and ripe apricots, with faint touches of hops, yeast, and sour dough thrown in for balance—this is an engaging nose that says precious little about grain, but volumes about hops and estery fruit; the taste, in a direction change, addresses grain, especially malt, in rich, weighty, and sweet terms—flavors of roasted barley, candied almonds, and baked pears headline the mouth presence—the texture is round, creamy, and medium-bodied; the aftertaste is intensely fruity (apples and pears) and remains in the throat long after the final sip; another drop-dead winner from the monasteries of Belgium.

RATING ★ ★ ★ ★   **Highly Recommended**

AFFLIGEM Tripel Abbey Ale (Belgium)

Handsome, solid, 14-carat-gold color, white foam, very good head retention; the nose opens with an intensely yeasty, honeyed bouquet—the second pass features a green-apple scent that's beguiling—the final two nosings merely shore up the positive impressions of the two earlier passes—a definitive abbey ale bouquet; on palate, it's lemon-snap taste gets things going for the taste buds—the midpalate is serenely balanced as the apple flavor harmonizes beautifully with the yeast and malt—a broad-shouldered, almost wine-like ale; the aftertaste is sour, crisp, and clean; in a word, luscious.

RATING ★ ★ ★ ★   **Highly Recommended**

ALGONQUIN Special Reserve Ale (Canada)

Very handsome tawny/deep-amber color, pure, solid beige foam, very good head retention; the strange nose reminded me of crayons, that waxy smell we all knew as children—but this is beer, not kindergarten, and the aroma perplexed me through the first two passes—in the last two nosings, I at last detected hints of sweet malt; there existed no such befuddlement with the flavor, as off-dry to sweet tastes of toasted cereal and honey-wheat bread made nice music together; the finish was medium-long, uncomplicated, silky, and off-dry; the pick of the Algonquin litter.

RATING ★ ★ ★   *Recommended*

ALGONQUIN Black & Tan (Canada)

Nearly opaque chocolate brown/blood red color, beige foam, no head retention; the nose is delightfully chocolatey, with a supporting cast of cherries in the first nosing, then the bouquet quickly diminishes with air contact from the second to the final passes—the last inhalation detects marginal traces of cocoa and coffee, but the fact is that by this juncture the aroma has pretty much bid adieu; it shows a decent malty bearing at palate entry, then the flavor shifts into coffee/cocoa mode at midpalate, finishing slightly bitter but rather flat; not at all an unpleasant experience, rather, an uninspired middle-of-the-road ride.

RATING ★ ★

ALGONQUIN Dark Ale (Canada)

Very handsome, luminous copper/orange hue, light-tan foam, brief head retention; the initial nosing reveals an understated maltiness that's off-dry to sweet, then, similar to the Black & Tan, the aroma gradually fades from the view finder, beginning at the second nosing—by the last pass there are still timid hints of brown rice and malt . . . and that's being kind; easy on the palate as simple, rudimentary flavors of lightly toasted malt and hops don't exactly conduct a flavor clinic, but they're affable and acceptable; the finely bitter finish is the best feature of this Everyman ale.

RATING ★ ★

ALTENMUNSTER (Bavaria-Germany)

Solid gold/hay color, no head to speak of; the rambunctious nose attacks right from uncorking, spewing no-nonsense scents of nut meat, herbs, hops, and wet grain in a full-throttle "Export" style; the texture is firm and creamy, with plenty of grip; tastewise, I detected all-out hops in the dry, almost tart flavor that goes slightly nutty in the long, mellow finish; I like the straight-ahead, round, chewy aftertaste; while solid overall, refreshing, and clean, it comes dangerously close to being too sour/lemony in the late palate and finish.

RATING ★ ★ ★   *Recommended*

AMSTEL Light Lager (Holland)

Soft, gold color, dirigible-sized bubbles, good purity, snow-white foam, good head retention; the nose is very yeasty and citrusy, but affable and rudimentary—there's a slight tinge of tanky-metal/sourness that shows up in the third pass—this is a nose that's as complex as Melanie Griffith; as advertised, Amstel is light in calories but also in aroma, texture, and flavor; it's not bad, just paper-thin and insipid; I will hand it to Amstel Light for being very refreshing, but then so is mineral water; for all the jive, one of the two or three lights I'd consider drinking if absolutely nothing else was available.

   RATING ★★

ANDES Cerveza (Venezuela)

Golden, harvest-yellow, but mildly turbid color, scant head; the bouquet is correct, pleasantly sweet, even ambrosial as compelling aromas of ripe pineapple, hops, honey, and brewer's yeast compete for dominance—the honeyed nose is a major plus; in the mouth, the impression is less engaging as mildly sweet, grainy flavors never quite fulfill the promise found in the nose; medium-long, off-dry, roasted finish; I wanted to like it more than it deserved.

   RATING ★★

AYINGER Brau-Weisse Helles Hefe Weissbier (Germany)

Sports a minor turbidity that makes the color a rich, sunrise-gold, really pretty, a snowy foam, exceptional head retention; the generous, but not effusive nose is a textbook study of what a wheat-beer bouquet should be— yeasty, moderately herbaceous, and earthy with that lovely forest-after-a-shower scent, plus backnote dashes of dried basil and oregano—this aroma alone earns two stars; creamy, delectable, and astonishingly fat on the tongue, this beauty has a first-class mouth presence that oozes sweet grain, herbs, maize, and yellow-fruit flavors from palate entry through the finish; a simply gorgeous, delicious, and superlative wheat that leaves most others in the dust.

   RATING ★★★★   **Highly Recommended**

AYINGER Altbairisch Dunkel (Germany)

Extremely comely color of deep chocolate brown/mahogany, the beige foam doesn't stick around too long; the nose is a lovely, complex mixture of coffee bean, vanilla extract, deep roasted barley, egg cream, brown sugar, molasses, and nougat—this is a layer-upon-layer affair that keeps the full attention of the drinker—a smashing nose; not as creamy or richly textured as I'd hoped for and projected after so vigorously embracing the bouquet; the coffee-bean taste influence is very evident in the entry, then the hops take over at midpalate as the bitterness factor takes firm hold of the flavor; the chocolatey aftertaste is long and smoky; the slight letdown in the flavor kept this better than average dark in the still respectable three-rating-star range.

   RATING ★★★   **Recommended**

AYINGER Celebrator Doppelbock (Germany)

Chestnut-brown/black-coffee hue, with no head retention whatsoever; the deep, but restrained nose is like dry roasted grain, black coffee, malted barley, honey, and even a smattering of herbs; in the mouth, it's firm, medium-bodied, and amply, but not overly, flavorful as dry, tasty flavors of wood smoke, cereal, and apples come together in a pleasing, bone-dry aftertaste; a sound double bock, but not nearly as majestic as Paulaner's awesome Salvator, which is a five-star classic.

   RATING ★★★   **Recommended**

B

Ba M'Ba BGI "33" Export (Vietnam)

Pale golden hue, big-beaded effervescence, very poor head retention; the nose is especially biscuity, nutty, and even spicy, with a keen yeastiness that I liked quite a lot—the later nosings reveal cake batter, intense maltiness, and yellow fruit; unfortunately, the next step is to taste it—it's at this critical point that this beer implodes—total devastation is the result—all the pluses admired in the nose are undercut by the spineless, flat, cardboard-like flavor and, as if that's not bad enough, the nonexistent aftertaste; the splooshy, basketball-sized bubbles should have given this lemon away, but like a fool I was swayed by the appealing bouquet and went on to taste the stuff; don't even think of buying it.

RATING ★

Bass Pale Ale (England)

Warm orange/amber-color/light-beige head, low-key, hoppy nose, which is moderately sweet—no heavyweight bouquet; medium-bodied, dry, and cereally on the palate; scant flavor follow-through in the finish; while technically sound and good on the palate, unlike other U.K. ales I've sampled and relished (for instance, Young's, Samuel Smith's, and the best of them all, Brakspears), Bass didn't have me pounding the tasting table in awe or delight; it simply seemed too compromised, too commonplace; being *correct* is a far cry from being *savory;* tasted at least a dozen times; upgraded.

RATING ★ ★

Bateman's XXXB Ale (England)

Very pretty orange/honey/amber hue, tan foam, very pure, average head retention; the nose is keenly floral out of the box, then it turns a bit woody/nutty in the second pass—the final passes reflect the first two with little dissipation; on palate, it's an unusual flavor, deep in hops, especially, on the surface as the manageably bitter taste obliterates all other flavor possibilities—subsequent samplings serve only to bolster and confirm the initial impression; more malt impact is detected in the finish, though hops still reign; for those sudsters who like their beers tight around the corners and snappily astringent.

RATING ★ ★ ★   **Recommended**

Bateman's Victory Ale (England)

Extremely deep, but not opaque, mahogany color, medium-beige foam, fair head retention; for all the depth of color, the opening stages of the nose are surprisingly meek and underdeveloped—the third pass reluctantly coughs up some mild maltiness (Gee, thanks)—after allowing in another ten minutes of aeration time, the fourth nosing unveils a wide panorama of aromas, including deep roasted malt, milk chocolate, brown sugar, toffee, and honey; in the mouth, the sweet malt headlines the flavor marquee—this is supported by secondary flavors of cola, cocoa, and dark fruit; the aftertaste is rich, sweet, and very pleasing.

RATING ★★★   **Recommended**

BAVIK White Beer—Bière Blanche (Belgium)

Pale golden color, bright white foam, long head retention, just slightly turbid; the vastly alluring bouquet is remarkably fruity, evoking in particular, yellow-orange fruit such as pears and apricots—there's a backnote of yeastiness that comes out in the second pass—the last two nosings reveal little, except for a distant hops note, past the aforementioned impressions; in the mouth, a mildly tart lemony/citrus taste highlights the entry—the lemony flavor stays with the flavor into midpalate; the finish is ethereal and short; hardly profound, but a nice, simple, warm-weather quaff.

RATING ★★★   **Recommended**

BECK'S Dark Pilsener (Germany)

Pretty chestnut/mahogany color, strong, foamy, beige head; unusually long head retention; multilayered, opulent, smoky, strawberry-like nose that also offers hints of wheat cereal, cream, and cocoa; full, chocolate mocha and fruit flavors meld beautifully with a taste of molasses; owns a toasted, honey-wheat finish that's very long and pleasingly off-dry; excellent brewing; this beer is as rich and flavorful as one could want.

RATING ★★★★   **Highly Recommended**

BECK'S Pilsener (Germany)

Sunny, hay-like, straw-gold color—shaving-cream-like, frothy white head, no head retention; clean, crisp, uncomplicated, oatmeal, pilsener nose with no surprises; on palate, this silky, feline beauty starts out off-dry and scrumptuously fruity; the long, sensuous finish is totally dry and mineral-like—so clean, it nearly crackles; Beck's creamy, plush bearing is downright regal, which is unusual for a mass-marketed pilsener; for a ubiquitous brew, tough to beat in terms of quality and flavor satisfaction.

RATING ★★★   **Recommended**

BECK'S Oktoberfest Lager (Germany)

Very attractive, orange-pekoe-tea/amontillado-sherry/tawny hue, topped with beige foam, fair head retention; the solid, toasty, pear-like, roasted-malt, and nut-like nose is generous and round in the first nosing pass and remains so through the subsequent three nosings—a rollicking, good, no-nonsense bouquet; on the palate, it's simple and properly malty, with fleet flavors of cola nut, hops, and nut meat; the finish is slightly weak as the flavors, which were faint to begin with, tailspin into the depths, never to be smelled or tasted again; the superb appearance and able, jolly bouquet were miserably let down by the too careful brewing approach in the flavor and aftertaste; a missed opportunity.

RATING ★★

BELHAVEN St. Andrews Ale (Scotland)

Astonishingly luminous look of a red ale—henna/auburn/tawny/chestnut/reddish-brown, eggshell foam, superb head retention; the nose exhibits solid, walnut/Brazil-nut, coffee-bean, roasted-malt, and old-saddle-leather aromas that are a touch sweet, earthy, and fruity—from the first to the fourth nosings, this thoroughbred bouquet streaks across the finish line barely out of breath—a genuinely accomplished, polished nose that has remarkable stamina; on the palate, it's racy and sinewy, but stately in bearing as fully endowed flavors of roasted chestnuts, orange peel, tangelo, and hoppy bitterness enchant the taste buds from entry to the delicately bitter aftertaste; simply an outstanding ale.

RATING ★★★★   *Highly Recommended*

BELHAVEN Scottish Ale (Scotland)

Very close in appearance to its sibling, the St. Andrews Ale—marginally darker and definitely redder—the off-white foam has better than average staying power; this nose is very roasted, yeasty, and malty, though I found the aroma of the St. Andrews Ale to be deeper and slightly more layered—interestingly, this aromatic nose is almost feminine, slightly musty, malty, husky, and plummy—amazing longevity from the first nosing to the last; among the most nimble of Scottish ales, Belhaven prefers to dance with the taste buds rather than conquer them; the finish is soft, long, and pleasingly hopped; the ideal partner to the St. Andrews, which is more muscular and assertive; try this dynamic, delicious Scottish duo.

RATING ★★★★   *Highly Recommended*

BELLE-VUE Kriek/Cherry Ale (Belgium)

Drop-dead gorgeous cherry-wood/ruby hue, faint white foam, no head retention; the predictable Bing-cherry nose is quite sweet, almost soda-pop-like in its bearing—beyond that there's not much more to address aromatically, even after four meticulous nosings; more sweet than sour, more uncomplicated than characterful, the flavor offers a one-track taste, just ripe red cherries; the aftertaste is limp, insipid, and virtually nonexistent; I wanted to like this lambic ale enough to recommend it, but the no-frills character wouldn't allow it; take a pass.

RATING ★★

BELLE-VUE Gueuze Lambic Ale (Belgium)

Very attractive appearance, deep amber/clover-honey hue, puffy white foam, extralong head retention; the nose is rather cagey and coy upfront, then it reluctantly shows some meager wheat-malt notes in the third pass, finally ending up with a dash of barley as well—an exasperatingly backward bouquet; the taste is somewhat sweetish, but with little definition or direction—it's simply a sweet, grainy, cereal-like taste that exhibits no real depth or character; the finish is lame and has a cereal-with-sugar taste at the very end; shapeless, paper-thin, and rudderless.

RATING ★

BELLE-VUE Framboise/Raspberry Ale (Belgium)

Garnet-red/cherry-wood tone, beige/pink foam, very long head retention; simplistic but pleasant nose that dies after the first nosing pass—it just vanishes completely; on the palate, the sour red-fruit flavor flashes a wee bit of red raspberry, but the confused fruit component could just as easily be loganberry or blackberry, so undefinable is it; no aftertaste to address; this anemic lambic is a prime example of how not to present this unusual type of beer; pass it by.

RATING ★

BERLINER KINDL Pils (Germany)

Very pretty marigold tone, crowned by a to-the-death white head of foam; the nose is rather subdued, prudently offering fragrances of sweet pine sap and hops; medium-bodied to the feel; the stone-dry flavor is remarkably crisp, I mean, it almost snaps with freshness; the finish is lean and dry; it's a good example of the austere side of German brewing, though I was hoping for a tad more dimension in the flavor department.

RATING ★★

BIG ROCK McNally's Irish Ale (Canada)

Handsome, bronze/rust/rich-amber tone, light-tan foam, very good head retention; this nose offers a generous hunk of malt in the opening pass, then it takes on a brown-rice note in addition to the malt in the second run—the last two passes are owned solely by the toasted malt; it shows a solid hoppy bitterness at midpalate after the entry comes off like cocoa and malt—medium-weighted texture—the final sampling has the hops and malt getting together in a strong, clean, and sweet finish, which topped off the entire experience with style and soundness.

RATING ★★★   *Recommended*

BINTANG Pilsener (Indonesia)

Golden hay color, fast deflating head, hardly any bubble activity at all—plus, on the negative side of the ledger, I detected minute suspended particles floating about in both sample bottles; the nose is properly doughy, if subdued, but all seems in order in the aroma category; the texture and weight are fine, but the tinny-metallic taste is an express ticket to troublesville; I suspect there's the chance that these two flat-as-a-pancake bottle samples are tired goods—when it comes to beer, freshness is everything; on the other hand, I doubt seriously that this beer is very palatable even at the peak of its lifecycle; no drinking date could be found on the label or the cap; avoid.

RATING ★

BODDINGTONS Pub Ale Draught (England)

I rarely take the chance of evaluating beer from a can, but here's an exception to that rule, mainly because of Boddingtons "draughtflow" system, which, strangely, works better in aluminum than it does in glass; the "draughtflow" thingamajig consists of a plastic ball inserted in the can/bottle of Boddingtons—when the can/bottle is opened, the ball shoots off a blast of nitrogen, which helps create a sensationally luxurious, whipped-cream-type of head; anyway, back to our story—the Pub Ale Draught seems almost identical to the bottled Pub Ale Export except in the aroma, which is far more malty, biscuity, and expressive in the canned version; go for the can.

RATING ★★★   *Recommended*

BODDINGTONS Export Ale (England)

Pouring this into the glass, I thought I was pouring an Irish Cream Liqueur, so viscous and milky is this export—the color is light amber/clover-honey/dirty-gold, unbelievably thick, off-white foam, the head lasts an eternity—it's quite a spectacle; the peculiar, but oddly alluring aroma speaks of ripe red fruit, caraway seeds, lightly roasted malt, and rubber pencil eraser—I found the strangeness of the nose to be a plus; regrettably, the flavor doesn't keep pace with either the remarkable appearance or the intriguing aroma—indeed, it's a refreshing, crisp, mildly bitter, light- to medium-bodied ale, but I didn't think that there was a lick of complexity in the smoky, roasted taste than lasted through to the finish; it lost its panache and momentum in the mouth.

RATING ★★

BOHEMIA Pilsener (Mexico)

Inviting, rich, harvest-gold color, excellent head retention; the nose is bountiful, grainy, off-dry, and mashy, with shadowy traces of metal and ground black pepper—it's an engaging nose that I've enjoyed numerous times in many Mexican restaurants; in the mouth, it's bone-dry, with a well-defined citrus-yeast flavor base that's medium-weighted and keenly refreshing; the finish is rather short, but clean and citrusy; Bohemia is not as grand as the great Negra Modelo, but it's one of the two Mexican beers that I invariably order (the other being golden Chihuahua) when the Negra Modelo runs out.

RATING ★★★ *Recommended*

BRAKSPEARS Henley Ale (England)

Prototypical Bitter tone, old-penny/copper/russet, lively tan foam, fair head retention; the bouquet is composed of round, roasted malt, light English toffee, nuts, nougat, coffee, and earthy hops—it's the stateliness and the finesse of the nose that make it so memorable—there's simply layer upon layer of aromatic charm; on the palate, it starts out malty-sweet as the cereal mashiness reaches its zenith at midpalate, whereupon the bitter hops converge, making it a totally harmonious flavor experience; certainly, this is one of England's premier Bitter aftertastes; a classic, complex, one-of-a-kind ale that serves as the benchmark of its category.

RATING ★★★★★ *Highest Recommendation*

BRASSEURS Bière de Paris Lager (France)

Russet/copper color, meek head; sweaty, yeasty, hoppy, one-dimensional nose; the pleasant, malty, citrusy flavor tries to redeem the questionable nose—but at the end of the day it's just a simplistic, limp attempt that's too off in the nose; you can't make good beer with smoke and mirrors; pure garbage.

RATING ★

BREUG Lager (France)

Medium-deep, gold/straw color, with a long-lived, firm, white pillow of foam; the alluring nose is spicy, hoppy (go lucky), and exhibits a pleasing snappiness—on the second and third passes I noted even a walnut-like quality that's very nice; regrettably, the lean, toasty, dry flavor isn't a topper to the delightful aroma—in fact, I was keenly disappointed by the sharp, austere taste; the aftertaste simply mirrors the biting flavor; what a pity after the strong showing by the appearance and bouquet that the taste and the finish should fizzle out; but the fine appearance and nose account for something; a ho-hum deal.

RATING ★ ★

BROKEN HILL Lager (Australia)

The intriguing gold color shows some copper highlights as it's being poured, the head is standard-issue white; the nose is assertive, crisp, clean, and grainy, resembling corn husk—there's a spicy/cedary/piney background in the bouquet that I find very appealing; on palate, it's firm, very clean, stone-dry, and straight-to-the-point—in other words, you needn't wade through layers of flavor and complexity in order to determine whether or not you like it—it's there in your face; a sound, honest performer.

RATING ★ ★ ★   *Recommended*

BUCKAROO Beer (Belgium)

Golden lager look, billowy white foam, long-lasting head; the unusual nose reminds me of damp wool, oatmeal, and steamed brown rice—I wouldn't term it offensive or "off," but neither would I describe it as an appealing aroma; in the mouth, it's clean, medium-weighted, moderately sweet in a grainy not a fruity way (almost like sweet corn), and it lies nicely on the palate; the aftertaste is austere, hoppy, and refreshing; this beer would have earned a third star and a recommendation had not the nose come off in so awkward a manner; really dumb name and even dumber label for a beer made in Belgium.

RATING ★ ★

C

CAESARUS Imperator Heller Bock (Switzerland)

Attractive light-orange/harvest-gold tone, white foam, short head retention; the nose is very concentrated and assertive without being aggressive or overbearing—there's a mild orange-peel quality that wraps around the steely, tanky, pork-loin, malty core aroma—although the nose was busy, I didn't particularly care for the minerally metallic bend in it; on the palate, there's a vigorous rush of heady alcohol that washes over the tongue like high tide—the flavors of cardboard, ginger, malt, and creamy hops are underdeveloped and unexhilarating; what's curious about this beer is that at one moment it seems to have lots of potential to soar, then in the next taste a mean, steeliness rears its head, canceling out the positive features; I come not to bury Caesarus . . . oh, hell, yes I do; nexxxxxxt.

RATING ★

CALEDONIAN Amber Ale (Scotland)

Opulent, utterly gorgeous amber/orange/russet tone, low head retention; the fabulously piquant nose oozes with large amounts of buttery, caramel-like, wood-smoke aromas that are delightfully juicy and complex—I liked the manner in which this bouquet comes right at you, no pussyfooting, no hesitation, no waltz-around-the-block while you wait for it to open up—this nose explodes from the glass; in the mouth, the smoky, seed-like, bitter, nut-meat taste is long and satisfying from entry through to the extended aftertaste; the splendidly toasty and vibrant nose alone is worth at least two rating stars; a dandy, robust ale from Scotland that's worth a serious search.

RATING ★ ★ ★ ★   *Highly Recommended*

CALEDONIAN Double Dark Ale (Scotland)

Dark reddish-amber/cherry-juice tone, meager head retention; the round, supple, bosomy bouquet is layered with a ripe cherry/berry top layer and a lactate/creamy-malt foundational layer—a sensational and highly memorable bouquet; on the palate, the fruit gives way to a solid, clean flavor of malt, with the slightest hint of wood smoke; the finish is slightly bitter, mildly fruity-nutty, and very extended; a rich, creamy winner on all fronts, in all aspects; find and purchase in enormous amounts.

RATING ★ ★ ★ ★   *Highly Recommended*

CALEDONIAN Golden Pale Ale (organically grown barley and hops) (Scotland)

Mildly hazy gold/marigold tint, white head that stayed around for a while, excellent purity; the handsome nose is yeasty, doughy, and malty in the first run-through, then in later passes the malt feature jumps into the lead in plump waves of sweet grain and honey notes—this is a dynamite, dynamic fragrance that puts a spotlight on the organically grown grain—lovely and fresh; in the mouth, I was disappointed in the lack of weight and gravity, but the flavors of hops and malt enchanted the taste buds, nevertheless; the aftertaste is a bit lean and short and very bread-like; good effort overall by a favorite Scottish brewer.

RATING ★ ★ ★   *Recommended*

CALEDONIAN Golden Promise Organically Produced Ale (Scotland)

Medium-fog, dusty-orange/honey hue, off-white foam, no head retention; the nose didn't impress me that much in the opening stages, as I found it hard-edged, kernel-like, stony, and steely—things improved as it warmed and aerated—the barley malt comes alive in the third pass, especially, bringing the warmth and roundness that it desperately needs—in the last pass, the bouquet comes to full flower in a hoppy, smoky, tobacco-like push; on palate, it comes across as being rather thin in texture and a trifle anemic taste-wise—subsequent tastings don't unveil any nuances that would pull it up into recommendable territory—the hardness in the aroma and the mid-palate are of a mineral kind; drinkable, unexceptional.

RATING ★ ★

CANADIAN BREWING COMPANY Black & Tan (Stout and Lager) (Canada)

Nearly opaque black/brown—it actually resembles a cola or a draught root beer, beige foam, little head retention, pure; the nose is muted at first blush, but I believe it to be too cold for the style—as this B & T warms and aerates, it rouses in the form of scents of dark caramel—the third and last passes reveal a distant nuttiness that's pleasing but elusive; on palate, there's a medium-bodied richness underlying the flavor part of the program—the soft taste of sweet, deep-roasted malt finds a nice counterpart in the hoppy twang that comes aboard at midpalate; the finish is rather quick, dry to bitter, and more hoppy than malty.

CANADIAN BREWING CO., ONTARIO, CANADA

RATING ★★★ **Recommended**

CARIB Lager (Trinidad, West Indies)

Textbook lager appearance—golden-hay/corn-yellow color, absolutely pure, pearl-white foam, very good head retention; the nose is a study in economical simplicity—it's tight, compact, a bit citrusy, only mildly malty, and clean; in the mouth, the facility noted in the nose is reprised and promoted as the surprisingly buxom texture forms the stable base for a sweet, cereally taste that ends up with a semibitter tang in the nearly plump aftertaste; runs rings around most premium American lagers because of the fullness; the quintessential beer for the steamy tropics.

RATING ★★★ **Recommended**

CARLSBERG LIGHT Lager (Denmark)

Deep gold color; medium-firm, brilliant white head; off-odor, sweaty, cheesy nose; medium-weighted, smooth texture; the dry, roasted-almond, toasted flavors come across nicely, then quickly fade in a very mild, faintly nutty aftertaste; attractive flavors and savory finish redeem the problem in the nose; certainly not the disaster that most of the domestic lights are.

RATING ★★

CARTA BLANCA Lager (Mexico)

Pleasant, golden color, puffy white foam; the nose has an intense citrus and mild nuttiness that is efficient and direct; on the palate, it's lean, very clean, and well balanced; the malty, on-line flavors are pleasing and simple; a solid, reliable, old-standby cerveza that does have charm, but fails to rise above mediocrity.

RATING ★★

CERVEZA-AGUILA Pilsener (Colombia)

Attractive golden-hay color, topped by a snow-white head; the clean, dry, malted-barley, corn-husk aroma comes straight to the point, nothing coy about this bouquet; the mouth presence exhibits a creamy texture that is delightful and mouth-filling; the taste reflects the qualities found in the nose—agile, forward, refreshing flavors of dry cereal and malted grains; the nicely done, effortless style owns considerably more character than most of its lame, golden North American counterparts.

RATING ★★★ **Recommended**

CHIHUAHUA Lager (Mexico)

Opulent, golden-hay appearance, snowy foam that quicky died; the substantial, honey-wheat-bread nose is really delightful; richly textured and silky to the feel; in the mouth, the husky, real, no-nonsense malt flavor is simultaneously generous and elegant; almost fine-wine-like in its bearing; underrated beer making; no one I know likes this beer as much as I do—I'm totally stumped by that; is anyone listening out there?

RATING ★ ★ ★   *Recommended*

CHIMAY Grande Réserve Trappist Ale (Belgium)

Similar to the Première in its rich bronze color, the steady storm of miniscule bubbles creates a thunderhead of tan foam; the melony-flowery aroma is spring-garden-fresh and simply one of the most beguiling beer bouquets I've yet encountered—it alone is worth the price and the search; almost wine-like in its bearing and alcohol content (9 percent), the opulent, sweet, honey-wheat flavor envelops the palate like a satin robe as refined tastes of pears, peaches, and plums go the distance; unbelievable quality; this is one to share with friends, so splendid is it; do what you have to do to snare a bottle or two of this outrageously luscious beer.

RATING ★ ★ ★ ★ ★   *Highest Recommendation*

CHIMAY Cinq Cents Trappist Ale (Belgium)

The burnished color is orange/copper, the foam is light tan and remarkably tight; an 8-percent alcohol brew bottled to commemorate the 500th anniversary (in 1986) of the Chimay principality—please note that it was created in 1986 and has of course had subsequent bottlings since that year; the engaging bouquet of this lush beer is noticeably drier and crisper than either the Première or the Grande Réserve, emitting hints of barley cereal and spice; on palate, the smoothness and elegance are totally captivating; the taste is direct and slightly fruitier (red fruits?) than the nose; the finish is full and even a bit smoky . . . *amen.*

RATING ★ ★ ★ ★   *Highly Recommended*

CHIMAY Red Trappist Ale (Belgium)

Rust color; mild beige, long-lasting head; the earthy, barnyard, musty, berry-like nose is soft but potent; immensely elegant, almost wine-like constitution and bearing; restrained, sweet, controlled flavors of ripe blackberries; it finishes fast, clean; very delectable; one of the more elegant, classy, cultured ales I've sampled from the Continent; while not my favorite Chimay, still a delicious ale of grace and finesse.

RATING ★ ★ ★   *Recommended*

CHIMAY Première Trappist Ale (Belgium)

Very pretty copper/russet color, topped off by an outrageously billowy beige head that explodes when poured into the center of the glass, an amazingly persistent bead; this is a 7-percent alcohol beer; the grainy/earthy nose is very brewery/yeasty/hoppy—a no-nonsense, softly fruity (honeydew melons?), freshly-tilled-soil bouquet that's a singular enchantment; on palate, the acute fruitiness holds court over the smoky grain quality in a cohesive flavor package that's completely European in demeanor—few American brewers could even approach this type of multilayered complexity; as all the Chimays, it comes packaged in a brown 750-milliliter bottle that's cork-sealed like champagne; well worth the search.

RATING ★ ★ ★   *Recommended*

CHRISTOFFEL Robertus Munich Lager (Holland)

Simply stunning, gorgeous, brilliant tawny/red/copper color, light-tan foam, average head retention; the nose is as sensational as the comely appearance, with finely roasted aromas of plums, sweet nut meat, and roasted malt enchanting the olfactory sense—the nose alone is worth two stars; satiny, medium- to full-weighted, intensely malty at palate entry—the sweetish midpalate oozes with plummy red fruit and malty flavors that envelop the taste buds in a velvety textural robe; the aftertaste leans to hops, moderate bitterness, and malt; a grand, elegant, and powerful Munich lager experience that stands at the top of the category.

RATING ★ ★ ★ ★ ★   *Highest Recommendation*

CHRISTOFFEL Blonde Ale (Holland)

Pretty, moderately turbid, gold/harvest-yellow/goldenrod color, thin, white foam, average head retention; the polite, mannered bouquet is doughy, hoppy, and acutely crisp; in the mouth, this lovely, medium-bodied pilsener takes off as rich, grainy/cereally flavors of lightly roasted malt and bitter hops give a clinic on how golden lagers should behave and taste; the finish is irresistibly clean, razor-crisp, and totally beguiling; as far as beers can get profound, Christoffel Blonde accomplishes the goal in a graceful, elegant fashion; a terrifically satisfying ale.

RATING ★ ★ ★ ★   *Highly Recommended*

CLAUSTHALER Non-Alcohol Brew (Germany)

Pale gold color, meekly effervescent, fair head retention; the pedal-to-the-metal nose makes me think that I'm walking through either a malting plant or a Scotch-malt-whisky distillery—there's very little to report on other than the gloves-off aroma of wall-to-wall barley malt; I have to say that the pallid, vapid flavor is eclipsed only by the clunky texture and the rank cereal finish; one of the worst N-A's to be found; stay away unless you're masochistic; see, I am liberal.

RATING ★

COOPER'S Black Crow Ale (Australia)

Medium amber/burnt-yellow/gold color, tan foam, admirably pure, excellent head retention; the fantastic nose is intensely malty and milky, offering pillowy wave after pillowy wave of cereal-with-honey aroma—it's a deep, plump bouquet in which the malt is king; in the mouth, it's not as chunky or layered as I'd hoped it would be, but it's a very alluring mouth presence all the same—again, the highlighted feature is the moderately roasted malt; the aftertaste introduces a hop component that balances the toasty malt.

RATING ★ ★ ★   *Recommended*

Cooper's Best Extra Stout (Australia)

Opaque, black/brown color, massive, dark beige foam, very extended head retention; this nose is a no-frills, all-business aroma that projects the dark malt right from the first pass in a dry to off-dry manner—in subsequent passes I pick up subtle secondary scents of molasses, brown sugar, tobacco smoke, and charred nuts; in the mouth, the firm textural foundation supports the pedal-to-the-metal malt thrust from entry to midpalate, where it enlarges its flavor scope by adding roasted chestnuts and burnt-toast tastes; the aftertaste is potent and dry.

RATING ★★★ *Recommended*

Corona Extra Pilsener (Mexico)

Brilliant sunshine-gold hue, white foam, moderate head retention; the restrained flowery/estery aromas emerge after ten minutes of aeration; the crisp, lean, tart, hoppy flavors finish fast; a light-bodied all-purpose quaff; the slightly roasted flavors are very appealing; the staple "glug back" in countless Mexican food joints across the country.

RATING ★★★ *Recommended*

Corona Light Pilsener (Mexico)

Very pale yellow color; medium-firm head; immediately identifiable as Corona, with its customary licorice, herbal, floral aromas; plenty of nutty, flowery, semisweet flavors carry on well through to the smoky aftertaste; not that much of a diminishment from regular Corona; one of the better lights around.

RATING ★★★ *Recommended*

Corsendonk Monk's Pale Ale (Belgium)

The volcanic effervescence billows up in the glass like it's going to take over my tasting room—the color is a golden hay-orange tone, pearl-white foam, unbelievable head retention; the in-your-face nose greets you with a rush of earthy fruit and nimble hops, then subsides into a mannered, malty, polite bouquet fit to take home for introduction to your mother; it's in the flavor department, however, that this sinewy thoroughbred takes flight as firm, full-bodied tastes of sweet, mashy malt, yellow fruit (pears mainly), and mild hops come in a creamy, decadent texture that envelops the whole of the tongue; the long, citrusy aftertaste is as impactful as the midpalate; if the nose had more definition and less wanderlust, this ale would comfortably be a five-star legend—as it is, it's a mere outrageously luscious four-star champ.

RATING ★★★★ *Highly Recommended*

Corsendonk Monk's Brown Ale (Belgium)

While the tan foam of this brown ale is active and long-lasting, it's no match for the explosive head of its rambunctious sibling, the Corsendonk Pale Ale—colorwise, you'll be looking at a medium-deep brown/oloroso-sherry type of hue—quite pretty; the lovely, generous bouquet is decidedly nutty, with background notes of tar, deep roasted malt, pumpernickel bread, mild yeast, and even an unusual touch of rye—I felt that this bouquet was marginally more evolved than that of the punkish Pale Ale; it's creamy, rich, and sweet in the mouth and medium- to full-bodied—in other words, grace-fully plump in the mouth—the soft, almost fat, sweet flavors range from milk chocolate to nut meat to chewy nougat; it finishes in a sweet and medium-long flourish, going a bit too thin at the very end; nevertheless, this is a su-perb brew and a stunning charmer right from the opening gun; buy at least three or four bottles.

RATING ★ ★ ★ ★   *Highly Recommended*

CREEMORE SPRINGS Premium Lager (Canada)

Honey/orange hue, with a frightfully short-lived, snowy head; intriguing sweet-sour, yeasty, bread-dough, barley-malt aroma; very roasted, toasted, doughy in the mouth—virtually no fruit/hop components show up here at all; it's exceptionally smooth and clean on the palate; finishes clean as a whis-tle, full, and with a dry hint of cereal; nice, correct, no flaws, but ultimately middle-of-the-road and average; on a retaste, I upgraded it to a two-star rat-ing.

RATING ★ ★

D

DELIRIUM Tremens Belgian Ale (Belgium)

Harvest-gold hue, billowy white foam, long head retention, great purity; the bouquet is sour and yeasty, with a heavy dose of clove right through all four passes—the last pass even has some lead pencil in it as the clove takes off like the Space Shuttle; in the mouth, all the tartness found in the nose becomes more focused on the tongue, to the point that it turns mildly sweet-sour à la Chinese cooking style—a metallic taste comes onto the scene at midpalate, taking something away from the flavor impression; it finishes cleanly, sour, and with the ever-present clove.

RATING ★ ★

DENTERGEMS Wit/Wheat Ale (Belgium)

More than properly turbid, in fact, majorly cloudy/muddy—looks like the color of a well-made margarita, that soapy yellow/green, white foam, little head retention; the nose offers up some sour yeastiness—sour as in un-ripened fruit, especially apples, not hoppy bitterness—the nose seems washed out and tired and was just plain unattractive, period; on the palate, where I hoped to encounter more in the way of style and substance, the lemony, doughy sourness persisted to the point of annoyance; I was glad when the limp-noodle finish came and went; an awkward dud, there's sim-ply no other way of putting it.

RATING ★

DE TROCH CHAPEAU Pêche/Peach Lambic (Belgium)

Gold/orange/peach nectar appearance, slightly cloudy, eggshell foam that's like whipped cream in consistency; the nose is true-to-fruit, supple, and succulent in its focus, which quite correctly is ripe, oozing peach—it's a superlatively expressive bouquet that exhibits sophistication and verve simultaneously; the incredible creaminess of the texture teams up with the ripe-peach concentration to produce one of the two or three finest lambic-taste and mouth-presence experiences of all; I can't recommend this superb lambic strongly enough; a bona fide, if unexpected, classic.

RATING ★ ★ ★ ★ ★   *Highest Recommendation*

DE TROCH CHAPEAU Mirabelle/Plum Lambic (Belgium)

The dusty gold/orange face is slightly turbid and topped by wispy white foam that doesn't hang around too long; the nose is difficult to pick up, since the plum scent is so faint as to be a mere shadow; however, this lambic works true magic in the mouth—this supple, creamy vixen of a lambic struts its finest stuff in the form of a gorgeous texture that fits over the tongue like a glove and a nuanced subtle, mildly sweet plum taste that's seductively distant—it's a mouth presence that teases; the aftertaste mirrors the midpalate; it's a fine lambic that skillfully balances the ripe fruit, soft malt, and velvety texture in a masterful fashion.

RATING ★ ★ ★   *Highly Recommended*

DE TROCH CHAPEAU Framboise/Raspberry Lambic (Belgium)

Cloudy, juice-like, dark-crimson/dirty-brown tone topped by a scattered pink foam that has no staying power whatsoever; the one-note bouquet is marked by concentrated berry fruit with a slight waxy backnote quality that I liked very much; on palate, it's fresh, simple, fruity, and straightforward—the malt content is not evident in the least, and again this brew like so many other lambics more resembles wine than beer; the aftertaste is extended, intensely berry-like, and clean; it's as refreshing a drink as one could hope for; a raspberry lover's dream come true.

RATING ★ ★ ★   *Highly Recommended*

DE TROCH CHAPEAU Gueuze Lambic (Belgium)

Deep honey/gold tone crowned by a frothing white foam that's very extended; the rice-like, stemmy, dank cellar-like aroma wouldn't be everyone's cup of tea, but I favorably responded to the grape-must quality found in the first two nosing passes—the third and fourth passes revealed deeper malt and yellow fruit (especially banana) aromas; the taste is so clean and refreshing you just want to keep drinking it—flavors of sweet, ripe yellow fruit mix perfectly with the lightly-roasted-malt taste; these two factors combine to make a softly sweet aftertaste that's simply brilliant; a tour-de-force lambic.

RATING ★ ★ ★   *Highly Recommended*

DE TROCH CHAPEAU Kriek/Cherry Lambic (Belgium)

Looks exactly like cherry juice—a foggy, flat red/purple color, the pink foam dissipates immediately; this aggressive nose jumps out at you, offering succulent, sweet-sour, black-cherry intensity with nary a hint of malt; in the mouth, the squeaky-clean/tart taste of just-picked black cherries is a real taste bonanza; from palate entry through to the finish, the only trace of malt is as a subtle underlying backnote flavor, but that's about it; whatever the case, this is a snappy, juicy lambic that deserves a try.

RATING ★ ★ ★   *Recommended*

De Troch Chapeau Fraises/Strawberry Lambic (Belgium)

Turbid, burnished red/auburn/red-fruit-juice tone, big bubbled foam, no head retention; the lovely, ambrosial, strawberry-shortcake bouquet delivers strawberry essence by the carload—huge, enticing, ripe-strawberry perfume fills the sampling room—delightful; I admit that my initial impression of the unripened taste was less than enthusiastic, but the second mouthful somewhat redeemed the first as the blockbuster strawberry flavor dominated the palate; it's only in the finish that a hint of malt was discerned; much more wine-like than beer-like due to the heavy-handed infusion of fruit juice; all right, but not something that I'd purchase.

RATING ★ ★

De Troch Chapeau Exotic/Pineapple Lambic (Belgium)

Dirty golden/honey hue, billowy white foam that lasts a very long time; the nose is slightly tanky, musty, fusty, and metallic in the first nosing pass, then the tart pineapple element comes into play in the second; in the mouth, the astringent, metal-coin quality detected in the first nosing reappears in the palate entry—the midpalate is clean, tidy, and compact, highlighting sour-pineapple notes as well as an herbal quality that's not complementary to the fruit; it's far from awful, but neither is it recommendable.

RATING ★ ★

Dos Equis (Mexico)

Trademark medium-dark-brown/caramel color; the coy, spicy hops/malty bouquet is always welcome—it's not a spectacular perfume, but it's workmanlike and honest; medium-weighted, pillowy texture; the proper, keen, malty flavors come wrapped in semirich texture; there's a slight nuttiness in the medium-long finish; the looks of it say top quality, the reality is that it's ordinary.

RATING ★ ★

Dos Equis Clara Special Lager (Mexico)

Amber-waves-of-grain color, limp, Milquetoast head; highly concentrated, tightly wrapped, malted-barley, mash-tun, corn-husk nose, which is one of the grainiest beer bouquets in memory—it really reminds me of the distillery smell I find when tramping about in Scotland's whisky country; the corn-like quality persists into the taste, which ends up being lame; there's finally a wee bit of toastiness in the dry to off-dry finish; overall, however, I was keenly disappointed, since I'm a mild fan of their tasty amber/red Dos Equis; a study in a flavor element that doesn't come close to fulfilling the promise found in the nose.

RATING ★

Double Diamond Burton Ale (England)

Pale amber/orange color, light-tan foam, low head retention; one of the most inviting suds noses I know of—the honey overtones meld beautifully with the ripe banana, juniper, flowers, and spice—it's a supremely confident bouquet that magically combines strength, depth, and finesse with aplomb; in the mouth, this well-crafted ale begins with a sweet lift at entry, then proceeds to get intensely fruity (especially key lime) and grainy (barley malt) by midpalate; the finish is firm, sure-footed, almost but not quite ambrosial, and very extended; this supple beauty is easily on a par with my other U.K. ale favorites from Young's, Samuel Smith's, and Whitbread; bravo, chaps.

RATING ★ ★ ★ ★   *Highly Recommended*

Dragon Stout (Jamaica)

Black-coffee color, with a low-retention tan head; it's difficult to pick up much of anything from this reticent, shy bouquet in the first and second nosings—finally some moderate estery aromas of black fruit emerge in the third pass; in the mouth, the opening impressions are highly favorable, as creamy, fruity flavors waltz onto the tongue—by midpalate, succulent, honey-like, wheat, and oatmeal-like flavors kick in; the aftertaste is sweet, ripe, and long as delightfully smoky and plummy tastes dominate; one of the maltier, rounder, fruitier stouts I've evaluated; delicious.

RATING ★ ★ ★   *Recommended*

Duvel Ale (Belgium)

One of the frothiest, most vigorous, cumulus-cloud, pillowy, whipped-cream, longest-lasting heads I've ever seen; pale gold/corn-yellow color; the intensely sweet, ripe-cherry, cedar, evergreen forest, minty nose is haunting; decidedly sweet, honeyed, voluptuous fruit flavors envelop the entire palate; finishes gently, with a malty-fruity encore; so cane-sugary-sweet in the mouth that it could be described as being a "dessert beer"; savory, but not for everyone, as it goes over the top with sweetness; I'll pass on it.

RATING ★ ★

E

Edelweiss Hefetrub Weizenbier (Austria)

Predictably foggy—the milky pale-gold hue is topped by an eggshell-colored foam that has remarkably great staying power; the delicate nose is very focused on the wheat element and, while admittedly one-dimensional, is quite pleasing in a simple, direct manner—in the background lurks a teasing citrus/herbal quality that significantly adds to the bouquet; has a solid, firm feel to it on the palate as the soft, barely discernable flavor wends its way down the throat with minimal impact; the finish is clean and a touch sour, even hoppy; the thinness of the flavor brought it down to two stars after I originally tacked on three—returning to it three times shook my confidence in it, as there simply didn't seem to be enough happening in the flavor to merit a recommendation.

RATING ★ ★

EDELWEISS Dunkel Weizenbier (Austria)

Even though I acknowledge that wheat beers can frequently look unappetizing, the cloudy brown appearance of this beer looks like dirty gutter water, light-tan foam, very extended head retention; the wheaty nose is quite sour, citrusy, and spicy (clove mostly)—beyond that there's nothing of consequence to add; once in the mouth, the clove-citrus quality jets forward, dominating the flavor to the exclusion of other flavors until the finish, when a sweet-sour, sweaty-wheatiness comes forth to shut down the entire operation; not one I'd go out to look for, but average in its execution.

RATING ★ ★

EKU Fest Bier Lager (Germany)

Brilliant, eye-catching, yellow/gold color, white foam, poor head retention; this nose is an instant winner as zesty, hoppy notes greet the sense of smell, then back off to allow the malty/cereally plumpness to come forth—every one of the four nosings is pleasant, fresh, hoppy, and mildly sweet; on palate, the flavor is malty-sweet and the texture is medium-full and silky smooth—while there admittedly isn't tremendous depth at midpalate, there is better than average refreshment; the finish is delightfully clean and nimble; unpretentious and very quaffable.

RATING ★ ★ ★   *Recommended*

EKU Hefe-Weizen (Germany)

Light amber/marigold/harvest-gold tone, white foam, very good head retention, no turbidity at all; the nose is somewhat closed down in the first pass, then it picks up speed in the second nosing as doughy, cracker-like scents emerge—the third and fourth passes run close to each other as a firm, clove-like, malted-wheat perfume permeates the air directly above the sampling glass; properly clean, even a bit sour at palate entry—at midpalate the sour-wheat taste edges out any other flavor possibilities; the finish is amiable and tart; not the best hefe-weizen around, but certainly not the worst either; drinkable and middle-of-the-road.

RATING ★ ★

EKU Rubin Dunkle Lager (Germany)

Stunningly gorgeous mahogany hue, medium-beige foam, average head retention, great purity; the nose is toasted, but not charred, and malty in the initial two nosing passes—the cereal sweetness found in the third nosing is more topical than substantial; on palate, it tastes nice, but there's no layering or authentic depth to it; this lager has the look of a round, chunky, meaty beer, but, while it's drinkable and even pleasant, it doesn't fulfill the promise noted in the appearance and is, therefore, something of a mild disappointment; a recommendation is out of the question.

RATING ★ ★

EKU 28 Kulminator Uptyp Hell (Germany)

Seriously attractive, luminous, new-copper-penny color, tan foam, no head retention to address; the alcoholic, hard-candy nose leaps from the glass at the outset—secondary scents of cedar/pine needles and wood resin intrigue, but do not charm my olfactory sense—the nose has a bit of a cleaning-fluid quality to it; in the mouth, this ultradense, high-gravity dopplebock is bittersweet, scoop-it-out-with-a-spoon thick, and not especially pleasant tastewise—the grain density is so elevated that I just come away with a resiny taste in my mouth; nowhere near as comely as Hurlimann's Samichlaus from Switzerland.

RATING ★

Elephant Malt Liquor (Denmark)

From Carlsberg Brewery; wheat-field/golden hue, fizzy white foam; the nose has a sweaty, locker-room, musty, dank quality on the first pass that had me considering a career change—subsequent nosings revealed no significant improvement—the bouquet is a technical mess; this peculiar brew thankfully tastes better than it smells; the palate entry is bone-dry and slightly bitter—this is followed by a potent wheat-like taste at midpalate that showcases a pleasant, focused maltiness all the way through the desert-dry aftertaste; if the nose was even neutral, the nice midpalate taste might have pulled it up to a two-star rating; as it is, skip it.

RATING ★

Elephant Red (Canada)

Beautiful, red/brown tone, tan foam, long head retention; the bouquet is rich, yet pleasantly astringent, with toasty, burnt layers of honey, dry-roasted peanuts, and grain crackers, especially Triscuits; the mouth-feel is medium-bodied and very satiny; the flavor ranges from off-dry to semisweet, as roasted tastes of cereal, barley malt, and sweet corn offer no hint of bitterness or hops—it's all warm, toasty, almost fruity cereal all the way downtown; the aftertaste is generous and medium-long; I recommend you pick it up when you see it.

RATING ★ ★ ★   **Recommended**

Erdinger Weissbier Hefetrub (Germany)

Moderately cloudy, banana-yellow/milky-straw hue, pearly foam, infinite head retention; the nose is firm, friendly, and sure-footed in its bearing—elemental scents of malted wheat, flowers, clove, Wheat Thin–brand crackers, and nutmeg are drawn together in an elegant bouquet that's supremely balanced and inviting—a prototype in the wheat-beer style; on palate, the texture is creamy and lush—the entry flavors include soft grain husk, spice, and malt—this is a mouth presence that prizes finesse and balance more than assertiveness and muscle; the finish is very soft, very controlled; truly a classic.

RATING ★ ★ ★ ★ ★   **Highest Recommendation**

Erdinger Pikantus Dunkel Weizenbock (Germany)

The opulent, mahogany/aged-tawny-port color is amazingly fetching, beige foam, extralong head retention; the intense nose zeroes in on dark-roasted, malted wheat in a manner that's simultaneously incisive and gradual—this is a bouquet that builds slowly, so that by the last nosing, all the aromatic pieces fit snugly together; on palate, the masterful brewing results in a polite mouth presence that's hardly short on firmness, but extraordinarily long on smoke and toasted maltiness—a honeyed background flavor complements the hops and malt perfectly; the finish is biscuity-sweet and long; simply luscious.

RATING ★★★★★ *Highest Recommendation*

ERDINGER Weissbier Dunkel (Germany)

Very deep brown/chestnut color, beige foam, exceptional head retention; the nose isn't nearly as pronounced from the outset as the Hefetrub's—by the third nosing, a caramel quality takes hold and stays in control through the final pass, eclipsing secondary aromas of chocolate malt, pecans, and honey; in the mouth, what strikes me first is the texture, a satin robe that envelops the tongue—the gentle taste spotlights toasted, malted wheat and honey; the aftertaste is smooth, off-dry to sweet, and medium-long; luxurious.

RATING ★★★★ *Highly Recommended*

EUROPA Lager (Portugal)

Standard-issue gold/straw lager color, the pearl-white head is short-lived; the attractive nose is round, full, fruity, and sweet—I liked this mushroomy, ripe-tropical-fruit bouquet very much; the taste echoes the nose with endowed fruitiness and a sweet and almost chewy texture; the finish is clean, roasted, buxom, and nutty; not a classic by any stretch of the imagination, but a solid performer that gives more than ample taste satisfaction.

RATING ★★★ *Recommended*

F

FISCHER D'ALSACE Amber Malt Liquor (France)

The medium amber appearance reminds me of apple cider, no head whatsoever; the closed-in, frightfully stingy fruit juice nose goes absoutely nowhere from the first nosing through the fourth; there's a definite malt quality in the mouth, with semisweet undertones, but beyond that it's barren; no aftertaste to speak of; not quite sure if this is a tired bottle or not; on palate, flavors are appley and mildly pleasant, but that's as far as it goes; where's the music? where's the character? where's the malt?

RATING ★

FISCHER D'ALSACE Bitter (France)

Bright golden color, fast, wimpy head; the annoyingly coy bouquet flashes a fleeting glance of rye-bread aroma then closes shop for the day—this nose is dead in the water; the crisp, clean entry shows some vital signs, then the astringent, rye flavor dominates the midpalate all the way through to the metallic, sharp finish; too exclusive for me; no depth of character or dimension; simply not my cup of bitter.

RATING ★

FOSTER's Special Bitter Ale (Australia/Canada)

Standard-issue, bronze/copper/rust orange color, eggshell-white foam, good head retention, excellent purity; this lively, spicy, off-dry bouquet needs no time to develop—it asserts itself right after the pour and remains pungent well into the second pass—by the third pass, the aroma vanishes; on palate, it's medium-bodied and only mildly bitter—the comely off-dry cereal flavor is never overwhelmed by the hoppy bitterness; the aftertaste is malty, yeasty, and moderately bitter; while I genuinely liked this ale, I got the feeling that Foster's reined in the hops so as not to have the beer end up being overly bitter, which is caving in to the assumption that the masses couldn't handle a true bitter.

RATING ★★★   *Recommended*

FOSTER's Lager (Australia/Canada)

Typical golden lager hue, with a huge cumulus-cloud head that stays for hours; the peculiar, highly individualistic but wholly satisfying nose of scrambled eggs (you read that correctly) and ripe kiwi also offers hints of almonds—a very uncommon but striking aroma that I really went for; the direct, focused, fleshy fruit component is off-dry to sweet from the slaty entry through midpalate, then goes abruptly dry, toasty, and malty in the austere aftertaste; this all-purpose beer offers a stunning array of flavors that work as a team; a quantum leap forward in the bleak world of mass-marketed lager; great job, Foster's.

RATING ★★★   *Recommended*

FOSTER's Light Lager (Australia/Canada)

Flaxen/gold/light-honey color, weak head; owns a sweet, round, herbal, but simple nose; pleasant, if meek, in the mouth as flavors of smoke, burnt bread, and chestnuts inhabit this taste; dry, medium-length finish; even though I despised the taste, considering how low it is in calories, it delivers more texture than some lights with much higher calorie counts. 88 calories.

RATING ★

FRAOCH Heather Ale (Scotland)

Very pretty amber/bronze hue, quick, beige head, pure as can be; the nose, which is not very forthcoming, teases the sense of smell with exotic, but underdeveloped, traces of flowers, distant malt, paraffin, and, strangely, resin—past the second nosing the aroma fades from sight; in the mouth, the fruity-sweet entry is followed closely by a fine malted-milk flavor at midpalate, which eventually gives way to a very mild hoppiness in the tail end; simple, indirect, more than drinkable, and enigmatic.

RATING ★★★   *Recommended*

FULLER's London Pride (England)

Fantastically brilliant, luminescent copper hue, low head retention; another superb English-beer perfume that offers keenly aromatic hints of almonds, hops, and tar; on the palate, it's medium-bodied, tarry, and dry at entry, then turns moderately bitter/dry in the hoppy aftertaste; a handsome, affable ale style that's more straightforward and less complex than those of Samuel Smith and Young.

RATING ★ ★ ★   *Recommended*

FULLER'S ESB—Extra Special Bitter Ale (England)

Autumn-brown color, tan foam, average head retention; the pungent, locker-room, honey-gone-bad nose that initially is quite offensive makes a turnaround in the third nosing and exhibits some appealing estery/red-fruit ripeness that almost rescued the bouquet; viscous, full-weighted texture; the honeyed, bitter, malty flavors are fundamental and hardly sophisticated, but present some minor charm—not enough, however, to correct the aroma problems and thus jack up the score.

RATING ★ ★

G

GAMBRINUS Lager (Czech Republic)

One of the deeper-colored lagers I've seen—an autumnal gold/honey color, topped off by a mountain of billowy white foam; the nose is deep, serious, toasty, nutty, and seriously luscious; the rock-solid, grainy texture is downright voluptuous and speaks volumes about the difference in brewing approach concerning lagers between most North American and European brewers; in the mouth, this sensational, big-boned lager explodes with lush walnut, wheat-like, and slightly honeyed flavors that escort one to beer nirvana; a great beer, period; I found myself searching my refrigerator for more sample bottles.

RATING ★ ★ ★ ★   *Highly Recommended*

GOSSER Export (Austria)

Standard-issue gold/hay hue, the meek white foam operates a convincing disappearing act; the intense, grainy nose smells exactly like rice pudding in the first pass, then steamed white rice in the second and third passes—it's the identical aroma that one comes across when walking through the malting rooms of distilleries and breweries; the palate follows suit as malty (perhaps a certain percentage of barley?) tones wipe out every other taste element (if there are any); it's clean, proper, and good, but way too lopsided in the malt factor; better balance in the flavor part of the show would have given this beer a third star; a close call.

RATING ★ ★

GRIFFON Extra Pale Ale (Canada)

Gold/harvest hay color that's really stunning—topped off with a volcano-like white head that seems to lead a life of its own; the charming off-dry nose is like sweet corn at the start, then with time out of the bottle it expands to include dry cereal and lemon peel; on the palate, it's buoyant and acutely effervescent, with whistle-clean flavors of corn (I failed to detect any trace of barley malt at all), yeast, and citrus; the finish is crisp and tart almost to the point of being astringent; it's one of the most explosively bubbly beers I've come across; but the fizziness doesn't take anything away from the quality of the beer.

RATING ★ ★ ★   **Recommended**

GRIFFON Brown Ale (Canada)

Very attractive mahogany tone with reddish core highlights, better than average head retention; the nose is restrained at first but by the second nosing turns delectably creamy, rich, and a tad smoky—this is a lovely, upper-bracket bouquet that comes off with a quiet confidence; on the palate, the texture is lighter than the creaminess in the aroma had promised—however, it's passable for a brown ale; the flavors are pleasant, persistent, off-dry, and show some mild bitterness in the aftertaste; while I do recommend this svelte Canadian ale, I feel, given the appearance and the nose, it should have earned four rating stars rather than three—the flavor didn't completely fulfill the potential suggested in the aroma.

RATING ★ ★ ★   **Recommended**

GROLSCH Premium Lager (Holland)

Deep honey/gold color, crowned by a remarkably billowy foam; the tanky, slightly medicinal nose didn't have my olfactory sense writhing in rapture; it does sport a lovely, endowed, sinewy body and texture; this beer is all business, no frills; it's intensely malty, but dry at the sleek entry, then by midpalate a luscious, sweetish, ripe-banana quality arises on the tongue; hazelnut takes charge in the lovely, succulent aftertaste; it then runs a little metallic in the tail, for which lapse I knocked off a fourth star; nevertheless, a bona fide, if uneven, beauty that offers layers of intrigue and complexity for a lager.

RATING ★ ★ ★   **Recommended**

GUINNESS Extra Stout (Ireland)

Opaque, black/brown/molasses color, beige foam, good head retention; the intense brown-rice, hoppy, and barley-malt nose titillates the olfactory sense with its inherent bitterness and layers of aroma; what begins at palate entry as a satiny-smooth bearing with intensely malty, cocoa-like flavors later explodes with coffee/mocha/espresso flavors at the back of the throat; a cocoa finish tops off this bracing and vivid stout experience; absolutely lovely and a rite of passage for beer lovers.

RATING ★ ★ ★   **Recommended**

GUINNESS Gold Lager (Ireland)

Glistening gold/amber color, the firm, snowy, vigorous head lasts a long time; the distinctive, malty, hoppy, grainy perfume is pleasingly uncomplicated and refreshing—not a killer nose, but appealing and clean just the same; light- to medium-weighted; well-crafted, simple, a sound, hot-day thirst killer of the first order that trots down the throat easily; alluring barley-malt aftertaste; awfully charming brew from start to finish; I didn't care too much for this beer when I first tasted it; a retaste changed my opinion.

RATING ★ ★ ★   *Recommended*

H

HAAKE BECK Non-Alcohol Brew (Germany)

Sunshine-golden color, with a billowy snow-white head and decent head retention; a shockingly true beer-like aroma of malt and hops; on palate, this fine malt brew shows genuine textural substance and a dry, grainy lager flavor sans the alcohol buzz; finishes long, crisp, and totally refreshing; stylistically speaking, it rivals some of the better real lagers out there; tasted blind, I thought I had been slipped a real beer ringer, that's how good it is; flat out, the pick of the N-A litter; many kudos to the talented, visionary Beck brewers.

RATING ★ ★ ★   *Recommended*

HACKER-PSCHORR Alt Munich Dark Ale (Germany)

Gorgeous mahogany/deep-brown color, beige foam, very good head retention, very pure; the nose is brown-rice-like at the start, then in the second and third passes a laser-like dark-roasted maltiness appears and dominates—there's not much beyond the soft, sooty quality of the toasty malt from then on; on palate, the dark malt feature carries this taste all the way into the midpalate—like the bouquet, even though the malt flavor seems to be the sole virtue, it works in an economical way—the malt feature is so pleasant and, in a sense, complete that expansion from that theme doesn't seem necessary; strange, but true . . . and highly recommendable.

RATING ★ ★ ★ ★   *Highly Recommended*

HACKER-PSCHORR Marzen Amber Ale (Germany)

Stunningly attractive copper-penny hue, light-beige foam, very good head retention, immaculate purity; the nose is lively and vibrant right off the pour, emitting supple but precise aromas of seeds (sesame?), peanuts, hay-in-a-barn, dry malt, and dark bread—more nosings don't reveal much new beyond the entrance of oatmeal in the final pass; in the mouth, this sinewy beauty slinks down the throat in nicely measured flavors of malty fruit, butterscotch, saltwater taffy, and genteel hops—the mouth presence is neatly arranged and very orderly; the aftertaste is mild, dry, and just a bit hoppy; highly enjoyable in an all-business kind of way.

RATING ★ ★ ★ ★   *Highly Recommended*

HACKER-PSCHORR Pschorr-Brau Dark Weisse (Germany)

Highly attractive, copper-penny/deep-amber hue, tan foam, extended head retention, clear, not cloudy; the vibrant, estery nose is all spice (cinnamon) and apples, especially red apples, right out of the bottle—this harmonious combination continues on through all four nosings; on palate, the malty wheat component rounds out the cinnamon and apple piquancy, making the midpalate rich, complex, and layered—I liked this dark wheat immensely on palate; the aftertaste highlights the creamy wheat; along with the Spaten, my favorite dark wheat from Germany.

RATING ★ ★ ★ ★   *Highly Recommended*

HACKER-PSCHORR Weisse (Germany)

Properly cloudy, soupy, broth-like straw/yellow color, voluminous white foam, infinite head retention; this sour nose is all clove and nothing but clove in the first pass after the pour—the second and third passes introduce wheat crackers and nectarine/tangerine scents, respectively—the last nosing puts them all together in a pleasantly spicy, unified way; shows a citrusy spritz at entry, then goes wheat-malty at midpalate; the aftertaste is sour, tart, but biscuity; thicker than you'd expect, yet not particularly complex.

RATING ★ ★ ★   *Recommended*

HACKER-PSCHORR Original Oktoberfest (Germany)

Medium-amber/pale-copper color, tan foam, medium head retention; the laid-back, shy nose is malty, mildly sweet, creamy, wine-like, bread-dough-like, and even a little nutty—it's so low-key, however, that it's difficult to get excited about it; on the palate, it's agile, but narrow in its flavor scope as modest tastes of nuts, hoppy bitterness, and citrus lurk in the background—it lacks a flavor leader; the finish is paper-thin and abrupt; there's nothing improper or distasteful about this beer, it's just that there's hardly anything to grip on to; I give it two stars because some people might want to give it a try; it's way too flaccid and lackluster to my taste, however, to recommend.

RATING ★ ★

HARP Lager (Ireland)

Gold, hay-like color is very attractive, active, frothy white foam, poor head retention; the dry, clean, malty nose has insipid hints of shredded wheat and little else; moderately full for a lager; it owns sufficient thirst-quenching dryness on the palate; the walnuty, quicksilver finish is all right but hardly earthshaking; unspectacular, plain, moderately tasty, mundane, and correct; if anyone thinks there's more to this middle-of-the-pack lager than this, they've been kissing the Blarney Stone too often.

RATING ★ ★

HEINEKEN Lager (Holland)

Flaxen/gold color, moderately strong head; the sedate, distinctive, clean, grainy, mildly hoppy nose hints of barley; the satiny texture, so characteristic of Continental lagers, leaves North American lagers in the dust; on palate, it gives off an undemanding taste of soft, sweet fruit, mostly apricot, then finishes like a champ—fast, crisp, decisive, and sweet; Heineken's sweetness element is more pronounced than either Beck's or Grolsch's; a really delicious, bountiful, and pleasurable beer that deserves its industry-leading position; next round's on me; bravo.

RATING ★ ★ ★ ★   *Highly Recommended*

Heineken Tarwebok Wheat Bock (Holland)

Beautiful copper/dark-honey/cherry-wood color, average head retention; the vigorous bouquet offers notes of bread dough, yeast, grain mash, and a subtle trace of spice in the initial two nosings, then with aeration it turns rather sedate and creamy—while the nose lost a minor amount of momentum with exposure to air, a sublime hoppy/nuttiness took over in the last nosing pass; on the palate, it feels good and tastes of grain and dark chocolate; the aftertaste is off-dry and shows no bitterness; I originally had it rated as a four-star entry, but after repeated tastings from two bottles, I determined that the flavor wasn't up to the smashing bouquet and dropped it back to a still respectable three stars.

RATING ★ ★ ★   *Recommended*

Heineken Special Dark (Holland)

Rich mahogany/chestnut color that's very pretty and inviting, the firm, khaki-colored froth dies an early death in the glass; I favorably responded to the curious, freshly-turned-earth, pumpernickel nose, which is subdued, but alluring; while it shows a substantial amount of finesse, it left me wanting more "guts," more "grip" and character; whereas the nose says "sweet," the taste says "off-dry" in wheat-like, malty flavors that are more calculated than expressive or evolved; the moderately long aftertaste of molasses is potent and heady; it's tasty, but my overall impression is of a reined-in dark beer whose producers didn't allow it room to run; give it more verve and animation and I'll recommend it.

RATING ★ ★

Hexen Brau Dunkel (Switzerland)

Beautiful deep-brown/tawny color that's flecked with ruby highlights, beige foam, scant head retention; the rich, bosomy aroma is rife with malted milk, chocolate milk, toasted pumpernickel, and molasses in the initial two nosings, then goes slightly downhill and muted by the third and fourth passes; decent presence in the mouth, though it could hardly be described as viscous; the mild (or is it bland?) flavor ranges from medium-roasted malt to an acceptable hoppy bitterness in the midpalate—no hints of fruit or smoke; the finish is neat and clean, but neither profound nor expansive; what began with promise ended up as an average, ho-hum dark.

RATING ★ ★

J

John Courage Amber Lager (England)

Pretty amber/pekoe-tea color; the shy, cola-nut, tangerine nose goes nowhere through the first two nosings, then blossoms into a pleasant, friendly bouquet; there's a razor-edged dryness at entry that I liked; the slightly bitter, road-tar flavors at midpalate didn't seem to have the gusto of the entry impact; emerging sweetness in the medium-length, cardboard finish; seems like it should have more bite and guts than it has; good, but ultimately uninspiring; the nose is the best part.

RATING ★★

Jubel (Germany)

Deep-amber/medium-brown hue, light beige foam, excellent head retention, pure; the nose isn't cooperative at all in the first two nosings—as it warms, the bouquet begins to peek out in scents of sour grain, medium-roasted malt, and very mild hops—one of the least expressive German beer bouquets I've come across—the last pass is the best, as soft caramel and dark-honey scents balance the sourness of the grain; in the mouth, the sour-grain feature continues to the point where I'd like to taste something beyond that or complementary to it—the midpalate is rather flat in terms of taste because no one aspect takes charge; the aftertaste is limp, malty, and dry; ho-hum.

RATING ★★

Julius Echter Hefe Weissbier/Wheat (Germany)

The amber/light-tawny hue is only mildly cloudy, light-beige foam, average head retention; the enticing bouquet is fresh, engagingly fruity, hoppy, and semisweet—it's a relatively deep aroma for a wheat beer—as it warms, there's a slight musty-mushroomy quality by the third pass, which disappears after another five minutes; in the mouth, the fruit element is heightened at palate entry, then that bows out in favor of earthy tastes of grain, dough, hops, and a touch of tangerine citrus; the aftertaste is quick and austere; I found this wheat likable, but something of a roller coaster ride in that at one moment it was soaring, the next it was mired in a quality lull; in spite of that, I believe there's enough overall quality to warrant the recommendation.

RATING ★★★   *Recommended*

K

Kaliber Non-Alcohol Brew (England)

Gold/amber color, topped by mountains of puffy white foam; the curious soy-sauce/sodium/Chinese-food nose also included a weird chicken-soup-and-egg-noodles aromatic backnote—this nose, while intriguing and inoffensive, is one of the most idiosyncratic aromas in the entire beer category; texturally, Kaliber has a very nice, medium-weighted feel to it; the flavor is bone-dry at entry, then goes off-dry at midpalate, as flavors of soy sauce, toast, and nuts take charge; the heavy-metal aftertaste really does it in, the last impression hardly being a pleasant one; it's an aggressive and complex non-alcoholic brew: it clearly has potential, but it needs to have the extremely metallic finish cleaned up before it can improve.

RATING ★

KINGFISHER Indian Lager (Brewed/Bottled in England)

Nice golden/hay/lager tone, fluffy white foam, little head retention; I liked the crisp, dry, hoppy, if simple, bouquet that evoked mild scents of barley mash and steamed white rice; once in the mouth, however, a dull sweetness emerges that detracts from the gains made in the pleasant bouquet—I found this lager flat-tasting (not in effervescence) and stingy in the midpalate and aftertaste; it began promising one thing and ended up delivering something else, which was inferior; it's neither bad nor offensive, just banal.

RATING ★ ★

KIRIN Lager (Japan/Canada)

Medium-deep gold/hay color, very active, voluminous, and extended head; lovely, round, generous malt aroma that is off-dry and has an alluring Brazil-nut quality in the background; the ethereal flavor left me disappointed after admiring the straightforward, well-developed nose; it finishes timidly; an inoffensive, eminently average lager, which came up short enough in the limp flavor and aftertaste not to be deemed recommendable—too bad, because the bouquet has a lot going for it.

RATING ★ ★

KIRIN Dry (Japan/Canada)

Pale gold color, huge, frothy white head; agreeably beery/hoppy in the nose—nothing complex or earthshaking in the aroma department, but an amiable bouquet nonetheless; in the mouth, it's clean, rather austere, unremarkable, but tasty as bone-dry flavors of slate and nuts make a late appearance; a quick, subdued, backseat finish; this is a decent, whistle-clean beer that due to its overall blandness is destined to be forgotten the moment the bottle is tossed away for recycling.

RATING ★ ★

KRONENBOURG Pale Lager (France)

Serious-looking, deep golden color that supports an off-white head that has real staying power; the distinctive, forest-floor, woodsy nose is reminiscent of springtime in the wild; a pleasant-enough quaff that is nutty, dry, and hoppy, but overall didn't impress me as being better than average.

RATING ★ ★

KROPF Dark Draft Lager (Germany)

Mahogany/chestnut/cola hue, with a long-lasting beige foam; the nose is surprisingly tame for a dark, showing equal parts bittersweet chocolate, honey-wheat bread, slate, and road tar; tastewise, it's off-dry, only slightly bitter, and only briefly commanding—it simply doesn't have the power you'd normally associate with this dark, brooding style of lager; like the timid bouquet, the flavor, while pleasing, is so low-key that it's almost shy; I liked it, I appreciated it, but I wouldn't necessarily cross the Alps to find it.

RATING ★ ★

KWAK PAUWEL Ale (Belgium)

The medium amber/vermilion-orange color is topped by a thick, creamy, sand-colored foam that almost needs a stick to control it; the nose is unmistakably Belgian in that the upfront aroma is expansive and like sour fruit, especially unripened grapes—the underlying aroma, however, is more nuanced and complex, revealing subtle hints of spice, malt, herbs, and yeast; on palate, the entry is full-throttle and almost sticky, as notes of grapes, red fruit, and maple syrup are never allowed to run oversweet by the solid acid spine—this ale almost reminds me of barley wine; acidic, fruity finish; not for everyone, but a source of joy for those of us who relish the wine-like beers of Belgium.

RATING ★ ★ ★ ★   *Highly Recommended*

L

LABATT 50th Anniversary Ale (Canada)

Pretty, solid, pale hay/straw color, with a full head of foam; very fresh, mown-hay nose that's robust and friendly when first poured, then rapidly dissipates; like most gold Canadian beers, the taste is firm, dry, straight at you, with the slightest hint of hops and herbs; the texture has plenty of grip; no aftertaste to speak of; pleasant enough, but uninspiring at the end of the day.

RATING ★ ★

LABATT Ice Beer (Canada)

Amber/gold color, with a firm white head and good head retention; this nose is intensely yeasty, grainy, tart, and to my olfactory sense, somewhat skunky—it's nowhere near as easygoing as the Molson Ice; limp on the palate—while the label says "smooth," I think a more apt term would be "vacuous"; just another case of a quicksilver, tasteless blast of alcohol for the thoughtless masses brought to us courtesy of the megabreweries; tasting this leaves little wonder why the Continent's microbrewery population is reaching new heights every month; consumers are tired of drinking these cardboard-like beverages that someone brazenly calls beer.

RATING ★

LA CHOULETTE Amber Ale (France)

Very pretty copper/rust hue, timid, splooshy, tan foam, enormous bubbles which make this beer go completely flat twenty seconds after pouring; the peculiar and unappetizing nose smells of wet dog, lead pencil, metal, yellow fruit, cardboard, and wet plaster—a horribly odd bouquet that's an unfortunate distraction; on the palate, it displays an appley, red-fruit entry, then all flavors mysteriously vanish by midpalate, which goes neutral; no aftertaste to speak of; the aroma is a major problem, since it's virtually impossible to work your way past its nearly unwholesome stench; sayonara, sweetheart.

RATING ★

La Trappe Quadrupel Trappist Ale (Holland)

The brilliant harvest-moon orange/rust/red/amber hue is crowned by a pillowy tan head; the heady, well-endowed bouquet talks eloquently of dark-bread dough, caraway seeds, medium-roasted malt, and a dash of flavorful hops—it's a controlled but abundant bouquet of the first order; the textural richness coddles the palate—the high-octane flavor erects a monumental taste experience that's equal parts malt and chocolate orange; the aftertaste is profound, multilayered, yet as with all classic beers, peerlessly elegant and self-possessed; one of Europe's hallmark ales.

RATING ★ ★ ★ ★ ★   *Highest Recommendation*

La Trappe Dubbel Trappist Ale (Holland)

Really attractive, sexy color of crimson/blood-red/deep-brown, firm, tightly wound, long-lasting, beige foam; the interesting bouquet had me guessing in the first and second passes, but by the third nosing a seed-like, melony, and extraordinarily nuanced perfume develops—I'm glad that I showed some patience with this nose, because it evolved deliberately into an ultrafine, delectable bouquet that spotlighted a dark-chocolate/marshmallow quality that I found provocative and deceptively decadent; in the mouth, the deep-roasted malt element is nicely backed by a black-coffee/cocoa underpinning flavor that's truly delicious and exotic; medium- to full-bodied texture; the aftertaste is yet another luscious progression to sensory reward; lovely, even stately.

RATING ★ ★ ★ ★   *Highly Recommended*

La Trappe Tripel Trappist Ale (Holland)

Lovely burnished-orange/medium-amber tone, mountains of fluffy tan foam sit atop this ale; the first nosing yields a sweet, fruited, sublimely malty burst that expands in the second and third nosings—this svelte bouquet is definitely on a roll here—it's a remarkably perfumed, feminine, and elegant aroma; once it's in the mouth, I realize that all the virtues celebrated in the nose are ably translated into layers of sweet, mildly citrusy/acidic/tart flavors of malt, hops, vanilla, and sugar-coated dry cereal; the aftertaste is splendid, very long, and enveloping; a terrific ale.

RATING ★ ★ ★ ★   *Highly Recommended*

La Trappe Enkel Trappist Ale (Holland)

Vermilion/deep-honey/iced-tea appearance, huge bubbles quickly dissipate the off-white head; the nose is assertive, sweet, flowery, and malty, with sturdy undertones of dough and fruit—by the third pass, however, much of the aromatic impact had given up the ghost; on the palate, this ale is agile, yet supple texturally, emitting very delicate, almost reluctant tastes of simple, lightly roasted malt and tropical fruit; the aftertaste is narrowly focused and meek; while it started off with a flurry, it lost the majority of its momentum by palate entry; okay, yet disappointing that it's merely okay.

RATING ★ ★

Liefmans Goudenband (Belgium)

Pretty, serious, deep-brown/oloroso-sherry/tawny hue, beige foam, below-average head retention; the nose is neither pronounced nor effusive in the first three passes, then with time and some warming a grainy opulence emerges so subtly that it could easily be missed through impatience—as it warms further, a scent of nut meat backs up the grain; the cleanness of it refreshes the palate completely as sweet, nuanced, biscuity flavors of dried fruit and sugary bread (like Christmas season cakes and breads, for example) take charge by midpalate; the aftertaste is very extended but elegant and stately; the combination of finesse and authority are a delight to admire … and consume; go for it.

RATING ★ ★ ★ ★   *Highly Recommended*

Liefmans **Frambozenbier/Raspberry Lambic (Belgium)**

Beautiful, deep, brackish, red/brown tone, beige foam, average head retention; the intensity of the ripe fruit aroma in the nose is a revelation, especially since I panned this lambic with a one-star rating back in 1991—beyond the raspberry rush is a firm, yeasty, wheat foundation; while I liked the bouquet more than the mouth presence, I still appreciated the true-to-fruit character of the tart, light-bodied taste; it finishes cleanly in a refreshing, slightly metallic-minerally fashion; I'm glad that I came back to retaste this lambic, because clearly my first meeting was tainted by a bad bottle.

RATING ★ ★ ★   *Recommended*

Liefmans **Kriekbier/Cherry Lambic (Belgium)**

I first evaluated this lambic in 1991 and disliked it intensely, but on retasting it I discovered a turbid, cherry-cola/ruby-cola tone and no foam; the nose here is much more vivid and varied than my initial encounter (which must have been a bad bottle)—this bouquet features the seed/pit side of cherry aroma with a slight tankiness-mustiness; the high point is the flavor, in which a focused, tart cherry taste outshines the grainy backnotes of malt and wheat; the aftertaste is clean and correct, turning sour at the tail end; more fruit fleshiness or intensity would have made it recommendable—as it stands, I like it more than I did five years ago, but I still perceive it as being mundane; it is certainly the weakest of the Liefmans lineup; it's a worthy two-star lambic.

RATING ★ ★

Lindemans **Pêche/Peach Lambic (Belgium)**

When I opened this lambic, its ambrosial perfume saturated my entire tasting room; the color is a mildly turbid, honey-gold/dusty-orange/medium-amber, white foam, below-average head retention; the most enticing aroma of any lambic I've evaluated—a ripe-peach, sweet fruit-meat fragrance that's both fruity and floral; velvety, medium-bodied texture; in the mouth, the peach flavor is appealingly acidic and tart at palate entry, then evolves into a succulently sweet, but never plump or cloying, presence that concentrates totally on ripe peaches; the finish is long, clean, crisp, and intensely peachy; this is a memorable libational experience of the first magnitude; go and buy lots of it for warm-weather quaffing.

RATING ★ ★ ★ ★ ★   *Highest Recommendation*

LINDEMANS Kriek/Cherry Lambic (Belgium)

Deep crimson/ruby/cherry-juice tone, pink foam, moderate head retention; this is a sweet, ripe-black-cherry aroma that's nuanced and seductive—what makes it so tempting a bouquet is the fact that it doesn't do much, like a great actor or actress who says lots with a small gesture—but you can sense that beneath the polite surface is a layered, concentrated core; in the mouth, that intense interior explodes, gushing hardcore black-cherry splendor in multiple waves that crescendo in the razor-edged, refreshing aftertaste; tasted alongside the kriekbiers of Liefmans and Belle-Vue, it blew them both off the table—the reason? much deeper flavor, quantums more intensity, and a more voluptuous texture; this is the kriekbier to work up to; get it.

RATING ★ ★ ★ ★   *Highly Recommended*

LINDEMANS Framboise/Raspberry Lambic (Belgium)

Clear, clean, tawny-port color, off-white foam, average head retention; this nose is surprisingly stemmy, vinous, and leafy in the first two nosing passes, then it finally gives off a faint red-raspberry aroma—the nose is not this lambic's zenith of quality, but it's acceptable; masses of true-to-fruit character are present and accounted for in the flavor as the sweet-sour, tangy taste of overripe raspberries enchants the taste buds; the aftertaste is delicious, clean, and very extended; a better, more expressive bouquet would have put a lock on a fourth rating star, but don't let that stop you from seeking it out.

RATING ★ ★ ★   *Recommended*

LINDEMANS Gueuze Cuvée René Lambic 1994 (Belgium)

Pretty, slightly foggy, golden amber hue, putty-white foam, superb head retention; the pungent, musty/fusty bouquet is heavy on the yeast—the foundational aromas include unripened yellow fruit, clove, citrus, and sourdough bread dough—this will never be entered into my personal beer aroma hall of fame; so sour at palate entry that my face twisted into a slipknot from which it barely recovered—I found the concentrated tartness so vastly unappealing that I actually hesitated before taking another sip—as I would regret soon afterward, I did take one more sip and found myself jotting down the symbol of one lonely star; the singlemost unappetizing lambic I've sampled; take heed and stay far away from this sourpuss.

RATING ★

M

MacANDREW'S Scotch Ale (Scotland)

The turbid, hazy brown color is very unappealing, beige foam, decent head retention; the coy, needs-to-be-coaxed-out nose of caramel and tar isn't worth all the effort; the raw, bittersweet, strangely rough flavors gnaw at, bite, and scrape the tastebuds; the pronounced lead-pencil finish doesn't quite make it with all the overlapping malty sweetness; too much of a metallic lead quality for my taste, too sweet, too heavily malted; as much as I love single-malt Scotch, I disliked this awkward, clumsy ale.

RATING ★

MACKESON Triple Stout (England)

Pours like thick midnight-black espresso into the glass, completely opaque, and is crowned with a mousse-like brown foam; heavy-duty chocolate perfume in the no-nonsense nose; the texture, though, is the real story here—it's an outrageously ropy, viscous, chunky stout that almost requires manipulation with a knife to get it moving out of the bottleneck; from the glass it uncoils onto the tongue and is actually heavy to the feel; smoke, cocoa, double-cream, road-tar, charcoal, and brownie-batter flavors all take turns impressing and steamrolling the taste buds in the sweet, succulent, syrupy flavor; it finishes in a surprisingly agile way as the concentrated flavor of rich cocoa bids adieu to the panting taste buds; it's like German chocolate cake in beer form; if you can handle it, go for it.

RATING ★ ★ ★ ★   *Highly Recommended*

MAMBA Malt Liquor (Ivory Coast)

Sturdy-looking, 14-carat-gold hue, eggshell foam, very good head retention; the nose is zesty, assertive, and estery—I think of yellow tropical fruit when smelling this appealing malt liquor from Africa's west coast—the last two nosings highlight both malt and fruit—a good, happy, snappy bouquet; in the mouth, the malt makes a strong play at entry, then in midpalate a succulently sweet, bread-dough flavor dominates; the finish is quite sweet, almost sugary, and very extended.

RATING ★ ★ ★   *Recommended*

MARSTON'S India Export Pale Ale (England)

Similar in appearance to the Pedigree Bitter—gold/honey/bronze hue, sand-colored foam, long head retention, pure; the nose, however, is completely different, mainly in the amount of malt aroma that's evident right out of the starting gate—subsequent nosings reveal dark caramel, roasted malt, and cedar—a great bouquet; on palate, the sinewy, muscular, medium- to full-bodied texture provides the perfect playground in which the voluptuous flavors of sweet malt, red fruit, and dry, flowery hops can freely play—the midpalate is especially rich, harmonious, and developed in the malt-hops balance; the aftertaste is very long, thirst-quenchingly bitter, but subtlely sweet; one of the few beers that I could enjoy every day of the week with all types of food . . . or simply on its own.

RATING ★ ★ ★ ★ ★   *Highest Recommendation*

MARSTON'S Pedigree Bitter (England)

Beautiful bronze/honey color, eggshell foam, long-lasting head, ideal clarity; a thrillingly prototypical bitter bouquet—loads of hops (my money is on Fuggles), spicy malt, and unripened yellow fruit—the nose says "British pub" all over it—an outstanding, classic aroma; in the mouth, there are traces of light caramel-toffee at entry, then the midpalate blossoms into full-scale hop bitterness, with just the slightest hint of cereal sweetness in the throat; the finish is big, dry, and very long; a prime example of why I believe the English produce more superb beer than any other country in the world.

RATING ★ ★ ★ ★   *Highly Recommended*

Marston's Oyster Stout (England)

Opaque, brown/black coffee tint, deep-beige foam, medium-long head, pure as far as I can tell; just like the vapid porter, this stout offers next to nothing in the opening nosing—what gives? Subsequent passes fail to register much in the way of aromatic character—a wasted opportunity, especially in light of their terrific Pedigree Bitter and India Export Ale—just skip the nose completely; on palate, the stout shows a smidgen more life than the porter, as semideep flavors of cocoa, espresso, and molasses keep the taste buds suitably entertained; texturewise, it sorely lacks creaminess and viscosity or, for that matter, anything at all to grab hold of, which is very much against the style; decent, if meek, aftertaste; the stout and porter are mere shadows of the lighter ales; pass on it.

RATING ★ ★

Marston's Albion Porter (England)

Chestnut-brown color, wet-sand-colored foam, long head retention, pure; the nose, oddly and disappointingly, shows very little aroma presence in the first two passes—to my amazement, aeration does little to help coax out any odors except for a dull maltiness—a major letdown; on palate, this porter offers a very pleasant, but hardly earthshaking, wine-like taste upfront, with subtler flavors of pine, malt, and cocoa coming in at midpalate—the texture is medium-full and not creamy at all; the finish is mildly sweet and medium-long; ho-hum and drinkable, but not all that enjoyable—maybe there was some bottle shock along the way, or, perhaps, it is past its prime—whatever the case, exercise caution.

RATING ★

McEwan's Scotch Ale (England)

Deep amber/chestnut-brown/mahogany hue, medium head retention; the soft, exotic nose displays bits of tar, hay, citrus, pineapple, and cardboard; it's very sweet, but agile to the taste, as brown sugar, honey, cola, cream soda, and plum flavors all take turns showing their best faces; the aftertaste is long, decidedly sweet, and easy; while complex and layered, the sweetness factor, which is never overbearing, makes this Scotch Ale undemanding and simple to quaff.

RATING ★ ★ ★   *Recommended*

McEwan's Export India Pale Ale (England)

Light amber tone, good head retention; the feisty, vivacious nose is vinous, grapy, hoppy, and alluringly floral, coming out like a lion before retreating into a soft, musty/dusty, attic-like, mildly honeyed, elegant bouquet that's very appealing; in the mouth, it shows ample weight, some tannic bite, citrus notes, and malt; the aftertaste is swift, clean, and off-dry where a curious taste of cola pops up in the end; an odd, but thoroughly likable, ale; come to think of it, that comment "odd, but thoroughly likable," applies to just about everything having to do with Scotland.

RATING ★★★　　*Recommended*

MEDALLA Pilsener (Puerto Rico)

Light, yellow/gold tone, snow-white foam, poor head retention; not much here in the way of aroma, except for a feeble rice scent way in the background—end of story; in the mouth, it's unforgivably flimsy—I've drunk stouter waters than this—one of the two or three worst beers of any style I've evaluated—gives new meaning to the term "puny"; this appalling garbage doesn't even deserve the one star.

RATING ★

MOLSON Ice (Canada)

Dark-straw/light-amber hue, milk-white foam with moderate head retention; the nose is sweet, malty, and slightly corn-husky—the bouquet could never be considered even moderately complex, but I found it pleasant in a simple estery/fruity sense; in the mouth, it's creamy, full-textured, and very quaffable—the round, contoured flavor includes a bread-dough/biscuity quality that is more than serviceable at entry, but the flavor ultimately falls back on its innocuous maltiness by midpalate; the finish is medium-long, bland, but for an Ice it's not bad; tough call.

RATING ★★

MOLSON Golden (Canada)

Amber/gold color, topped by a puffy, long-lasting, blanched head; not a powerhouse in the aroma, but a pleasant, slightly sweet/malty nose; carries a bigger flavor stick than either the neutered Export Ale or the flimsy Light; has a feeling of round, chewy, substance on the tongue; flavors of cream, nuts, slate, and smoke present ample drinking pleasure; hardly memorable, but a decent middle-of-the-road lager.

RATING ★★

MOLSON Light (Canada)

Corn-yellow/gold color; both samples were absolutely flat, no head to speak of; unappealing, sweaty, footlocker nose; round, velvety, orange flavor dominates on entry, then gives way in the mildly nutty aftertaste; the genuinely enticing flavor element is sandwiched between a disagreeably malodorous nose and an easy, toothsome finish; it's a shame that the horrid nose detracts so much from the taste; both bottles smelled bad. 109 calories.

RATING ★

MOLSON Export Ale (Canada)

Pretty harvest-gold color, frothy, firm, chalky-white head; the interesting, substantial, steamed-rice nose has moderate appeal; in the mouth, you taste a bit of fruit, but it's weak at best; what you're left with in the mouth is a beer that's bland and lackluster; clean? yes; refreshing? to a degree, yes; flavorful? hell, no; I remember when Molson offered some giddyap and sturdiness in the flavor department; this flaccid, rickety version runs like a gelding; Molson, we hardly knew ye.

RATING ★

Molson Exel Non-Alcohol Brew (Canada)

Standard-issue gold color, very vigorous, full, snow-white head; soupy, rice-like nose that, like Kaliber, possesses a strange saltiness to it, though I hasten to add that it's not offensive at all, just unorthodox; Exel owns one of the more beer-like textures for an N-A; stone-dry to the taste; the steamed-white-rice quality continues on the palate; tastes like saltine crackers in the finish; certainly not in the same league as the dazzling Haake Beck; has a few good things going for it, but on balance it's unacceptably salty.

RATING ★

Molson Red Jack Ale (Canada)

Prototypical red-ale bearing, auburn/henna hue, blimp-sized bubbles that first form, then immediately dissipate the tan head; the pleasantly roasted, malty, nutty bouquet shows real promise in the first pass, but by the second nosing a noticeable aromatic diminishment begins—by the third nosing, a shift to the malt takes hold and stays firmly in place well into the last pass; on the palate, an off-dry, clove-like spiciness greets the taste buds—the midpalate offers mildly spicy notes that alone can't support the weight of this deficient ale; it doesn't taste bad, it just barely tastes at all; the lame-duck quacker of an aftertaste does zero to bolster the fleeting flavor; too bad that the ale inside the bottle isn't as appealing as the great label slapped on the outside of the bottle; am I turning into a bitter curmudgeon?

RATING ★

Moosehead Canadian Lager (Canada)

Standard golden-lager color, active, pearl-colored head, decent head retention; banal, unspectacular, run-of-the-mill, grainy nose, with a barely discernable hint of citrus; nice, full-bodied, satiny texture; off-dry taste that has a subtle nuttiness to it that's quite appealing; ends in a soft maltiness; what it lacks in bouquet it somewhat makes up for in texture and the malty aftertaste; just the same, one would be safe to assume that it's not destined for the suds hall of fame.

RATING ★

Moretti La Rossa Doppio Malto Lager (Italy)

Very attractive "red" look as ruby/mahogany shades form the core color, on top of which rests a meek, tan head; the toasty bouquet is heavily malted, with side attractions of nougat, hazelnut, and even a faintly sweet touch of molasses/brown sugar way in the back recesses of the aroma; this sinewy lager hits you like a thick slice of pumpernickel bread at palate entry and through the midpalate—beyond that there's not an abundance of taste characteristics except for coffee; the sweetish, coffee-like aftertaste is clean, roasted, and quite extended; I liked this simple amber, especially in the comforting finish.

RATING ★ ★ ★   *Recommended*

MORETTI Birra Friulana Pilsener (Italy)

Rich, gold/honey color, monster-sized bubbles, thin, quick head; the shy, grainy nose speaks to me of white rice, lightly roasted malt, walnut meat, and a bit of juniper and honeysuckle—the main event in the nose, make no mistake, is the nicely beery rice/malt tag team; very pleasant at palate entry as the dry nuttiness/grapiness makes for a good opening—unfortunately, the flavor doesn't broaden or deepen one iota at midpalate or in the aftertaste—it's simply more of the same from the bouquet; it's a decent thirst killer with which to wash down a pastrami on rye just before you're mugged in the park on a June afternoon; broaden the scope, give it a layered flavor with some animation and it garners a third star—until then, a worthy two-star beer.

RATING ★ ★

MORRELL'S Oxford Castle Ale (England)

Simply gorgeous pale-ale color of burnished orange/copper, off-white foam, average head retention; the delicious bouquet is all about digestive biscuits in its ultragrainy, granola, dried-banana, dried-guava, and brown-sugar layers—an outstanding Bitter bouquet; on the palate, the flavors of roasted malt, crisp hops, and hazelnuts almost, but not quite, match the splendor of the aroma; nevertheless, the aroma/flavor impact is significant enough to land four very well-deserved stars; the finish is compact, austere, and cleansing; buy it.

RATING ★ ★ ★ ★   *Highly Recommended*

MOUSSY Non-Alcohol Brew (Switzerland)

Orange/harvest-gold color, the insipid head rapidly disappears, which is something of a lapse, since the word "moussy" means a rich and creamy head in French; the pleasing, hoppy, off-dry, sweet-corn nose has a foundation of toasted malt, honey, and oat-bran cereal; the slender promise suggested in the aroma gets dashed on the tonsils as the anemic, washed-out, watery flavors limply try to impress the taste buds; the awkward, steely, tongue-on-penny finish is too heavy on the malt; say goodnight to this one. 50 calories.

RATING ★

MURPHY'S Irish Amber (Ireland)

Very attractive, medium amber/bronze color, eggshell-colored foam, good head retention, very pure; the compelling nose is so nutty, chocolatey, and doughy that it makes me think of chocolate-chip cookies with nuts—this is a seriously decadent bouquet; in the mouth, there's a minor letdown at entry as the texture seems at first to be a bit watery—that amends itself at midpalate as rich, creamy, but dry tastes of roasted malt and hops pick up the brief slack; the aftertaste is round, chewy, and long, highlighting the hops more than the malt; more textural substance would have assured a fourth rating star.

RATING ★ ★ ★   *Recommended*

MURPHY'S Irish Stout Draught (Ireland)

Black-as-your-hat appearance, long-lasting, sand-colored foam; the heavy nose is thick with cigarette smoke, milk chocolate, cocoa, black coffee, and dark malt—very nice, if slightly pedestrian, through all four nosings; where this stout crumbled to the ground was in the mouth—all the toasty/roasted promise found in the fragrance went to the boards on palate as paper-thin flavors were supported by an overly lean texture—whither the creaminess? whither the black-tar taste? whither the door?

RATING ★

N

NEGRA MODELO Dark Ale (Mexico)

Tawny/amber/russet color, ample, tan head, long head retention; the robust, decadent, off-dry to sweet nose offers effusive scents of toasted barley, guava, candied almonds, and cocoa—it's a superlative bouquet that's both abundant and elegant; the enticing, luxurious, and opulent texture is perhaps its greatest asset; on palate, its creamy and rich flavors are buttressed by savory elements of molasses, milk chocolate, and honeyed oatmeal; it finishes quietly and sweetly in a satiny honey-wheat flavor that's long, accomplished, and very satisfying; by far, the classiest, most polished Mexican beer and one of the world's most delectable dark ales; it's always my first choice in any restaurant that specializes in Mexican or Southwestern cuisine.

RATING ★★★★   *Highly Recommended*

NEWCASTLE Brown Ale (England)

Medium amber color, tan foam, low head retention; the nose of this sexy brown ale is all about milk chocolate and cocoa—I find it seductive and decadent; in the mouth, what this ale lacks in depth, complexity, and richness, it makes up for in a fruity-estery flavor burst that resembles grapes and berries all the way into the off-dry to sweet malt finish; in retrospect, I realized that the midpalate impression was almost like that of a light red wine from Provence; an intriguing, approachable ale that satisfies totally without being ponderous or profound.

RATING ★★★   *Recommended*

NIAGARA FALLS Eisbock Ice Beer (Canada)

Handsome, vermilion/burnished-orange hue, tan head, good head retention; the nicely toasted, mildly malty bouquet is quite compelling in the first pass, then it settles down into a simple, nut-like aroma that remains steadfast through the fourth and final nosing pass; on the palate, the steely/salty style of the brewery is immediately sensed at entry, then the midpalate displays an intriguing, if brief, red-fruit fling that is quickly overshadowed by the malt element; the medium-to-full finish highlights the hops and malt; nice brewing.

RATING ★★★   *Recommended*

NIAGARA FALLS Brock's Extra Stout (Canada)

The soupy, viscous body is painted a dark-brown/almost-black color, topped by a long-lasting, beige head; the piquant, heady nose is all about chocolate malt, egg cream, dark toffee, molasses, and sweet cereal—I liked the bouquet mostly for the creamy/milky quality; once in the mouth, this stout's heavily roasted, keenly bitter maltiness makes itself known, but what disappointed me was the loss of the creaminess, the disappearance of the textural silkiness by midpalate; the aftertaste is like the taste left in your mouth after you've smoked a cigar—smoky and bitter; what began as a broad-shouldered stout ended up on the leaner, excessively bitter side of the scale.

RATING ★★

NIAGARA FALLS Kriek/Cherry Ale (Canada)

Pretty copper/rust/medium-amber hue, pink/white foam, good head retention; the seedy, pit-like nose is stingy after the initial nosing, emitting only a fruit-stone tang in the painfully anemic second, third, and fourth nosings; on the palate, this is one of the worst fruit-beer mouth presences I've encountered, as wispy, paper-thin flavors of sour cherries, fruit acid, metallic tartness, and hints of quinine work hard to distress the taste buds; the finish merely echoes the totally unpleasant midpalate experience with a sickly sour-cherry-candy taste that has neither finesse nor depth of character; a complete, unmitigated disaster of the first rank . . . with the emphasis on "rank."

RATING ★

NIAGARA FALLS Apple Ale (Canada)

The appearance is akin to ginger ale or apple juice, light amber tone, raucous fizz, silvery foam, decent head retention; the nose is a delicate, delightfully curious cross between ripe apples, applesauce, and bread dough, particularly sourdough—the bouquet is neither full-throttle sweet nor tart and regrettably loses much of its panache by the third nosing pass; the palate entry is clean but strangely stony/steely, showing bits of apple and lots of acid dryness—the midpalate is bland and somewhat cardboard-like; the finish is meek, flat, and disappointingly lackluster; what little steam this generated at the outset was completely released by midpalate.

RATING ★

NIAGARA FALLS Maple Wheat Ale (Canada)

Light amber/honey color, splooshing, huge bubbles form the unstable foam; the mildly pleasant nose holds some minor charm in a caramel/nougaty manner as the brown-sugar/maple-syrup character reluctantly peeks out; in the mouth, the maple taste is evident, especially in the midpalate, where the thin body fails to support the flavors in an adequate or acceptable fashion; by the aftertaste, this ale implodes, leaving behind a tinny, tanky, rancid flavor to cover the skeletal frame; a weak-kneed mess once you get past the bouquet; avoid.

RATING ★

NOCHE BUENO Winter/Christmas Amber (Mexico)

Lovely, tawny/deep-copper hue, beige foam, good purity, flat effervescence; the nose is waxy, nutty, and dense in its maltiness, but it takes considerable coaxing to maintain, since it keeps fizzling out after each pass; pleasantly malty at entry, with a biscuity/doughy/yeasty quality that expands at the cocoa/chocolate-tasting midpalate; this bottling seemed fatigued, but it still held enough charm, substance, and integrity to receive a recommendation.

RATING ★★★   *Recommended*

NORDIK WOLF Light (Canada)

Pale gold color, sickly, white froth, no head retention; the good news is that the firm, full, hoppy, sweet-pineapple nose is leagues ahead of most other light-beer aromas; unfortunately, the full-fruited quality admired in the bouquet slips through the cracks in the far less enjoyable taste—in the mouth, the flavors of minerals, tartness, and stainless steel betray the attractive appearance and decent nose; too bad for the belly flop in the taste.

RATING ★

O

OBERDORFER Weiss Wheat Beer (Germany)

Rich gold/straw color, with a snowy, billowy head, very good head retention; the perfumy, sweet, intoxicating nose is waxy and grainy in the same way as Nabisco's Triscuit crackers are or even Shredded Wheat cereal—it's a very intense aroma that doesn't mask its origin; in the mouth, it's like liquid cereal initially, then goes wildly citrusy at midpalate; the lemon/pineapple taste continues on through the sour and unpleasant aftertaste; while refreshing and clean, it comes off as being too sour/lemony in the late palate and finish for my taste; missed the boat.

RATING ★★

OBERDORFER Dark Weissbier (Germany)

Very appealing, reddish-brown/cherry-wood color, beige foam, average head retention; the nose immediately lets you know it's a wheat by the clove/nutmeg perfume, which has a secondary scent of lemon peel—the middle passes discover little more, while the fourth nosing detects a peppery note; in the mouth, it's manageably citrusy and sour at palate entry, then it turns ridiculously sour at midpalate—the mouth presence is more like a citrus soda pop than a beer; nearly undrinkable.

RATING ★

OKOCIM O.K. Pils (Poland)

Admirable, medium-gold/yellow hue, perfectly pure, snow-white foam, average head retention; hold on, somebody has stolen the aroma—there's no aroma that closely resembles anything having to do with beer—it's a vacuum; on palate, only a tanky, mild bitterness greets the taste buds—there's no complexity, no flavor, just a pool of medium-bodied, virtually tasteless liquid; get it away from me.

RATING ★

OLD GROWLER English Ale (England)

Ochre/tawny color,with a soft wheat-colored foam, fair head retention; the pumpernickel nose is loaded with accessible scents of cracked bran, honey wheat, and black cherries—a feast for the olfactory sense—aromatically, a good show; surprisingly dry, focused, and dry-cereal-like—it reminds me of plain Wheaties-brand cereal; the aftertaste is completely dry, with measured bits of wheat toast and brewer's yeast; I really liked this toasty, roasted, fully concentrated but never awkward ale from Suffolk, England, because its makers have achieved an excellent balance of character and drinkability.

RATING ★★★   *Recommended*

OLD GROWLER Porter (England)

Deep mahogany/brown/cola color, covered with a medium-beige, moderately long-lived head; the rather sedated aroma has traces of molasses and road tar—not the blockbuster, chunky, estery, malty nose that one frequently gets confronted with in an English porter; the flavor is all roasted grain and burnt rye toast—please note that this observation is not meant in a negative way, since I have a feverishly developed fondness for charred toast, and this smoky flavor experience is definitely akin to that; not a soupy/ropy type of porter, texturewise; quite nice and well-behaved, a gentlemanly porter with a bit of flair.

RATING ★★★   *Recommended*

OLD PECULIER Yorkshire Ale (England)

Please note that the name is not misspelled; dark amber/chestnut-brown color, deep-beige foam, moderate head retention; the sublime nose is like an infectious melody, sweet and harmonious, as coy hints of mint, honey, bacon fat, and egg cream make themselves known—it's a fabulous bouquet that doesn't lose intensity with time; tastewise, it's full-throttle egg cream from the velvety entry through to the sensuous finish; while in one sense, it's one-dimensional in terms of the taste, the intensity level of the rich creaminess is so highly notable that this is one of those rare instances in which a singular purpose is successfully pulled off and quite sufficiently; takes its place among my twenty favorite imported beers.

RATING ★★★★   *Highly Recommended*

ORVAL Trappist Monastery Ale (Belgium)

Bright orange/amber color, sudsy, whipped-cream head, good head retention; the semisweet, generous, floral, herb-garden, sandalwood, rosewood, amazingly complex, multilayered nose is unique and compelling; on palate, it abruptly and disappointingly shifts gears and turns rather dry and stony, with an overly bitter, road-tar quality that erases any hint of sweetness; long, dry, black-licorice finish; I enjoyed the vivacious nose and disliked the flavor and aftertaste, which were diametrically opposed to the aroma.

RATING ★ ★

P

PACIFICO CLARA Pilsener (Mexico)

Golden color, white foam, soft head retention; the malty/fruity aroma is simplistic to the max—just simply nothing happening here; meek and wimpy on the palate as the waxy texture underscores the lack of taste dimension; not unpleasant, but monumentally forgettable, because of lack of character, more than anything.

RATING ★

PAULANER Salvator Doppelbock (Germany)

The deep mahogany color is gorgeous as it flashes ruby highlights, beige/tan foam, medium-long head retention; the sweet, concentrated, raspberry bouquet is a dazzler—there's a ripe-fruit aromatic core, wrapped in a smoky, molasses-like exterior scent that's remarkably cocoa-like—one of my four or five favorite beer bouquets, period; in the mouth, this velvety classic starts out as chocolate-covered cherries, then advances dryly into a bittersweet-chocolate mode; the aftertaste is endless and fathomless as the biscuity, hot-chocolate, marshmallow, roasted-nut, and whipped-cream flavors meld into one of the most harmonious finishes in the beer category; show me a more satisfying total beer experience and I'll make it worth your while; the best dark beer from the Continent.

RATING ★ ★ ★ ★ ★ *Highest Recommendation*

PAULANER Lager (Germany)

Pretty golden hue, crowned by mountains of white foam, average head retention; the nose reminds me of only two things—steamed white rice and malted barley; in the mouth, the creamy texture combined with the concentrated maltiness brings to mind malted milk; the aftertaste is stately and refined, reflecting the finest hops (probably Hallertau) and malt; this is a textbook lager from Munich's biggest and most influential brewer; a supremely good beer worthy of a search.

RATING ★ ★ ★ ★ *Highly Recommended*

PAULANER Oktoberfest Lager (Germany)

Fantastic, new-copper-penny/burnt-orange color, beige foam, long head retention, perfect clarity; the intense, concentrated, doughy/malty opening aroma is beguiling—the second pass features the introduction of pumpernickel and yeast—the third and fourth passes are relatively timid by comparison, but still exceedingly pleasant; in the mouth, what comes to the fore is the thick, velvety texture, which acts as the foundation for the potent, pungent, and wholly satisfying flavors of roasted malt, dark bread, caramel, and coffee bean; the finish is long, but compact and focused on the malt; yet another dazzler from this superlative brewery.

RATING ★ ★ ★ ★   *Highly Recommended*

PAULANER Bavarian Alpine Extreme Ale (Germany)

Has the medium amber/bronze look of a pale ale from the U.K., light-tan/sand-colored foam, superb clarity, excellent head retention; the nose is muted and muffled for the first two nosings—with warming and aeration, appealing scents of sour dough, malt, and saltine crackers emerge in the third and fourth nosings—not Paulaner's most memorable bouquet, but serviceable; it's much more expressive on palate than in the nose—a caramel-like, candied, and intensely malty entry leads to a satisfying, though not brilliant, midpalate; a sturdy, blue-collar, and densely malted amber ale.

RATING ★ ★ ★   *Recommended*

PAULANER Hefe-Weizen (Germany)

Very pretty, harvest-gold/medium-amber hue, mildly turbid, the cumulo-nimbus-like head is composed of eggshell-colored foam; ridiculously long head retention; the potent, assertive nose reeks of cracked wheat, eggs, sour mash, clove, flowers, and wet vegetation—it's an earthy, elemental bouquet, one that threatens to go a bit too egg-like in the final pass; on palate, the sour, clove flavor is faithful to the style and very refreshing; the aftertaste is quite full, hoppy, and sour; I rode the ratings fence on this one because of the egginess in the last stages of the aroma.

RATING ★ ★ ★   *Recommended*

PERONI Lager (Italy)

Pale gold/apple-juice color, snowy foam, excellent head retention; the nose bursts forth from the sampling glass immediately after the pour and fills my tasting room with malty, digestive-biscuit, and sugar-cookie aromas—the bouquet isn't as perfumed and pronounced in the second pass, but it's still animated and vivacious—the last two nosings spotlight the malty/biscuity core aroma; the palate entry is medium-bodied—the mid-palate offers sweet (like sweet corn), hoppy, and slightly metallic/slaty flavors that never seem to develop or deepen; the finish is brief and regrettably thin; this lager lost much of its momentum by midpalate, ending pleasantly, but limply; I was disappointed with the skeletal flavor and the timid aftertaste after admiring the spirited bouquet; still, it's middle-of-the-road.

RATING ★ ★

PETER'S BRAND Pilsener (Holland)

Eye-appealing, sunshiny golden, flaxen-like color, big, splooshing bubbles, low head retention; the clean, hoppy, uncomplicated nose is basic, but pleasing; this deliciously dry, lean, razor-edged, thirst killer pleases from start to finish; on palate, the flavor is neatly laced with a soft hazelnut taste; medium length and weight, with a stone-dry, intensely hoppy finish; a to-the-point pilsener that gives its fellow countryman Heineken a very serious run for the money; pick up both and compare them.

RATING ★ ★ ★   *Recommended*

PETRUS Triple Ale (Belgium)

Mildly cloudy, harvest-gold/yellow/amber tint, mountains of long-staying white foam; the bouquet is intensely malty, very much like dry cereal fresh out of the box—it doesn't grow much beyond that in subsequent nosing passes, however; I really responded to this Triple once it was resting on my tongue—it has a firm, rock-solid flavor of mildly sweet grain and fruity hops, supported by a sturdy texture that nicely underpins the whole mouth experience—the body is the glue to this ale; good finish, though it vanishes a bit quickly; overall, very pleasant.

RATING ★★★ **Recommended**

PETRUS Oak-Aged Dark Beer (Belgium)

Eye-catching chestnut-brown, mahogany color with a beige foam; medium-long head retention, excellent purity; the intriguing nose is almost wine-like in the opening pass—the second nosing focuses on a sour fruit–hops combo that I'm not sure I like—the third and fourth nosings reveal nothing new; in the mouth, the wine aspect accelerates as a sourness dominates the entry, then subsides slightly at midpalate, allowing for a subtle introduction of oak resin to come aboard—the sour wine/grape taste wasn't a huge turn-on for me taste buds, matey; winey finish, some hops, a bit of malt; drinkable, so perhaps I could become accustomed to it.

RATING ★★

PETRUS Speciale Ale (Belgium)

Attractive bronze/medium amber hue, very extended head retention, pretty eggshell foam, good purity; only scant aromas of barely discernable hops and light-toasted malt make fleet appearances in the first two nosings—with aeration, the malt aspect picks up some strength in the third pass, but even then I would consider it meek, at best; on palate, there are small bursts of malt in the entry, then they fade rapidly by midpalate, where there's very little to talk about other than a mundane, rudimentary maltiness but virtually nothing behind it; aside from the fact that's there's nothing to grip onto, there's little technically wrong about this beer—it's simply a Belgian snorefest; don't bother with it.

RATING ★

PILSNER URQUELL Pilsner (Czech Republic)

Gorgeous harvest-gold/medium-amber hue, snowy-white foam, average head retention; the dry nose is the deepest, most profound, and most layered of any of the world's golden lagers—the fragrant bouquet is so supple, round, voluminous, and evolved that you can almost chew it—the complex network of aromas, including dry, flowery Zatec hops, lightly toasted malt, corn husk, brown rice, and kid-leather gloves, keeps the olfactory sense focused and thoroughly entertained through all four nosings—one of my top five all-time favorite beer bouquets; as concentrated and regal in the flavor as it is in the aroma—the midpalate bitterness is moderate, behaved, and the ideal foil for the opulent maltiness; this savory classic is the benchmark for pilseners and, in my opinion, is a perfect beer; the aftertaste is long, properly bitter, and impressively elegant; here is the real "King of Beers."

*RATING ★ ★ ★ ★ ★   **Highest Recommendation***

Pinkus Home Brew Munster Alt (Germany)

Pretty, rich amber/orange color, tan foam, fairly long head retention; the nose talks to me of seeded dark bread, moderately roasted malt, and a bit of tankiness (perhaps that's from the beer's long maturation period of six months)—as it opened with time and warming, an estery, ripe-black-fruit element briefly appeared, only to give way to a tarry, wood-smoke aroma in the final nosing—there's a lot happening in this fascinating and sexy bouquet; in the mouth, the smoke and tar flash themselves at the palate entry, then recede and are replaced by a mildly bitter, hoppy, malty, and creamy midpalate of considerable charm; long, smoky aftertaste; a superb, prototypical alt.

*RATING ★ ★ ★ ★   **Highly Recommended***

Pinkus Home Brew Wheat Beer (Germany)

A rare translucent wheat beer—deep harvest-gold color, off-white foam, extralong head retention; the bouquet is pleasantly earthy, grainy, and nutty, with wee traces of herbs, citrus, and wheat—I liked this supple, sure-footed nose very much, especially in the final passes as it warmed, emitting floral, wet-earth, and doughy fragrances for a grand aromatic finale; the flavor is crisp, dry, and carries more weight than most wheat beers; the aftertaste is keenly refreshing and gently zaps you with a kiss of bitterness right at the tail end; far from your typical wheat, Pinkus is a delightful break from the banal pack.

*RATING ★ ★ ★   **Recommended***

Pinkus Muller Ur Pils Organic Home Brew (Germany)

Harvest-gold/dark-straw color, pearl-white foam, decent head retention; this gloriously estery nose is steeped in sweet cereal, banana, honey, melon, and pear scents—it's a first-rate, inviting perfume that's in passing gear right from the start, but so much for the good news; in the mouth, the gains made in the terrific nose are suddenly abandoned in a wildly bitter, lightish flavor whose virtue eluded me completely—I found the taste and the finish distressingly coin-like, metallic, and just plain awful; it's a shame that such a sexy, vivacious fragrance was neutered by an over-the-top, disgustingly bitter flavor and penny-like aftertaste; don't go near it, it may bite.

RATING ★

Port Royal Export Pilsener (Honduras)

A murky gold/amber color, little head retention; even allowing for the mild turbidity in the appearance, the bouquet is sweaty, stinky, mushroomy, and metallic—in short, it's a hideously disagreeable nose that reeks of somebody's perspiration; I hesitated to sample it, but when I did I found the taste sour, paper-thin, and soapy; now, I understand that I may have bought a bad bottle, but since most consumers buy their own beer in stores, I urge you to avoid this hostile mongrel at all costs; from the dating code on the bottle, this megalemon was not old goods; adios, El Bow-wow.

RATING ★

PRESIDENTE Pilsener (Dominican Republic)

The medium gold color is topped off by billowy, puffy mountains of silver white foam; little head retention; the nose is grainy, more oats than barley, and off-dry; admirably clean on the palate, with a slight touch of metal and citrus in the midpalate before going all citrusy/astringent in the finish; while I didn't swoon over it, not a bad brew just the same; could actually envision it going very well with spicy Mexican, Cajun, or Caribbean cuisine.

RATING ★ ★

R

RADEGAST Original Lager (Czech Republic)

Peach/golden tone, with a deflated head; the aroma is lovely, hoppy, herbal, and assured—typical of rock-solid brewing, while commonplace in Europe, Radegast is only now taking hold in the U.S.; on the palate, the bearing is acutely crisp, dry to off-dry, refreshing, nutty, and sublime; the finish shifts the spotlight back to the flowery hops in gentle waves of flavor; like its Czech lager brother, Gambrinus, this is a top-notch beer, period.

RATING ★ ★ ★ ★   *Highly Recommended*

RAZOR EDGE Lager (Australia)

Luminous, 18-carat-gold/straw-yellow hue, white foam, big bubbles, very good head retention; the bouquet is quite tame out of the bottle and only develops in the third pass as lemony, rice-like, pineapple scents barely reach the rim of the glass—the last nosing returns to the land of the meek; on palate, it's admirably clean, properly crisp, but it shows little in the way of character, leaning to the watery end of the flavor spectrum; I'm sure that Razor Edge Lager is a very welcome libation when it's 110 in the outback, but ultimately it's a middle-of-the-pack offering.

RATING ★ ★

RED HORSE Malt Liquor (Philippines)

Deep gold color, but I detect to my utter amazement black specks and various other brown/gray particles floating about—doesn't make you want to jump right in; the appealing nose is like sweet red onions, with just a hint of hoppiness; the flavor takes the taste buds on a trip to no-man's-land— nothing there to speak of; San Miguel Brewing clearly had a bad filtering day when this was bottled; makes for rather rocky public relations.

RATING ★

RED STRIPE Lager (Jamaica)

Pretty gold/hay color; owns a mildly fragrant, hoppy, yeasty nose, flecked with scents of malted grain, earth, and even wax; has a sensuous, full texture that generously coats the palate; the flavor is a bit muted but from what I could detect offers a delicate nuttiness; this rather timid, inoffensive beer sits on the bench, opting not to get involved in the action; I kept waiting for something to happen with it.

RATING ★ ★

RODENBACH Red Ale (Belgium)

Without a doubt one of the prettiest red ales I've seen—a deep, blood-red/aged-tawny-port hue that's an utter knockout, beige foam, little head retention; the spicy, snappy V-8 Juice nose is loaded with intriguing elements, not the least of which are black pepper, cayenne, Worcestershire sauce, jalapeno pepper, and onions—I'm not saying I liked it, but it certainly put a lock on my attention; so sour as to make my lips purse—the sour-apple flavor is splashed with equal parts yeast and vinegar; the finish is spicy, sour, and unrepentant; even though I wouldn't order it or buy it, I admit to a grudging appreciation of its uniqueness and its ability to cleanse and entertain the palate; I'll give it a try again in a year.

RATING ★ ★

ROMAN Dobbelen Bruinen (Brown) Ale (Belgium)

The deep-auburn/henna-colored appearance is nearly opaque, whipped-cream-like foam, seemingly eternal head retention; the sensuous, come-hither nose reeks of chocolate, road tar, molasses, and charred malt—it's a multilayered bouquet that's simultaneously classy and powerful; the palate entry is bitter, intensely chocolatey, and malty, then the off-dry to semi-sweet midpalate exposes some interesting backnotes of fruit and tobacco smoke; the aftertaste displays a keen hoppy bitterness that closes the circle; the texture is full and creamy; this satiny beauty should be high on the list of any aficionado of robust ales.

RATING ★ ★ ★ ★   *Highly Recommended*

ROMAN Ename Dubbel Abbey Ale (Belgium)

Beautiful, dark mahogany/chestnut-brown tone, long-lasting beige foam—a genuinely splendid bearing; the doughy, pumpernickel nose is a dazzler, not so much because it clubs you into submission (it does not) as much as it charms you, seduces you with its grainy/bread-like subtlety; the wonderful, off-dry to sweet, grain/bread concentration continues in the flavor; the aftertaste is polished, nimble, and long; a classy ale with loads of finesse and maltiness that I found to be as delightful as a warm hunk of just-baked pumpernickel bread; dynamite.

RATING ★ ★ ★ ★   *Highly Recommended*

ROMAN Ename Tripel Abbey Ale (Belgium)

Golden/hay color, aggressive, cumulus-cloud-like white foam that will only be harnessed with the help of a firehose; the delicately sweet nose offers ample doses of hops and malt, but not much beyond that; in the mouth is where this sweet ale does its best work as the plump, velvety texture buttresses the moderately hoppy, floral, malty, and slightly herbal flavors that last well into the refreshing aftertaste; the judicious use of hops really pays off as the rich malt character grips the taste buds early and soon makes them believers; elegant, layered, well-endowed, and luscious.

RATING ★ ★ ★ ★   *Highly Recommended*

ROYAL Extra Stout (Trinidad, West Indies)

Semisweet-chocolate brown color, opaque, smoky-brown foam, very good head retention; the nose zips right along in fourth gear as it offers scrumptious aromas of wood smoke, dark caramel, and tobacco leaf from start to finish—by the third pass, warming and aeration encourage the molasses/chocolatey sweetness to dominate—this seductive bouquet is like being in a bakery and sniffing the best chocolate cake they have—I adored this aroma; it's unabashedly sweet and lip-smacking-decadent in the mouth—you almost want to scoop it out with a spoon as though it's mocha-chocolate ice cream; it's one of the most hedonistic beer experiences I've had; I also found it roughly similar to malmsey Madeira; an absolute must-have ale.

RATING ★ ★ ★ ★ ★   *Highest Recommendation*

ROYAL OAK Pale Ale (England)

Pale amber/copper hue, alabaster foam, long head retention; the nose is mesmerizing in its sweet, biscuity, cake-like perfume—a barely discernable trace of cinnamon/nutmeg exists way down below the citrus fruit, woodsy, pine, cedar top layer of aroma—it's a complex, multilayered nose that alone is worth two ratings stars; the flavor is off-dry to sweet and shows up a bit one-dimensional compared to the bouquet—the creamy texture supports zesty, vivid flavors of hops and cereal grain; it finishes up on the bitter/dry side of the chart; a very pleasant pale ale indeed.

RATING ★ ★ ★   *Recommended*

RUSKI Lager (Russia)

Pretty goldenrod color—weak, dissipated foam, no head retention to speak of; to my amazement, samples from both bottles had minute suspended particles floating in the glass—I have no idea what the particles were; in comparison to the other beer samples, all of which were whistle-clean, the Ruski beer obviously needed some filtering; due to the particles, I have to say that I hesitated in my tasting, but decided to try it anyway; the nose is more pilsener-like than lager-like; the flavor is quite refreshing with an orange-peel quality that's agreeable; it finishes crisply, dryly, and cleanly; if it's cleaned up, the Russians may find a niche here; several points off for the highly suspicious appearance; nevertheless, it definitely shows promise; formally evaluated thrice.

RATING ★ ★

S

St. Ambroise Pale Ale (Canada)

Brilliant, luminous, copper/orange hue, off-white foam, average head retention; the biscuity bouquet is nicely accented by moderate hops and malt—the first pass right out of the bottle provides the most aromatic meat as later the nose gradually fades from the second through the last pass, finally resting in a delicate, floral scent of hops; on the palate, it's clean, crisp, properly but not overly bitter; medium-weighted texture; solid finish of keen hops and subdued malt; I liked this blue-collar Pale Ale more than the same brewery's Oatmeal Stout and as much as their two "Griffon" bottlings; able brewing from Montreal.

RATING ★ ★ ★   *Recommended*

St. Ambroise Oatmeal Stout (Canada)

Black/dark-chocolate-brown tone, with a whispy beige head and virtually no head retention; the full-throttle bouquet clubs the nasal canals with thick layers of big-time molasses, wood smoke, road tar, and pumpernickel bread aromas—this is no lacey, delicate, tip-toeing beer; on the palate, concentrated, bitter flavors of burnt wheat toast, metal, charred barley malt, and cigar smoke mercilessly assault the taste buds; actually, the deep, cereally flavor is quite palatable once you get past the tidal waves of intense bitterness; it finishes stone-dry, smoky, heavy, and grainy; only for the already converted "stout-hearts"; while nice, this stout isn't in the same arena or even the arena car park as those from England (i.e., the legendary Samuel Smith's)—the reason is the lack of balance between the intensity of the bitterness and the sweet-tar quality of the grain.

RATING ★ ★

St. Feuillien Blonde Abbey Ale (Belgium)

Pretty flaxen/amber tone, off-white head, extralong head retention; the assertive bouquet has an intensity rarely found in domestic beers—layers of brewer's yeast, sour dough, hops, pineapple, grapefruit, and paraffin all come together in an extraordinary aroma that's simultaneously elegant, intense, and forward; in the mouth, the resemblance to bread and tropical fruit celebrated in the bouquet is underscored in the flavor by an opulent creaminess that's dazzling, complementary, and supremely confident; the long, leisurely aftertaste is gracefully accented by the grain and the light usage of hops; this is easily one of the best beers from continental Europe.

RATING ★ ★ ★ ★ ★   *Highest Recommendation*

St. Feuillien Brune Abbey Ale (Belgium)

Really handsome tawny/burnished red/brown hue, deep beige foam, moderate head retention; this cereal-like, off-dry nose is slightly coy, but round, and shows some tar, roasted nuts, and deep-roasted malt—while solid, it's nowhere near as bountiful or gregarious as the Blonde Ale; off-dry at palate entry, this virile ale displays its best side in its sweet, toasty, honey-wheat, malty midpalate; the aftertaste is fruity, sweet, velvety, and malty; a very palatable ale that offers ample virtue wrapped in a very pretty robe.

RATING ★★★   **Recommended**

St. Georgen Brau Kellerbier Lager (Unfiltered) (Germany)

Mildly turbid, foggy orange/copper color, beige foam, the strong, steady opening effervescence diminishes quickly, good head retention; the nose is alluring and concentrated more on hops than on cereal as biscuity and mildly bitter scents rise from the glass—I don't know how else to say this other than it's a very "beery" aroma, with the accent on hops; on palate, it's dry and intensely hoppy at entry, then a slow introduction of malt is made at midpalate—it's delightfully full and totally refreshing; the finish is floral, hoppy, and just a bit malty; superb, minimalist brewing.

RATING ★★★★   **Highly Recommended**

St. Landelin Blonde Abbey Ale (France)

Solid, pretty harvest-gold/amber color, enormous, splooshing bubbles lazily float to the surface, creating a short-lived pearl-white foam; the engaging, sweet nose is pleasantly malty, yeasty, and French-bread-like, showing a bit of sugared dry cereal—a sound, even plump, intensely grainy bouquet that really developed into a rousing, characterful nose by the final pass—bravo; in the mouth, this medium- to full-bodied ale mirrored all the positive findings identified in the nose, as bread-like, biscuity flavors of malted barley and oats more than amply satisfied the cravings of the taste buds; nice, firm, deeply grainy aftertaste that put the final fine touches on this sophisticated ale; highly recommended; this gentleman prefers this Blonde.

RATING ★★★★   **Highly Recommended**

St. Landelin Amber Abbey Ale (France)

Extremely handsome color of deep copper/chestnut-brown is topped off by a beige head that hung tough for an extended period; to my surprise, this nose is not nearly as pronounced as that of the Blonde, but it's moderately appealing in the first two nosings, offering willing signs of malt, then the grain element takes off with warming; the lightly roasted flavors are better than average—the 6.8-percent alcohol gives you plenty of giddyap beneath the sweetish, grainy, red fruit flavor; the finish falls off a bit; overall, a sound, supple ale that could have been better, but definitely worth a try nonetheless.

RATING ★★★   **Recommended**

St. Landelin Brown Abbey Ale (France)

As deep as most porters in color, the gorgeous dark-chocolate/black-coffee brown tone is crowned by a remarkably creamy/thick beige foam that displays good staying power; the nose is almost completely closed off in the first two passes, then emits a slightly tanky/steely odor in the third nosing, finally saving itself in the last pass by giving off charming scents of deep-roasted malt, milk chocolate, and even an innocent dash of tar; the palate entry is firm, but not opulent as mild reined-in tastes of dark-roasted malt, pumpernickel, and black fruit (plums?) show up for work but refuse to get effusive; the aftertaste is about as controlled as the midpalate; don't get me wrong, it's a good, recommendable ale that's worth trying, but it will never be accused of being generous or expansive.

RATING ★★★   *Recommended*

St. Paul Triple Abbey Ale (Belgium)

Nice, light new-copper-(penny)/medium-amber tone, off-white foam, average head retention; the perfumy nose is acceptably sour, stylish, and very malty in each nosing pass; it's in the mouth that this svelte Triple earns its stars, however, as the silky, medium-bodied texture forms the foundation for the fruity/malty flavor that enlivens the taste buds with the exotic taste of tropical fruit; this otherwise snappy ale fell down a bit in the finish, but overall the flavor impact was sufficient to garner a recommendation; a far more satisfying experience than the awkward, capricious Double.

RATING ★★★   *Recommended*

St. Paul Double Abbey Ale (Belgium)

The milky-brown appearance is crowned by a persistent beige foam; the thick nose speaks of little else but malt, with a very subtle backnote of citrus that wasn't identified until the third pass—in the fourth pass, cocoa is added to the list of aromatic positives; there's a huge malty rush at the palate entry that abruptly turns sour by the midpalate point—I didn't care for the mouth-puckering, sour-candy directional change in the taste because it wasn't at all complementary to the bouquet or the palate entry; I found myself puzzled and disappointed in the midpalate and the extremely tart aftertaste; the slowly evolving aroma had promised much finer things in the flavor than what you actually got; the nose wins the two stars; much to my surprise, this over-the-top Double has done well in some competitions.

RATING ★★

St. Paul Blonde Abbey Ale (Belgium)

Mildly foggy, golden hay/amber color, bright white foam, good head retention; the full-throttle nose assertively offers a top-drawer aroma of biscuity malt in the first two nosings, then it quiets down into a soft, harmonious perfume consisting of nuts, tropical fruit, and steamed white rice; the palate entry is clean and malty—the midpalate flavors range from toasted cereal to barley mash to oatmeal to rice cakes—in other words, it's a high-flying grain harvest in the mouth; the aftertaste is crisp from the hops; a good but not great Blonde, which would have been recommendable if it had had more body and intensity; the bread-like mouth presence garnered the two stars.

RATING ★★

St. Paul Special Abbey Ale (Belgium)

Beautiful, henna/rich-auburn color, mountains of long-lived beige foam; the nose isn't very expansive directly out of the bottle, but then with warming it picks up the pace by sending out delicate aromas of cracked grain, new coins, and dry hops—I didn't rate this bouquet highly because on balance there wasn't much depth to analyze; the hoppy taste was seriously lacking in depth (à la the nose), as right from the palate entry there was only meager hops and malt to deal with, no subtleties, no nuances; while there's nothing technically wrong with this Special, stylistically it possesses no flair or élan; it's a one-note melody.

RATING ★

St. Pauli Girl Pilsener (Germany)

Fine straw/gold color, with a vigorous, pearly-white, long-lasting froth; the particularly fragrant nose of flowers, hops, and damp cork is a definite winner—it shows a veiled elegance that's alluring and inviting; it comes off slightly sour and astringent on palate, but is, in spite of that, refreshing and clean; good, correct, clearly better than average; gives ample satisfaction; if the taste and finish had matched the heights reached by the enticing bouquet, I would have happily rated it higher; I've evaluated this pilsener three times—it's received one upgrade.

RATING ★★★   *Recommended*

St. Sebastian Dark Ale (Belgium)

Remarkably appealing appearance, highlighted by the smashing tawny port/cherry-wood color, which is crowned by a tan foam that has average head retention; the nose is not very well developed until the third pass, when it blossoms into a balanced, fruit/malt perfume of memorable impact; but it's in the mouth that this silky, handsomely textured, layered ale soars, with sweet flavors of plums, cherries, moderately roasted malt, and mild, floral hops; the aftertaste is harmonious, fruity/sweet, and very focused; a very satisfying brew.

RATING ★★★   *Recommended*

St. Sebastian Golden Ale (Belgium)

Light honey color, white, short-lived foam; the bouquet is seriously malty, chewy, and even a tad fruity right from the first pass—with time and warming, the intense maltiness diminishes only slightly—this is a round, biscuity perfume that I found alluring; I wasn't as moved by the taste as I was by the opulent, vivacious bouquet—the taste highlights the malt component, but only that, leaving behind all other traces of flavor; the finish is clean and neatly wrapped; I yearned for more dimension on the palate, something texturally or tastewise that would parallel the fine aroma.

RATING ★★

Saku Olletehas Originaal Pilsener (Estonia)

Solid, gold color, snowy-white foam, superb head retention; the nose is a trifle subdued right out of the bottle—the second pass offers meager hints of white rice, malt, yeast, and hops—the third nosing remains shut down—in the final pass, the rice and malt components at last make an effort, but not enough to make me a convert; on palate, the play is on the hops, as a bitter upfront flavor holds sway over everything else in the taste—even after three passes, it doesn't get its engine revved up, and very little flavor impact is noted except for a bit of hops and stale rice; don't bother with it.

RATING ★

SAKU OLLETEHAS Estonian Porter (Estonia)

Shows more of a henna/auburn-red ale look than a nut-brown porter, beige, billowy, root-beer-like foam, exceptional head retention; the nose has a peculiar rubbery top layer—just underneath that is a foundation of malt—no depth or dimension, though, aromatically; on palate, it definitely offers more in the way of character as flavors of cocoa, bittersweet chocolate, prunes, and dark fruit come alive—the chocolate and fruit tastes dominate throughout; the aftertaste is charred, grainy, and bittersweet, but fails to bring the taste experience to a positive ending; pedestrian and overly charred.

RATING ★

SAMICHLAUS Dark Lager (Switzerland)

Pretty, bright, deep amber/red-ale/tawny hue, fast beige head; the nose is intensely fruited as waves of sweet-sour red fruit (primarily Red Delicious apples, cherries, and plums) mix well with backnotes of molasses and hops; it's on the palate that this high-alcohol (14 percent), port-like lager cuts against the grain, with high-flying, heavily textured flavors of black grapes, molasses, chocolate cake frosting, jet black-roasted malt, and ripe plums suggesting that you're really sipping either a madeira or a cream sherry; the finish is surprisingly beer-like in that there's a closing rush of sweet malt and hoppy bitterness; once the strongest beer in the world in terms of alcohol content (now, it's America's own Samuel Adams Triple Bock), Samichlaus remains a delicious, unique, fortified-wine-like brewing novelty that's more than worth several tries.

RATING ★ ★ ★ ★   ***Highly Recommended***

SAMUEL SMITH'S Oatmeal Stout (England)

India-ink/jet-black tone, long, long head retention—wow!; the captivating, succulent, and intense nose is chocolate-covered cherries, malted barley, road tar, dark caramel, molasses, and, most desirable of all, CocoPuffs, the American chocolate-flavored kids' cereal—hey, c'mon, I was a kid once; texturewise, it's like liquid satin, plush and thick; at palate entry, the flavor drips with sweet wood smoke and tar, then by midpalate the chocolate cherries make another appearance followed by a superb sweet-cereal rush that has no peer in the entire stout subcategory; the aftertaste is like cocoa butter; it's my choice as one of the world's five best dark beers and, if pushed to the wall, I'd most likely make this my all-time favorite beer, domestic or imported, period.

RATING ★ ★ ★ ★ ★   ***Highest Recommendation***

SAMUEL SMITH'S Taddy Porter (England)

Root-beer color, crowned by an amazingly frothy head; the peerlessly complex, multilayered, opulent, cola-nut, licorice, semisweet, burnt-toast, buttery nose is one of the great beer bouquets that you or anyone will find;

sports a heavy body and consequential bearing; fruity, almost wine-like (or is it port or sherry?) in its generous grapiness; concentrated, somewhat sour flavors that are utterly delicious from stem to stern; luscious aftertaste that fades fast and clean; the mesmerizing bouquet itself is worth the search for it; excellent, high-quality example of a beer style that has been passed over in favor of stout by brewers; what a mouthful of pleasure.

RATING ★★★★   ***Highly Recommended***

SAMUEL SMITH'S Imperial Stout (England)

Deep brown/black color, beige foam, average head retention for the style; the cigar tobacco, sweet-william, heavily floral, bread-dough, rubber-eraser nose is sweet, decadently voluptuous, and rich; the viscous, velvety texture envelops the entire palate and takes no prisoners; cocoa, bittersweet, licorice, molasses, chocolate flavors dominate but don't throttle the palate; surprisingly lean, clean herbal/fruity finish; a top-flight, mouthwatering stout for those people who are willing to take the plunge into serious beer drinking.

RATING ★★★★   ***Highly Recommended***

SAMUEL SMITH'S India Ale (England)

The enormous sand-colored head sits atop this bronze/copper beauty like a cloud, excellent purity; the exotic, surprising nose offers an opening wave of pear/citrus, followed in the second pass by a deep maltiness that is both round and refreshing—in the third pass, the red-fruit creaminess of the foam absolutely knocks out the olfactory sense—this is a superbly crafted bouquet from top to bottom; the customary Sam Smith fullness is there right from the entry—layered, tart, bitter flavors hops, sour mash, toasty malt, and cereal excite and satisfy the palate—the midpalate features a heightened bitterness that cleanses the tongue; the finish is keenly astringent and smoky to the point of almost making the lips pucker; wow—I loved it.

RATING ★★★★   ***Highly Recommended***

SAMUEL SMITH'S Pale Ale (England)

Iced-tea color, with a long-lasting, frothy, beige head; outstanding, rich, yeasty, sour-apple, fresh-spring-garden, firm nose; sweet, raisiny, full-throttle flavors that caress the taste buds, then leap down the throat and conclude quietly with a dash of coffee flavor; loaded with malty character; one of the most delicious pale ales I've sampled; a stately, vastly elegant ale that is akin to a fine wine; English brewing at its best.

RATING ★★★★   ***Highly Recommended***

SAMUEL SMITH'S Nut Brown Ale (England)

Deep amber/orange/ochre color, tan foam, medium head retention; the juicy, malty, estery, ripe pear, ripe peach nose is disarming, firm, and elegant—like that of the Pale Ale and the Taddy Porter, the bouquet is irresistible and earns two rating stars on its own—in the fifth and sixth nosings, the marvelous bouquet expands into a chocolate-cherry, honey-wheat masterpiece; in the mouth, off-dry, sinewy flavors of maple, cane sugar, cream, malted milk, and raspberries welcome and coddle the taste buds; the finish is full, very long; I admit that I missed the "nut" factor, but when everything else works so spectacularly, who gives a damn? if I were to choose one brewery in the U.K. that I wouldn't mind being trapped inside of for a year, it would be Samuel Smith's, hands down.

RATING ★ ★ ★ ★   **Highly Recommended**

SAMUEL SMITH's Lager (England)

Golden hay-like color; the fruit quality in the invitingly sweet nose is miles ahead of any domestic lager; medium-weighted, full, round, nicely textured; the fruity, nutty palate entry is delightful, fresh, and clean; the dry, hoppy, commanding finish is firm yet unimposing; this is a lovely, unpretentious lager that is well balanced and harmonious; well done.

RATING ★ ★ ★   **Recommended**

SAMUEL SMITH's Winter Welcome Ale 1995-1996 (England)

Golden/amber/russet hue, with an infinite head that refused to diminish; the beery, malty nose warmly welcomes you but doesn't really proceed much further than only moderate complexity or depth of aroma—scents of barley malt and grain husk run the entire race in the nose; the palate is treated to the expected Samuel Smith's creamy, satiny texture and gentlemanly bearing—the off-dry flavors highlight the grain, showing only a trace of fruitiness; the aftertaste is dry and mildly bitter; give the classic texture more guts in the way of taste and it would garner four rating stars—until then, it's a strong-three-star brew.

RATING ★ ★ ★   **Recommended**

SAPPORO Original Draft Pilsener (Japan)

Straw/gold color—moderately active head, extended head retention; the curious, key-lime-like nose is simultaneously strange and charming—in the second pass the nose kicks into a savory maltiness that is very welcome and charming; this is definitely one of the more lush Pacific Rim lagers in terms of texture; it owns a silky, mannered presence on the palate as the dry, astringent flavors of citrus expertly cleanse the palate; medium-long finish of citrus goes toasty in the tail; very palatable beer by any standard.

RATING ★ ★ ★   **Recommended**

SCALDIS Special Ale (Belgium)

Absolutely dazzling honey/amber tone, eggshell foam with long head retention; the well-behaved nose is off-dry to semisweet and speaks of nuts and barley malt, with a perceptible underlying layer of honey/caramel; ultimately, though, it's on the palate that this opulent, lushly textured, and regal ale scores its biggest points as sweetish flavors of candied nuts and rich malt are balanced by a lactic-acid-like intense hoppy crispness; the lovely, plump finish is grainy and hoppy as a slight bitterness closes the door on it; this is a huge, multilayered ale that would be suitable with a rich dish like beef Wellington or, even better, served after the main course; a dynamite ale.

RATING ★ ★ ★ ★   **Highly Recommended**

SCALDIS Noël Special Ale (Belgium)

Really pretty, rich copper/bronze hue, beige foam, excellent head retention; the aroma has punchy notes of caramel corn, dried fruit, heavily roasted malt, and even double cream—the last two passes expose nothing further; in the mouth, it's sweet at entry in a grainy rather than a fruity way, then it runs bitter and road tarry in midpalate as the hops and malt aggressively come at you with all barrels blazing; the finish is surprisingly lackluster, considering the giddyap found in the bouquet and mouth presence, but it is sweet and malty; not right enough for my holidays.

RATING ★★

SCHIERLINGER Roggen Bavarian Rye Beer (Germany)

Stunningly beautiful red/sorrel/chestnut hue, thick tan foam, long head retention; the pleasing nose is top-heavy on the grain, which to me smells more like malted wheat than rye—there's no fruit element to speak of in the aroma, just a husky, dark bread/graininess—I liked this aroma, but I expected something else; the stand-out quality is the layered texture, which somehow feels like rye bread; tastewise, the rye backbone is acutely evident at midpalate as round, chewy flavors of rye, red fruit, and dill combine nicely; good, solid aftertaste; a delicious, top-flight dark that's both unique and difficult to locate in the U.S.

RATING ★★★★ *Highly Recommended*

SCHNEIDER Weisse Hefe-Weizen (Germany)

Surprise! no turbidity, light amber/orange-pekoe-tea color, thick, off-white foam, very extended head retention; the nose is tidily grainy, clove-like, and fresh—add traces of orange and lemon peel in the third pass—the final nosing exhibits some very pelasant biscuitiness; on palate, the citrusy entry gives way to a yeasty midpalate—the medium-weighted texture is silky and fine; the finish belongs to clove and lemon; the grain element was played down in this fine hefe-weizen.

RATING ★★★ *Recommended*

SCHNEIDER Aventinus Wheat Doppelbock (Germany)

Mildly foggy, deep rust/burnished-orange color, beige foam, extended head retention; the nose is deep, citrusy, and only mildly clove-like right out of the bottle—with aeration, the bouquet broadens to include a sour yeastiness and a cracker-like wheat element—there's lots happening aromatically; the palate entry is sour, then the flavor does an about-face at midpalate, featuring tastes of sweet, ripe plums, honey, and malted wheat; the finish is intensely grainy, long, and off-dry to semisweet; this doppelbock takes you on an intriguing ride, which includes a hairpin turn or two; atypical, tasty.

RATING ★★★ *Recommended*

SHEAF Stout (Australia)

Jet-black, opaque appearance, little head retention; the tantalizing nose emits delightful scents of dark chocolate, malted milk, and Ovaltine—no fruit, no grain, all cocoa and milk—I loved the simple, no-frills, straight-ahead bouquet; the flavor is properly bitter and medium-weighted as tastes of honey-wheat toast, oloroso sherry, and tobacco tar acquit themselves nicely; what I hoped for and didn't receive was a tad more texture, but overall I think this is a well-crafted stout that's most worthy of a try.

RATING ★★★   *Recommended*

SHEPHERD NEAME India Pale Ale (England)

Truly beautiful new-copper-penny color, tan foam, very long head retention, immaculate purity; the nose is delightfully and fetchingly fragrant in a bread-dough way—while it's not as hoppy in the bouquet as you'd expect for the style, the round, doughy aroma is so irresistible, you forget about style; in the mouth, the sweet-malt component greets the taste buds at entry, then takes them on a jolly ride to the midpalate, where the floral hops take the helm; the aftertaste is measured, medium-long, and properly bitter; had the body/texture been fuller, I'd have given it a fifth rating star.

RATING ★★★★   *Highly Recommended*

SHEPHERD NEAME Masterbrew Premium Bitter Ale (England)

Striking honey-amber/copper hue, whipped-cream beige form, very long head retention, pure as can be; I love this nose because there's so much substance to it—waves of lightly toasted malt, spicy grain, paraffin, and flowery hops make for an engaging aromatic experience from the first nosing through the last—in the later nosings, a mashy background note accents the other aromatic features; on palate, it's clean, properly bitter without being overly astringent, and mildly malty—the texture is sound and firm, creating the perfect foundation for the flavor; the finish is lovely, whistle-clean, and hoppy; this ale begs for a bag of chips doused with malt vinegar.

RATING ★★★★   *Highly Recommended*

SHEPHERD NEAME Spitfire Ale (England)

Soft amber/clover honey/iced-tea hue, creamy foam, extended head retention, minor suspended particles; the orange-biscuit, butter-cookie aroma dazzled my sense of smell in the first two nosings—the unbaked dough and citrus qualities continued in the last two passes—the malt element carried the load in the sublime nose; on palate, I really got into the creamy, honey-wheat entry taste, then the hoppy bitterness enters the scene and acts to counterbalance the lovely grainy sweetness—what a delight in the mouth; the aftertaste highlights the hops rather than the malt; I just shake my head time after time with pleasure over these marvelous ales from England.

RATING ★★★★   *Highly Recommended*

SINGHA Lager (Thailand)

Beautiful, brilliant, 18-carat-gold color, crystal-clear, powerful, persistent bubbles, snow-white foam, superb head retention; the nose is a lager lover's dream—crisp, clean, off-dry, and richly malted in the first two passes—it settles down into a substantial hop/esters/malt bouquet in the final two nosings; on palate, Singha owns an impressive opulence that you rarely come across in golden lagers that aren't made in the Czech Republic or Germany—the midpalate is a lager banquet, complete with sweet malt, dense,

bitter hops, bread dough, and even a dash of white rice in the finish; refreshing, off-dry, and simply dazzling; a must-have item for lager mavens.
RATING ★ ★ ★ ★   *Highly Recommended*

SLEEMAN Cream Ale (Canada)

Brilliant, luminous, pale amber hue, with a rocking and rolling billowy head that doesn't know anything about the term "quit"; the assertive, clean, fresh, sea-air, wheat-field-in-the-spring nose is totally captivating; the mouth presence is nutty, dry to off-dry, intensely hoppy, creamy, and mannered on the palate; it has a well-defined nut-like, citrus quality as it descends the throat; a lovely, compact ale that I could quite zestily guzzle all afternoon long and feel all the better for it.
RATING ★ ★ ★   *Recommended*

SOL Especial Pilsener (Mexico)

Pale gold/straw color, off-white foam, meager head retention; the nutty, burnished aroma is most like steamed white rice—no depth to speak of aromatically; in the mouth, this pathetic piece of garbage is virtually flavorless, totally characterless; the aftertaste is flat and vapid; a mess from Mexico; get me out of here; should get a no-star rating.
RATING ★

SPATEN Lager (Germany)

Light-gold/new-corn yellow hue, brilliant clarity, silvery foam, excellent head retention; the luscious nose reeks of forest pine, sweet malt, and bits of orange peel—the hops don't reveal themselves until well into the second pass—the last two nosings are devoted to the interplay between the light mashiness of the malt and the soft nibble of the hops; but it's in the mouth where the true greatness of this classic is fully realized—the rich, velvety texture acts as the platform on which a genuine flavor extravaganza unfolds—beautifully melded, totally harmonious tastes of fine, off-dry malt and precise, brisk hoppy bitterness dazzle the palate; superb, clean, medium-long aftertaste; one of continental Europe's two or three finest lagers, period, case closed.
RATING ★ ★ ★ ★ ★   *Highest Recommendation*

SPATEN Dark Hefe-Weissbier (Germany)

Gorgeous, eye-poppingly attractive red/vermilion/tawny color, crowned by a frothy, creamy foam, head retention reaches "eternity" on the longevity meter; this bouquet is considerably rounder than that of the light Hefe-Weissbier, a quality that has mostly to do with the added element of the smoky malt, which contributes an endowed, roasted-nut quality to the nose—this is a truly splendid nose; in the mouth, the texture luxuriously coats the tongue as an opulent, deep-roasted, wheat/maltiness/red-fruit flavor impresses the taste buds from the point of entry through midpalate; the aftertaste is silky, chewy, supple, and fruity; solid from start to finish, this lovely dark wheat is at the head of its class.
RATING ★ ★ ★ ★   *Highly Recommended*

SPATEN Optimator Doppelbock (Germany)

The cherry-cola/mahogany/sorrel color is not quite opaque, but very dense nevertheless, ideally pure, sand-colored foam, excellent head retention; the nose is subdued and off-dry, offering only a trace of deep-roasted malt in the opening pass—with warming, the bouquet comes alive, emitting controlled aromas of hops and toasted whole-wheat bread—I found this nose very stingy; on palate, it's medium-rich, pleasantly roasted/toasty, and moderately creamy—medium- to full-bodied; the aftertaste is charred, hoppy, and suitably malty; a very nice Old World double bock, not a serious rival to Paulaner's magnificent Salvator.

RATING ★★★ **Recommended**

SPATEN Ur-Marzen Oktoberfest Lager (Germany)

Gorgeous, medium amber/honey color, with mountains of sustained beige suds—so billowy you almost need a ladder to get past them to the lip of the glass; the nose is delicate, though hardly timid or shy and emits mild, woodsy scents of earth, leaves, and even some cedar and spice; I admire the round, supple texture—it feels plush on the tongue; flavorwise, it shows polite, well-crafted tastes of hops, yeast, and malted milk; it's very beery and isn't trying to masquerade as a wine or a cordial, which more than a few beers make attempts at, as though suffering a case of identity crisis; this beauty is easy to drink and offers a completely satisfying beer experience.

RATING ★★★ **Recommended**

SPATEN Hefe-Weissbier (Germany)

Only a tad cloudy, a rich honey/amber/gold color is topped by creamy mountains of foam that last a lifetime; the assertive bouquet is predictably like cracked wheat in the initial nosing, then the spice/clove element takes over and dominates into the third pass—the final nosing offers a bit of yellow fruit and truckloads of clove; immensely refreshing at palate entry—by midpalate the grain-clove tandem achieve total domination, but that's all right with me, since they're so complementary—it seems as though the interplay of the wheat and clove is sufficient; the finish is slightly melony and banana-like; the wheat-clove harmony and definition make this beer recommendable.

RATING ★★★ **Recommended**

STAROPRAMEN Pilsener (Czech Republic)

Handsome, deep gold color, stark-white foam, excellent head retention; the nose is disturbingly stale right off the pour, but that sweatiness blows off with time, revealing a pleasantly crisp maltiness by the third pass—the final nosing doesn't fare well, as a steely tankiness appears from nowhere; on palate, it's decent as a razor-like hoppiness tries valiantly to redeem the dubious aroma and damn near succeeds; the finish is nicely malted; this beer tried to make a comeback; not every pilsener from the Czech Republic can rival Pilsener Urquell.

RATING ★★

STERKENS Bokrijks Kruikenbier Ale (Belgium)

Moderately cloudy orange/honey color, off-white foam, poor-to-fair head retention; the nose is zesty and piquant right out of the bottle, then it turns sedate and somewhat coy as a nuanced maltiness underlies the more prominent aroma of spice; very pleasant going at palate entry as citrusy/tart tastes of desert-dry hops and malt don't try to be something they're not—what they are is amiable; the finish is lightish, very crisp, keenly hoppy, acceptably bitter, and dry to off-dry; a more than decent quaff that expects little but gives enough of itself in waves of fundamental pleasure to be recommended.

RATING ★★★ *Recommended*

STERKENS Poorter (Belgium)

(Please note that this ale is no relation to the traditional porter style of beer—the term "Poorter" means "freeman" and refers only to the freeing of the region's serfs in the Middle Ages.) Gorgeous tawny-port/medium-brown color, light-beige foam that quickly dissipates; this good-looking ale offers a modest but pleasant bouquet of red fruit, fragrant malt, and dark toffee in understated amounts; clearly, this ale's best face is found in the taste and mouth presence, as highly delectable flavors of black cherries, black plums, and overripe grapes are highlighted in the medium-bodied midpalate experience; the finish is clean, agile, and medium-long; the fruit focus makes for an intriguing ale.

RATING ★★★ *Recommended*

SUNTORY Draft Pilsener (Japan/Canada)

Attractive, deep amber/harvest-gold tone, off-white foam and little head retention; the appealing nose is sweet, sugary, malty, and delightful, though hardly profound or multidimensional—it just has a sexy, ripe-fruit quality that I found interesting; once in the mouth, however, a good portion of the charm I noted in the aroma vanishes as a flat, cardboard-like, neutral, and only faintly malty flavor took the lead; the aftertaste was limp, reflecting the lackluster taste; the disappointment of the taste and the finish relegated this woeful beer to one-star territory; don't even consider it for a second.

RATING ★

SUPERIOR Clasica Pilsener (Mexico)

Appearancewise, it's bright-golden in color, pearly-white foam, low head retention; the singular, roasted-nuts aroma is quite nice, if a bastion of simplicity; to my disappointment, this frail pilsener unravels in the mouth with a cardboard-like flavor that is grossly unappealing, and, worst of all, it hangs around well into the aftertaste; the liquid must be given some recognition, nonetheless, for the moderately pleasing bouquet.

RATING ★

T

Taj Mahal Lager (India)

Dark gold color, with cumulus-like clouds of pasty-white foam—I thought for a minute that I'd have to evacuate my tasting room, the foam was flowing over the glass so furiously; the pleasing nose highlights the floral character of the hops—the aromatic layer beneath the hops offers sugar-cookie batter; it's in the taste that this particular cookie crumbles, however, as agonizing flavors of glue and stale bread dominate the disastrous palate from entry to aftertaste—this is really an awful-tasting beer and there's no other way to put it, there's no point in glossing over it; it bears no resemblance to hops, yeast, or barley malt whatsoever; another candidate for the no-star category.

RATING ★

Tangle Foot Ale (England)

Attractive, golden/orange/vermilion color, eggshell foam, quick head retention; the bouquet is all hops from start to finish—it's a floral/garden-like hoppiness, not a bitter hoppiness—this is not a monster nose, neither is it a flirt—it's solid, steady, and workmanlike; in the mouth, it hits the palate with affable, open, even generous tastes of off-dry malt and dry cereal—the hoppy bitterness quotient enters for keeps at midpalate; the finish is clean, refreshing, and mildly bitter; very nice, uncomplicated drinking.

RATING ★ ★ ★   **Recommended**

Tecate Pilsener (Mexico)

Deep amber/harvest-gold tone, white foam, average head retention; the nose is floral, fresh, and appealing in a simple way—it's clear right off the bat that this is no Samuel Smith's Lager competitor, but, hey, they all can't be; in the mouth, this pilsener's best attributes come out—uncomplicated, yeasty, hoppy, and mildly doughy flavors that don't consume lots of analysis time; I've evaluated this beer three times, with the final examination upgrading it to two stars; middle-of-the-pack, functional.

RATING ★ ★

Thames Welsh Bitter Ale (Wales)

Slightly milky/foggy, soft copper hue, tan foam, average head retention; the strange but not unpleasant aroma features red cherries and red currants in the opening salvo, then turns in on itself and goes dumb in the second pass—the cherry/berry duo reemerges in the third pass and it finishes on this one-note melody of fruitiness; on palate, it's estery/fruity, off-dry to sweet (this is a bitter?), and exceedingly refreshing—I think what perplexes me is the lack of bitter hoppiness—the ripe-red-fruit component dominates the taste; while I didn't find this very nice beer bitter at all, I'm giving it three stars anyway because it's so drinkable; but, buyer, beware, this beer is not a bitter by any stretch of the imagination.

RATING ★ ★ ★   **Recommended**

Thomas Hardy's Ale Vintage 1994 (England)

Stunningly fetching chestnut-brown tone with reddish highlights, virtually no head retention; the distinctive, honeyed, cake-batter, red-fruit bouquet is one of the more compelling ale aromas in existence—the fruit element is remarkably sturdy, yet graceful—this is a nose that alone earns two rating stars; on the palate, the entry taste is like cocoa, then at midpalate it rings more like cherry cola; by the heavy malt aftertaste, there's a bit of short-lived coffee-bean bitterness, then a cake-frosting sweetness that rounds out the whole experience with finesse; multidimensional, luxurious, textured, and sublime; bravo, encore, encore.

RATING ★ ★ ★ ★   *Highly Recommended*

Thomas Hardy's Ale (England)

Comes in a small 6.33-ounce bottle at a very dear price; cloudy appearance, throws some sediment, reddish/brown color; cardboard, anise, dill, cherry, intensely herbal nose, which also has nuances of dried roses, sweet licorice, and molasses; flavors of charcoal, cola, and nuts tweak the taste buds; endless road tar, licorice, herbal finish; while I didn't love it to death, I really appreciated its complexity and uniqueness, especially in the thought-provoking bouquet; I suspect that this bottle was beginning to grow stale, hence the cardboard-like aroma, which in my experience is the first sign of chemical diminishment in beer.

RATING ★ ★ ★   *Recommended*

Thomas Hardy's Country Bitter (England)

Standard-issue pale-ale/Bitter appearance—pretty medium-amber/sienna/copper hue, tan foam, better than average head retention; the fresh nose is particularly zesty, lively, and forward as ripe, honeydew-melon, red-fruit (plums), malty (like Ovaltine), and hoppy aromas indulge the nasal cavity with a genuine treat—I delighted in this admirable bouquet; on the palate, however, I was seriously disappointed as the light- to medium-weighted texture knocked the legs out from under the flavor, resulting in a meek, malty taste that left the great promise implied in the nose totally unfulfilled—the taste was damn near neutral; sour, thin finish; the two stars were earned by the fine appearance and the superstar-level aroma.

RATING ★ ★

3 Monts Flanders Golden Ale (France)

Seriously attractive, 18-carat-gold color, amazingly fizzy, ivory foam, infinite head retention; the first stage of the nose is like when you cut open a package of baker's yeast when making bread—it has that tangy, almost sour, twang—by the third pass, the yeastiness mostly blows off, and what remains is a delicious, underripe fruitiness (apples, pears, and kiwi)—an exciting, unfolding, multilayered bouquet that keeps the nose guessing; on palate, the big, yeasty flavor quickly takes charge of the willing taste buds—the textural heft alone of this ale makes it memorable—the midpalate features flavors of apple, spice, and very sweet malt; complex, engaging aftertaste; you may need a whip and a chair to control it after opening.

RATING ★ ★ ★ ★   *Highly Recommended*

Tolly Cobbold IPA (England)

Gorgeous harvest-gold/honey hue, eggshell foam, superb head retention, immaculate purity; the nose isn't the most pronounced bitter ale bouquet from the U.K. I've come across—there's a hoppy snap immediately following the pour, then a soft maltiness takes over and doesn't relinquish its hold through the remaining nosings—a bit one-dimensional; in the mouth, the lightness of the texture plays against it, because there's not a solid enough base on which to build a lot of flavor—the flavor highlights the hops rather than the malt as a moderately bitter taste carries the entire mouth experience; the aftertaste is clean, quick, and whispy; drinkable, but for an IPA from the U.K., it's a tad too meek.

RATING ★ ★

Tsingtao Pilsener (China)

Standard gold color, very long-lasting, billowy white head; very aromatic, enchanting, concentrated, malt-laden nose with background notes of pencil eraser, hops, and ripe fruit, especially kiwi; the one-note, dry—verging on off-dry—taste of hops is pleasant enough, though; I wished it would have shown more oomph after the singular nose; finishes clean and fast; God knows I've downed plenty of this middle-of-the-road, refreshing lager in the Chinatowns of New York and San Francisco; unfortunately, it lacks in the flavor and aftertaste the necessary character follow-through that ultimately separates the average beers from the recommended ones; recently upgraded to two stars.

RATING ★ ★

Tuborg Gold Label Pilsener (Denmark)

Very-pale-gold/yellowish, wimpy color, bubbles the size of the Goodyear blimp ensure that the head lasts approximately three nanoseconds—golly, thanks; the odd nose is like bubblegum, ripe grapes, sugar, pencil eraser, and plums—it's a strange but appealing bouquet that keeps you on your toes wondering what other weird aromas are in there; on palate, I found this beer to be overly hopped (which I didn't like), somewhat green and underripe, yet remarkably fruity (which I did like); the finish is clean, crisp, and short; too inconsistent in its personality to be recommended.

RATING ★ ★

Tucher Kristall Weizen (Germany)

Brilliant pale-gold color, firm white head; for a wheat beer, the bouquet is surprisingly off-dry to sweet as a pleasant, ripe-apple fragrance wafts up from the sampling glass; in the mouth, again an engaging, sweet tang meets the palate—it's hardly a complex beer, but it owns nicely rounded, fruited flavors that last into the medium-long aftertaste; this is a borderline judgment, so I'll go in favor of recommendation because I believe there's enough quality and charm here to warrant a nod.

RATING ★ ★ ★ **Recommended**

Tucher Bajuvator Doppelbock (Germany)

Medium-to-dark amber color, no head retention to speak of; the off-dry nose is quite mild and lazy, with hints of wood smoke, brown rice, quinine, slate, minerals, and biscuits—hardly succulent, but pleasant nonetheless; texturewise it's not in the same league as the viscous Paulaner Salvator or Ayinger Celebrator, being medium-bodied at best; tastewise it shows cola nut, vanilla bean, coffee with cream, and a smidgen of molasses; the finish is clean, almost lean, and long as a roasted-walnut quality nicely sums up the experience; not an inspired double bock, but sound, presentable, and better than average.

RATING ★★★　*Recommended*

TUCHER Hefe Weizen (Germany)

Slightly deeper gold color than the Kristall Weizen, no head worth talking about; the appley nose is a tad musty, even though the freshness dating indicator is well within the safe range; on the tongue, I don't find this beer to be as agile as its sibling; the taste picks up a bit on the second pass, almost redeeming the anemic, attic-like bouquet; finishes cleanly, simply; too fundamental to recommend.

RATING ★★

TUCHER Dunkel Hefe Weizen (Germany)

Hot-tea color, white, puffy head, poor head retention; the nose is sweet, fruity (red grapes, red plums), minty, and even wine-like—one of the more beguiling bouquets in the Tucher portfolio; unfortunately, a good portion of the charm found in the aroma mysteriously escapes through the back door in the flavor as little of the svelte fruitiness comes across on the palate—really what you're left with is a flimsy, Wheat Thins–tasting libation that's anything but intriguing or satisfying; the finish is wham-bam fast; a disappointment; the aroma earns the stars.

RATING ★★

TUSKER Premium Lager (Kenya)

Pleasant appearance of medium gold, huge, planet-sized bubbles, off-white foam, fair head retention; there's an inviting sweetness to the faint nose, a kind of pine-nut/cedar, elemental aroma—I just wish that there was something greater to grab a hold of—it's a very thin, some might say delicate, bouquet; mildly appealing in the mouth as a meager flavor of malt (from equatorial barley) provides the majority of the music; the medium- to full-bodied texture is a high point; the aftertaste is keenly tart and refreshing; I liked it more as I kept going back to it—I finally upgraded it to three stars on the final sampling; it expanded and filled out with aeration.

RATING ★★★　*Recommended*

V

VELTINS Pilsener (Germany)

Medium gold color, with a blizzard of white foam, better than average head retention; the assertive nose reeks of toasty barley malt and flowery hops—I greatly like this straight-ahead, in-your-face type of bouquet that's compelling and friendly; in the mouth, the hops get intense as the flavor goes into an off-dry, astringent mode that's remarkably refreshing and enlivening; the aftertaste is sleek, hoppy, and medium-long, with a dash of bitterness in the tail end; easily one of my favorite German beers.

RATING ★ ★ ★ ★   ***Highly Recommended***

W

WATNEY'S Cream Stout (England)

Opaque/black, beige foam, low head retention; the blockbuster nose is like chocolate milk, tobacco smoke, and roasted chestnuts, with subtle supporting hints of malt, tar, and even spearmint; the texture justifies the use of the word "cream"; flavorwise, what we have here is a brawny, deep, walnut-like, sweet stout that offers tantalizing, smoky, opulent flavors of burnt toast, vanilla beans, egg cream, caramel, and dried plums; the finish is thick, long, and lavish; fasten your seatbelt, matey, before you sample this muscular beauty.

RATING ★ ★ ★ ★   ***Highly Recommended***

WATNEY'S Red Barrel (England)

Has the medium-amber/burnished-orange hue that's frequently associated with amontillado sherry, admirably pure, sand-colored foam, good head retention; the estery nose displays a beguiling array of sweet, charred-malt, red-fruit, cotton-candy, and cherry-cola fragrances—I liked the bouquet a lot, largely because of the ripe fruitiness; medium-bodied and satiny to the touch, but neither viscous nor bosomy; the mouth presence mirrors the aroma as the sweet, mashy malt element is complemented by a fruitiness that expands into a nut-meat quality by midpalate; the aftertaste reveals more of the hop influence as a mild nip of bitterness caps the experience.

RATING ★ ★ ★   ***Recommended***

WEIHENSTEPHAN Weizenbier (Germany)

Looks like ginger ale, huge, devouring head; the very focused, apple-like, and intense aroma speaks of wheat in capital letters—it's a sour, tart, grainy nose that simply didn't arouse me; it's true to form in the mouth as the keenly tart flavor of sour apples cleans the palate, but leaves little room for anything else; finishes meekly and very dryly; while I understand and appreciate the innate qualities of wheat beers, I can't force myself to like this lean, even austere, unripe green-apple taste; claims to be the world's oldest brewery, circa 1040 A.D.

RATING ★ ★

WHITBREAD Traditional Pale Ale (England)

Pretty, rich, rust/coral-red/honey/amber color that's topped by a cream-colored head—what an eyeful; nosewise, this supple beauty brings to mind ripe plums, black cherries, candied almonds, and muesli cereal; on the palate, the accented red-fruit flavors bedazzle the gleeful taste buds in decadent waves of malted-barley comfort; the cherry quality reemerges in the fruity, then steely, dry finish; a well-mannered, scrumptious, fruity pale ale from the country that does justice to this beer style better than anyone.

RATING ★ ★ ★ ★   *Highly Recommended*

WICKULER Pilsener (Germany)

Standard medium-gold color, but with a very extended, billowy head of creamy-white foam; the amazingly varied nose reminds me all at once of raisin bran, grapes, wet slate, minerals, wet pavements, roses, and barley—I love this type of flowery, elegant bouquet; in the mouth, a stony dryness dominates, with satellite flavors of dry cereal, roasted chestnuts, and yeasty bread vying for attention as they orbit around the prime taste of bitterness; finishes long and minerally in the throat; the nose alone is worth the experience.

RATING ★ ★ ★   *Recommended*

WURZBURGER HOFBRAU May Bok (Germany)

Very pretty copper/burnished-orange/amontillado-sherry/honey tone, beige foam, quick-to-leave head retention; the first burst from the aroma was alluring as ripe red fruit and barley malt wafted gently up from the glass—by the second pass only moments later, however, only timid, fleeting fragrances of sweet mash and honey wheat could be discerned—little aroma registered by the final nosing—whither the bouquet?—quite pleasant, if simple, on the tongue as polite, toasted-malt, and lightly fruited flavors converge at midpalate; the aftertaste exhibits a nice display of hoppy twang, bringing a sense of closure to the experience; an average, middle-of-the-road, but on the whole, uninspiring bock.

RATING ★ ★

WURZBURGER HOFBRAU Bavarian Light (Germany)

Pleasant, opulent, golden tone, billowy white foam, good head retention; it took me a long time to coax anything from the closed-off, blunted aroma—by the third nosing, bits and pieces of hops, dry bitterness, and white rice peeked out—not a candidate for my all-time top 5,000 beer bouquets; even worse on the palate, this sorrowful excuse for a beer is metallic, tanky, unpleasantly astringent, and undrinkable; it finishes as rudely as it begins; don't even consider it; it left a taste of keys in my mouth; horrible.

RATING ★

WURZBURGER HOFBRAU Fallfest Beer (Germany)

Attractive, deep tawny/brown color with dark-red highlights, beige foam, average head retention; once again as with other beers from this brewery, I found the bouquet to be meek and miserly, at best, in its spirit of giving—by the third pass, I at last noted some weary scents of tobacco smoke, hop-related tartness, roasted malt, and dry cereal—I allowed as much time as necessary for the aroma to develop, and it failed to do so; on palate, there's marginally more evidence of character, as some baked, toasty flavors barely emerged—the midpalate experience involved considerable bitterness and frightfully little else; lean, austere, astringent finish; don't waste your time or money.

RATING ★

WURZBURGER HOFBRAU Original Bavarian Holiday Beer (Germany)

Lovely, tawny/red/cherry-wood tone, beige foam, very good head retention; this terrible nose is sweaty, steely, unclean, and reminds me of the smell of coins—not an auspicious beginning; strangely, in the mouth it's sweet, roasted, and medium-bodied, with flavors of road tar, nougat, and candied almonds, all of which make some attempt at respectability; the aftertaste is more bitter than sweet; I scored it so low because it was so tough getting past the gross aroma; a bomb for the holidays.

RATING ★

WURZBURGER HOFBRAU Bavarian Dark (Germany)

Sound, medium brown color, tan foam, little head retention; in keeping with the feeble house style, this dark, which you'd think would offer something more in the way of aroma than its siblings, ended up being among the most vapid aromatically of this dismal bunch—the neutrality of the bouquet boggled my mind; not all that much improved or animated in the mouth, as skimpy, lifeless flavors of moderately roasted barley and wood smoke are the best that this niggardly beer can produce; the finish is flat as a pancake; just plain lousy.

RATING ★

X

XINGU Black Beer (Brazil)

Cola-colored, opaque brown/black, with no head to speak of; the intriguing bouquet is sweetish and has hints of egg cream, rye bread, pumpernickel bread, and road tar—I liked the hodge-podge bouquet quite a bit though I really had to work at discerning any definable aromas; in the mouth, there's a surprising and disappointing thinness to the texture; sour flavors of smoke, tar, and citrus also disappointed me; to make matters worse, it ended up with an astringent, paper-thin finish; I can't recommend it in terms of quality, but I did find it an interesting beer experience all the same, especially the exotic aroma.

RATING ★ ★

Y

Young's Special London Ale (England)

Tawny/brown color; firm, ample tan foam, good head retention; this ale's clean, subdued, and elegant nose highlights yeasty, ripe-fruit aromas—a lovely, well-behaved bouquet; on the palate, apples and pears abound in fruitbasket flavors, which are simultaneously rich, assertive, and classy; ideally paced finish of nuts, cake, and fruit; perfectly balanced, medium-weighted; unquestionably, one of the nicest, most satisfying ales I've ever tasted; it simply has everything going for it: a delightful, fragrant, and fresh bouquet; approachable, fulfilling, nicely melded flavors; and a crisp, clean finish that leaves one feeling very well indeed; get out there and find it.

RATING ★ ★ ★ ★   *Highly Recommended*

Young's London Porter (England)

Deep mahogany color, topped by a beige, frothing head; the extraordinarily alluring nose ripples with heady scents of sourdough bread, vanilla extract, and cream-custard (flan)—the nose is layered, lush, and so profound that you simply can't stop sniffing it—the nose easily earns two of the rating stars on its own; the texture is satiny and medium- to full-weighted; savory flavors of fruit, nuts, and licorice surround the taste buds in a silky jacket of flavor; the long, fruit-salad finish completes this stunning thoroughbred in elegant fashion; a brilliant porter that's a must-have item for any serious beer lover.

RATING ★ ★ ★ ★   *Highly Recommended*

Young's Ram Rod Pale Ale (England)

Light-catching orange/pekoe-tea-with-lemon color, firm off-white foam, superb head retention; the divinely aromatic elements of toasty, sweet cereal, caramel, and rich cocoa combine beautifully in this perfumy, grainy, slightly bitter nose; on palate, the bone-dry, roasted-barley, anise flavors are not as primly melded as in the nose; the potent, long finish of roasted barley lasts all night; this is a very pleasant pale-ale winner that would have scored higher had it offered as much in the flavor as it did in the aroma.

RATING ★ ★ ★   *Recommended*

Young's Old Nick Barley Wine Style Ale (England)

Impressive, dark-ale appearance, deep chestnut/nut-brown hue, pure, medium-beige foam, long head retention; the rich, perfumy bouquet offers subtle scents of berries, deep-roasted malt, and nuts in the first aromatic burst after the pour, then it substantially diminishes in the second and third passes—it settles down in the final nosing, emitting barely perceptible aromas of sweet malt and grain husk; on palate, it's moderately astringent at entry and stays so through to midpalate, where a benign maltiness emerges just prior to the aftertaste; the finish is a nicely balanced duet that features malt and hops; I found this confusing ale to be more in the style of nut-brown ale than what I know to be barley wine; that aside, it's still very pleasant.

RATING ★ ★ ★   **Recommended**

YOUNG's Oatmeal Stout (England)

Opaque, dark chocolate-brown color, the foam is the color of wet sand, extended head retention; the nose is lovely and elegant as heavily grained, roasted, and mashy aromas keep the olfactory sense charmed for the first two nosings and, regrettably, somewhat bored for two more passes as the aroma lost considerable steam with aeration—there was a final gasp of creaminess in the last nosing; in the mouth, the thick, creamy texture gives a sturdy foundation for the moderately dense flavors of dark malt, oats, and bittersweet chocolate; the finish is long, semisweet, and grainy; very nice, indeed, but not in the same league as the style benchmark, the Oatmeal Stout from Samuel Smith.

RATING ★ ★ ★   **Recommended**

YOUNGER'S Tartan Special Ale (Scotland)

Deep amber/amontillado-sherry/tawny/brown color, tan foam, great purity, average head retention; the zesty nose leaps from the glass right after the pour in delectably inviting waves of sour dough, mashy malt, and wet fabric—subsequent passes aren't as dynamic as that first rush, but they are still quite vibrant—the third pass reveals a supple maltiness that's very similar to wheat-based cereal with honey—it's a sweet, lovely bouquet; in the mouth, it's not as rich or sweet as the nose would have you believe, but it's solidly delicious and malty nonetheless; the finish is round, showing a healthy dose of hops; a tad more meat on the bones of the flavor would have been welcome.

RATING ★ ★ ★   **Recommended**

Z

ZIEGEL HOF Non-Alcohol Malt (Switzerland)

Gold/honey color, medium-frothy head, good head retention for an N-A; the aromatic, sweet-sour, soy-sauce nose has undercurrent elements of ripe berry fruit, honey, nuttiness, and wheat toast; on the palate, the charming qualities found in the nose take a backseat to an almost wine-like taste at the back of the throat; the peculiar grapiness slowly fades in the aftertaste, but its impression remains behind in the midst of the honey/sweet-malt-flavored tail; it's not a taste that I'd search out, but the fruity component might please some alcohol-conscious drinkers; on balance, a good effort; evaluated three times with the same score.

RATING ★

APPENDIX A

Complete Alphabetical Domestic Beer Ratings Summary by Rating Category

CLASSIC—HIGHEST RECOMMENDATION

CELIS White Hefe Weizen ★★★★★
GEARY'S London Style Porter ★★★★★
LAKEFRONT BREWERY Riverwest Stein Beer Amber Lager ★★★★★
LAKEFRONT BREWERY Klisch Pilsner ★★★★★
NOR'WESTER Blacksmith Porter ★★★★★
SAMUEL ADAMS Double Bock Dark Lager ★★★★★
SAMUEL ADAMS Honey Porter ★★★★★
SEA DOG Riverdriver Hazelnut Porter ★★★★★
SIERRA NEVADA Stout ★★★★★

SUPERB—HIGHLY RECOMMENDED

ALASKAN Smoked Porter ★★★★
ANCHOR Old Foghorn Barley Wine Style Ale ★★★★
BREWERY HILL Cherry Wheat Ale ★★★★
BROOKLYN BREWERY Black Chocolate Stout ★★★★
CELIS Pale Bock ★★★★
DOCK STREET Illuminator Bock ★★★★
DORNBUSCH Alt Ale ★★★★
DUBUQUE STAR Big Muddy Red Ale ★★★★
ELM CITY Blackwell Stout ★★★★
ERIN'S ROCK Stout & Amber Lager ★★★★
GRANT'S Scottish Ale ★★★★
GRANT'S Perfect Porter ★★★★

GRITTY McDUFF'S Best Bitter Ale ★★★★
GRITTY McDUFF'S Best Brown Ale ★★★★
HEARTLAND BREWERY Indiana Pale Ale ★★★★
JACK DANIEL'S 1866 Classic Amber Lager ★★★★
JACK DANIEL'S 1866 Classic American Ale ★★★★
JUAN PISTOLA'S Acapulco Gold Pale Ale ★★★★
KATAHDIN Red Ale ★★★★
LAKEFRONT BREWERY Cream City Pale Ale ★★★★
LAKEFRONT BREWERY ESB OCIA Certified Organic Ale ★★★★
LAKEFRONT BREWERY Eastside Dark Lager ★★★★
LAKEFRONT BREWERY Holiday Spice Lager 1995 ★★★★
LATROBE Bohemian Pilsner ★★★★
MAGIC HAT Irish Style Red Ale ★★★★
MILL CITY Oatmeal Stout ★★★★
NAKED ASPEN Raspberry Wheat ★★★★
NEW AMSTERDAM New York Amber ★★★★
NEW AMSTERDAM New York Ale ★★★★
NORTH COUNTRY Fat Bear Stout ★★★★
NOR'WESTER Hefe Weizen ★★★★
NOR'WESTER Raspberry Weizen ★★★★
OLD COLUMBIA Strauss Stout ★★★★
OLD COLUMBIA America's Finest Pilsener ★★★★
OLD THUMPER Extra Special Ale ★★★★
OREGON Nut Brown Ale ★★★★
PETE'S Gold Coast Lager ★★★★
RED HOOK ESB ★★★★
RED HOOK Blackhook Porter ★★★★
RHINO CHASERS Dark Lager ★★★★
RJ'S RIPTIDE Oatmeal Stout ★★★★
ROGUE American Amber Ale ★★★★
ROGUE Mogul Ale ★★★★
ROGUE Smoke Rauch Style Ale ★★★★
ROGUE Shakespeare Stout ★★★★
ROGUE Old Crustacean Barley Wine Style Ale ★★★★
RUFFIAN Extra Special Bitter ★★★★
SAMUEL ADAMS Dark Wheat ★★★★
SAMUEL ADAMS Triple Bock 1994 Brew Reserve ★★★★
SAMUEL ADAMS Scotch Ale Triple Malt ★★★★
SARANAC Adirondack Amber Lager ★★★★
SARANAC Chocolate Amber ★★★★
SARANAC Season's Best Nut Brown Lager ★★★★
SAXER Three Finger Jack Stout ★★★★
SEA DOG Old Gollywobbler Brown Ale ★★★★
SEA DOG Windjammer Blonde Ale ★★★★
SIERRA NEVADA Porter ★★★★
SLO BREWING CO. Cole Porter ★★★★
STEGMAIER 1857 Lager ★★★★
STOUDT'S Golden Lager ★★★★

WILD BOAR Special Amber Lager ★★★★
WIT Amber ★★★★

ABOVE AVERAGE—RECOMMENDED

ALASKAN Amber Beer ★★★
ALMOND BROTHERS Amber Ale ★★★
ANDERSON VALLEY Boont Amber Ale ★★★
ANCHOR Liberty ★★★
BADERBRAU Bock Beer ★★★
BADERBRAU Pilsener ★★★
BALLANTINE India Pale Ale ★★★
BELMONT Marathon Ale ★★★
BERGHOFF Dark Beer / Dortmunder Style ★★★
BLUE MOON Nut Brown Ale ★★★
BLUE RIDGE ESB Red Ale ★★★
BREWER'S CAVE Black Barley Ale ★★★
BREWER'S CAVE Golden Caramel Lager ★★★
BREWSKI Bar Room Ale ★★★
BROOKLYN BREWERY East India Pale Ale ★★★
BROOKLYN BREWERY Lager ★★★
BUFFALO Lager ★★★
BUFFALO BILL'S Pumpkin Ale ★★★
CATAMOUNT Bock ★★★
CATAMOUNT Porter ★★★
CATAMOUNT Christmas Ale 1995 ★★★
CATAMOUNT 10th Anniversary Ale Special Edition IPA ★★★
CELIS Ale Grand Cru ★★★
CELIS Golden Ale ★★★
COORS Winterfest ★★★
DEVIL MOUNTAIN BREWERY Railroad Ale ★★★
DEVIL MOUNTAIN BREWERY Porter ★★★
DIXIE BLACKENED VOODOO Lager ★★★
DOCK STREET Bohemian Pilsener ★★★
DOCK STREET Philadelphia Amber ★★★
DRYTOWN Susquehanna Gold Ale ★★★
ELM CITY Connecticut Ale ★★★
GEARY'S Pale Ale ★★★
GEARY'S Hampshire Special Ale Winter 1995–1996 ★★★
GEORGE KILLIAN'S Irish Brown Ale ★★★
GEORGIA PEACH Wheat Beer ★★★
GEORGIA Wild Raspberry Wheat Ale ★★★
GRAIL Amber Ale ★★★
GRANT'S Imperial Stout ★★★
GRANT'S Weis Beer ★★★
GRANT'S Celtic Ale ★★★
HARPOON India Pale Ale ★★★
HARPOON Octoberfest ★★★

HARPOON Pilsner ★★★
HEARTLAND BREWERY Red Rooster Ale ★★★
HELENBOCH Holiday Ale ★★★
JACK DANIEL'S 1866 Classic Pilsner ★★★
JAMAICA BRAND Red Ale ★★★
JUAN PISTOLA'S Baja Tan Brown Ale ★★★
LATROBE Bavarian Black Lager ★★★
LATROBE Pale Ale ★★★
LEINENKUGEL'S Red Lager ★★★
MAGIC HAT 9 Not Quite Pale Ale ★★★
MANHATTAN Gold Lager ★★★
MCSORLEY'S Ale ★★★
MICHAEL SHEA'S Blonde Lager ★★★
MICHAEL SHEA'S Irish Amber Lager ★★★
MICHAEL SHEA'S Black & Tan ★★★
MIDDLESEX Brown Ale ★★★
MIDDLESEX Raspberry Wheat ★★★
MILLER Reserve 100% Barley Draft ★★★
MYSTIC SEAPORT Pale Ale ★★★
NAKED ASPEN Apricot Ale ★★★
NARRAGANSETT Lager ★★★
NEPTUNE Premium Ale ★★★
NEUWEILER Stock Ale ★★★
NEW AMSTERDAM Black & Tan ★★★
NEW AMSTERDAM Winter Anniversary Dark Ale 1995–1996 ★★★
NEW ENGLAND Oatmeal Stout ★★★
NEW ENGLAND Atlantic Amber ★★★
NEW YORK HARBOR Amber Ale ★★★
NEW YORK HARBOR Dark Ale ★★★
NORTH COAST Ruedrick's Red Seal Ale ★★★
NORTH COUNTRY Whiteface Pale Ale ★★★
NOR'WESTER Best Bitter Ale ★★★
OLD COLUMBIA Karl Strauss' Amber Lager ★★★
OLD COLUMBIA ESB Ale ★★★
OLD PECONIC Hampton Ale ★★★
OLD SLUGGER Pale Ale ★★★
OREGON Honey Red ★★★
OXFORD Raspberry Wheat Ale ★★★
PETE'S Wicked Lager ★★★
PIG'S EYE Pilsener ★★★
PIG'S EYE Red Amber Ale ★★★
PYRAMID Best Brown Ale ★★★
RED FEATHER Pale Ale ★★★
RED HOOK Ballard Bitter India Pale Ale ★★★
RED HOOK Rye Ale ★★★
RED HOOK Wheat Hook Ale ★★★
RHINO CHASERS American Ale ★★★
RHINO CHASERS Amber Ale ★★★
RHINO CHASERS Peach Honey Wheat ★★★

RHINO CHASERS Winterful ★★★
RJ's RIPTIDE Original Honey Ale ★★★
RJ's RIPTIDE Two-Berry Ale ★★★
RJ's RIPTIDE Charger Gold Ale ★★★
ROGUE-N-BERRY Ale ★★★
ROGUE Mexicali Ale ★★★
ROGUE Ale ★★★
ROGUE Dead Guy Ale ★★★
ROGUE/ST. ROGUE Red Ale ★★★
ROGUE Maierbock Ale ★★★
RUFFIAN Copper Ale ★★★
RUFFIAN Porter ★★★
RUFFIAN Blonde Bock ★★★
SAMUEL ADAMS Boston Lager ★★★
SAMUEL ADAMS Winter Lager ★★★
SAMUEL ADAMS Boston Ale ★★★
SAMUEL ADAMS Boston Lightship Light ★★★
SAMUEL ADAMS Cream Stout ★★★
SAMUEL ADAMS Golden Pilsner ★★★
SARANAC Golden Pilsener ★★★
SARANAC Pale Ale ★★★
SAXER Three Finger Jack Hefedunkel ★★★
SEA DOG Old East India IPA ★★★
SIERRA NEVADA Pale Ale ★★★
SPANISH PEAKS Black Dog Pale Ale ★★★
SPANISH PEAKS Peaches & Cream Ale ★★★
STAR Raspberry Wheat Ale ★★★
STOUDT'S Fest Marzen Style Lager ★★★
THE SHIPYARD Longfellow Winter Ale ★★★
WEINHARD'S Red Lager ★★★
WHITE KNIGHT Light Ale ★★★
WILD BOAR Classic Pilsner ★★★
WILD BOAR Wild Winter Spiced Brown Lager ★★★
WILD GOOSE Porter ★★★
WILD GOOSE Amber Ale ★★★
WIT Black ★★★
WIT White ★★★
WOODSTOCK Arnold's Amber Lager ★★★
YUENGLING Porter ★★★
YUENGLING Lord Chesterfield Ale ★★★
ZIP CITY Vienna Amber Lager ★★★

AVERAGE—NOT RECOMMENDED

ALASKAN Pale Ale ★★
ANCHOR Porter ★★
ANCHOR Steam Beer ★★
ANDERSON VALLEY Belk's Extra Special Bitter Ale ★★
BELMONT Strawberry Blonde Ale ★★

BLUE MOON Belgian White ★★
BLUE MOON Honey Blonde Lager ★★
BLUE MOON Raspberry Cream Ale ★★
BLUE RIDGE Golden Ale ★★
BOULDER Extra Pale Ale ★★
BREWER'S CAVE Amber Wheat Ale ★★
BREWERY HILL Honey Amber Ale ★★
BREWERY HILL Pale Ale ★★
BROOKLYN BREWERY Brown Dark Ale ★★
BUNKER HILL Lager ★★
CATAMOUNT Amber ★★
CATAMOUNT American Wheat ★★
COLD SPRING Export Lager ★★
COLD SPRING Honey Almond Lager ★★
COLD SPRING Blackberry Bramble Ale ★★
CRESTED BUTTE White Buffalo Peace Ale ★★
ELK MOUNTAIN Amber Ale ★★
ELM CITY Golden Ale ★★
GEORGE KILLIAN'S Irish Red Lager ★★
GRANT'S India Pale Ale ★★
GRITTY MCDUFF'S Black Fly Stout ★★
HARPOON Alt Ale ★★
HARPOON Winter Warmer ★★
HARPOON Golden Lager ★★
HEARTLAND BREWERY Cornhusker Lager ★★
HEARTLAND BREWERY Harvest Wheat Ale ★★
HEURICH'S Maerzen Lager ★★
IRON CITY Beer ★★
J.J. WAINWRIGHT'S Evil Eye Raspberry Wheat ★★
JUAN PISTOLA'S Sangria Ale ★★
KOCH'S Golden Anniversary Beer ★★
LAKEFRONT BREWERY Fuel Café Coffee-Flavored Stout ★★
LITTLE KINGS Cream Ale ★★
LITTLE KINGS BRUIN Pale Ale ★★
LOWENBRAU Special Pilsener ★★
MICHELOB Lager ★★
MICHELOB Dry Lager ★★
MIDDLESEX Porter ★★
MILLER Reserve Velvet Stout ★★
MOOSE Brown Ale ★★
NANTUCKET Island Amber ★★
NEUWEILER Traditional Lager ★★
NEUWEILER Porter ★★
NEUWEILER Black & Tan ★★
NEW AMSTERDAM Blonde Lager ★★
NEW AMSTERDAM Light Amber ★★
NEW ENGLAND Gold Stock Ale ★★
NORTH COUNTRY Maple Amber Ale ★★
O'DOUL'S Premium Non-Alcoholic Brew ★★

OLD COLUMBIA First National Bock ★★
OLD COLUMBIA Ed's Hoppy Birthday Pilsener ★★
OREGON ESB ★★
PETE'S Wicked Winter Brew ★★
PETE'S Wicked Honey Wheat ★★
PETE'S Wicked Red Amber Ale ★★
PIKE PLACE Pale Ale ★★
PINK TRIANGLE Light Beer ★★
RED BARON Cherry-Flavored Beer ★★
RED BONE Red Lager ★★
RHEINGOLD Light ★★
RJ'S RIPTIDE Dunkel Weizen ★★
RJ'S RIPTIDE Red Ale ★★
ROCK ICE Amber Lager ★★
ROGUE Golden Ale ★★
ROGUE Mo Ale Belgian Style ★★
ROLLING ROCK Extra Pale Lager ★★
ROLLING ROCK Bock ★★
RUFFIAN Irish Red Ale ★★
SAMUEL ADAMS Cherry Wheat Ale ★★
SAXER Three Finger Jack Amber Lager ★★
SAXER Lemon Lager ★★
SCHAEFER Pilsener ★★
SIMPATICO Amber Lager ★★
SPANISH PEAKS Black Dog Ale ★★
STEGMAIER Porter ★★
STEELHEAD Extra Stout ★★
YUENGLING TRADITIONAL Amber Lager ★★
ZIP CITY Oktoberfest Amber Lager ★★

POOR—NOT RECOMMENDED

AUGSBURGER Golden Lager ★
BELMONT Unfiltered Wheat ★
BELMONT Top Sail Amber Ale ★
BELMONT Long Beach Crude Nut Brown Ale ★
BEVERLY HILLS Palimony Bitter Ale ★
BREWERY HILL Raspberry Red Ale ★
BREWERY HILL Black & Tan ★
BUDWEISER Lager ★
BUD Light ★
BUDWEISER Ice Draft ★
BUSCH Lager ★
CARLING BLACK LABEL Light ★
CATAMOUNT Pale Ale ★
COORS Pilsener ★
COORS Light ★
COORS Cutter Non-Alcoholic Brew ★
COORS Red Light ★

Dixie Jazz Amber Light ★
Dixie Slow-Brewed Lager ★
Downtown Brown Ale ★
Ed's Cave Creek Original Chili Beer ★
Elk Mountain Red Lager ★
Genesee Cream Ale ★
Heartland Brewery Farmer Jon's Oatmeal Stout ★
Heurich's Foggy Bottom Ale ★
Hudson Lager ★
Jack Daniel's Oak-Aged Winter Brew ★
J. J. Wainwright's Evil Eye Ale ★
J. J. Wainwright's Evil Eye Honey Brown Ale ★
J. J. Wainwright's Evil Eye Oktoberfest ★
J. J. Wainwright's Black Jack Black & Tan ★
Juan Pistola's Amber Ale ★
Lone Star Lager ★
Magic Hat Blind Faith IPA ★
McMahon's Irish Style Potato Ale ★
Meister Brau Light ★
Michelob Amber Bock ★
Michelob Light Lager ★
Miller Lite ★
Miller Genuine Draft Cold-Filtered ★
Miller Genuine Draft Light ★
Miller Icehouse Ice Beer ★
Naked Aspen Pale Ale ★
North Coast Blue Star Great American Wheat Beer ★
Old Columbia Karl's Cream Ale ★
Old Columbia Karl Strauss' Light Lager ★
Oregon Hefeweizen ★
Oregon IPA ★
Oregon Raspberry Wheat ★
Oxford Class Amber Ale ★
Perry's Majestic Lager ★
Rattlesnake Lager ★
Red Dog ★
Red Tail Ale ★
Red Wolf Lager ★
Riverside Brewing Golden Spike Pilsner ★
Riverside Brewing Pullman Pale Ale ★
Riverside Brewing Victoria Avenue Amber Ale ★
Riverside Brewing Raincross Cream Ale ★
Rogue Mocha Porter ★
Rolling Rock Light Lager ★
Slo Brewing Co. Blueberry Ale ★
Slo Brewing Co. Brickhouse Extra Pale Ale ★
St. James Ale ★
Samuel Adams Wheat Brew ★
Schmidt's Light ★

SCRIMSHAW Pilsner ★
SHARP'S Non-Alcoholic Brew ★
SIMPATICO Golden Lager ★
SPANISH PEAKS Honey Raspberry Ale ★
SPANISH PEAKS Black Dog Wheat Ale ★
SPORTS Light ★
STOUDT'S Honey Double Mai Bock ★
TELLURIDE Lager ★
THE SHIPYARD Export Ale ★
THE SHIPYARD Goat Island Light Ale ★
THE SHIPYARD Bluefin Stout ★
WEINHARD'S Blue Boar Pale Ale ★
WILD GOOSE India Pale Ale ★
WILD GOOSE Spring Wheat Ale '96 ★
YUENGLING PREMIUM Light Lager ★
ZIMA Clearmalt ★

APPENDIX B

Complete Alphabetical Imported Beer Ratings Summary by Rating Category

CLASSIC—HIGHEST RECOMMENDATION

AECHT SCHLENKERLA Rauchbier (Germany) ★★★★★
BRAKSPEARS Henley Ale (England) ★★★★★
CHIMAY Grande Réserve Trappist Ale (Belgium) ★★★★★
CHRISTOFFEL Robertus Munich Lager (Holland) ★★★★★
DE TROCH CHAPEAU Pêche Lambic (Belgium) ★★★★★
ERDINGER Weissbier Hefetrub (Germany) ★★★★★
ERDINGER Pikantus Dunkler Weizenbock (Germany) ★★★★★
LA TRAPPE Quadrupel Trappist Ale (Holland) ★★★★★
LINDEMANS Pêche/Peach Lambic (Belgium) ★★★★★
MARSTON'S India Export Ale (England) ★★★★★
PAULANER Salvator Doppelbock (Germany) ★★★★★
PILSNER URQUELL Pilsner (Czech Republic) ★★★★★
ROYAL Extra Stout (Trinidad, West Indies) ★★★★★
ST. FEUILLIEN Blonde Abbey Ale (Belgium) ★★★★★
SAMUEL SMITH'S Oatmeal Stout (England) ★★★★★
SPATEN Lager (Germany) ★★★★★

SUPERB—HIGHLY RECOMMENDED

ADNAMS Nut Brown Ale (England) ★★★★
AFFLIGEM Dobbel Abbey Ale (Belgium) ★★★★
AFFLIGEM Tripel Abbey Ale (Belgium) ★★★★
AYINGER Brau-Weisse Helles Hefe Weissbier (Germany) ★★★★
BECK'S Dark Pilsener (Germany) ★★★★

BELHAVEN St. Andrews Ale (Scotland) ★★★★
BELHAVEN Scottish Ale (Scotland) ★★★★
CALEDONIAN Amber Ale (Scotland) ★★★★
CALEDONIAN Double Dark Ale (Scotland) ★★★★
CHIMAY Cinq Cents Trappist Ale (Belgium) ★★★★
CHRISTOFFEL Blonde Ale (Holland) ★★★★
CORSENDONK Monk's Pale Ale (Belgium) ★★★★
CORSENDONK Monk's Brown Ale (Belgium) ★★★★
DE TROCH CHAPEAU Mirabelle/Plum Lambic (Belgium) ★★★★
DE TROCH CHAPEAU Framboise/Raspberry Lambic (Belgium) ★★★★
DE TROCH CHAPEAU Gueuze Lambic (Belgium) ★★★★
DOUBLE DIAMOND Burton Ale (England) ★★★★
ERDINGER Weissbier Dunkel (Germany) ★★★★
GAMBRINUS Lager (Czech Republic) ★★★★
HACKER-PSCHORR Pschorr-Brau Dark Weisse (Germany) ★★★★
HACKER-PSCHORR Alt Munich Dark Ale (Germany) ★★★★
HACKER-PSCHORR Marzen Amber Ale (Germany) ★★★★
HEINEKEN Lager (Holland) ★★★★
KWAK PAUWEL Ale (Belgium) ★★★★
LA TRAPPE Dubbel Trappist Ale (Holland) ★★★★
LA TRAPPE Tripel Trappist Ale (Holland) ★★★★
LIEFMANS Goudenband (Belgium) ★★★★
LINDEMANS Kriek/Cherry Lambic (Belgium) ★★★★
MACKESON Triple Stout (England) ★★★★
MARSTON'S Pedigree Bitter (England) ★★★★
MORRELL'S Oxford Castle Ale (England) ★★★★
NEGRA MODELO Dark Ale (Mexico) ★★★★
OLD PECULIER Yorkshire Ale (England) ★★★★
PAULANER Lager (Germany) ★★★★
PAULANER Oktoberfest Lager (Germany) ★★★★
PINKUS Home Brew Munster Alt (Germany) ★★★★
RADEGAST Original Lager (Czech Republic) ★★★★
ROMAN Dobbelen Bruinen (Brown) Ale (Belgium) ★★★★
ROMAN Ename Dubbel Abbey Ale (Belgium) ★★★★
ROMAN Ename Tripel Abbey Ale (Belgium) ★★★★
ST. GEORGEN BRAU Kellerbier Lager (Germany) ★★★★
ST. LANDELIN Blonde Abbey Ale (France) ★★★★
SAMICHLAUS Dark Lager (Switzerland) ★★★★
SAMUEL SMITH'S Taddy Porter (England) ★★★★
SAMUEL SMITH'S Imperial Stout (England) ★★★★
SAMUEL SMITH'S India Ale (England) ★★★★
SAMUEL SMITH'S Pale Ale (England) ★★★★
SAMUEL SMITH'S Nut Brown Ale (England) ★★★★
SCALDIS Special Ale (Belgium) ★★★★
SCHIERLINGER Roggen Bavarian Rye Beer (Germany) ★★★★
SHEPHERD NEAME India Pale Ale (England) ★★★★
SHEPHERD NEAME Masterbrew Premium Bitter Ale (England) ★★★★
SHEPHERD NEAME Spitfire Ale (England) ★★★★
SINGHA Lager (Thailand) ★★★★

SPATEN Dark Hefe-Weissbier (Germany) ★★★★
THOMAS HARDY'S Ale Vintage 1994 (England) ★★★★
3 MONTS Flanders Golden Ale (France) ★★★★
VELTINS Pilsener (Germany) ★★★★
WATNEY'S Cream Stout (England) ★★★★
WHITBREAD Traditional Pale Ale (England) ★★★★
YOUNG'S Special London Ale (England) ★★★★
YOUNG'S London Porter (England) ★★★★

ABOVE AVERAGE—RECOMMENDED

ADNAMS Broadside Ale (England) ★★★
ADNAMS Suffolk Extra Ale (England) ★★★
ALGONQUIN Special Reserve Ale (Canada) ★★★
ALTENMUNSTER Export Lager (Bavaria-Germany) ★★★
AYINGER Altbairisch Dunkel (Germany) ★★★
AYINGER Celebrator Doppelbock (Germany) ★★★
BATEMAN'S XXXB Ale (England) ★★★
BATEMAN'S Victory Ale (England) ★★★
BAVIK White Beer—Bière Blanche (Belgium) ★★★
BECK'S Pilsener (Germany) ★★★
BIG ROCK McNally's Irish Ale (Canada) ★★★
BODDINGTONS Pub Ale Draught (England) ★★★
BOHEMIA Pilsener (Mexico) ★★★
BROKEN HILL Lager (Australia) ★★★
CALEDONIAN Golden Pale Ale (Scotland) ★★★
CANADIAN BREWING COMPANY Black & Tan (Stout and Lager)
    (Canada) ★★★
CARIB LAGER ★★★
CERVEZA-AGUILA Pilsener (Colombia) ★★★
CHIHUAHUA (Mexico) ★★★
CHIMAY Red Trappist Ale (Belgium) ★★★
CHIMAY Première Trappist Ale (Belgium) ★★★
COOPER'S Black Crow Ale (Australia) ★★★
COOPER'S Best Extra Stout (Australia) ★★★
CORONA Light Pilsener (Mexico) ★★★
CORONA Extra Pilsener (Mexico) ★★★
DE TROCH CHAPEAU Kriek Lambic (Belgium) ★★★
DRAGON Stout (Jamaica) ★★★
EKU Fest Bier Lager (Germany) ★★★
ELEPHANT Red (Canada) ★★★
EUROPA Lager (Portugal) ★★★
FOSTER'S Special Bitter Ale (Australia/Canada) ★★★
FOSTER'S Lager (Australia/Canada) ★★★
FRAOCH Heather Ale (Scotland) ★★★
FULLER'S London Pride (England) ★★★
GRIFFON Extra Pale Ale (Canada) ★★★
GRIFFON Brown Ale (Canada) ★★★
GROLSCH Premium Lager (Holland) ★★★

GUINNESS Extra Stout (Ireland) ★★★
GUINNESS Gold Lager (Ireland) ★★★
HAAKE BECK Non-Alcohol Brew (Germany) ★★★
HACKER-PSCHORR Weisse (Germany) ★★★
HEINEKEN Tarwebok Wheat Bock (Holland) ★★★
JULIUS ECHTER Hefe Weissbier (Germany) ★★★
LIEFMANS Frambozenbier/Raspberry Lambic (Belgium) ★★★
LINDEMANS Framboise/Raspberry Lambic (Belgium) ★★★
MAMBA Malt Liquor (Ivory Coast) ★★★
MCEWAN'S Scotch Ale (England) ★★★
MCEWAN'S Export India Pale Ale (England) ★★★
MORETTI La Rossa Doppio Malto Lager (Italy) ★★★
MURPHY'S Irish Amber (Ireland) ★★★
NEWCASTLE Brown Ale (England) ★★★
NIAGARA FALLS Eisbock Ice Beer (Canada) ★★★
NOCHE BUENO Winter/Christmas Amber (Mexico) ★★★
OLD GROWLER English Ale (England) ★★★
OLD GROWLER Porter (England) ★★★
PAULANER Bavarian Alpine Extreme Ale (Germany) ★★★
PAULANER Hefe-Weizen (Germany) ★★★
PETER'S BRAND Pilsener (Holland) ★★★
PETRUS Triple Ale (Belgium) ★★★
PINKUS Home Brew Wheat Beer (Germany) ★★★
ROYAL OAK Pale Ale (England) ★★★
ST. AMBROISE Pale Ale (Canada) ★★★
ST. FEUILLIEN Brune Abbey Ale (Belgium) ★★★
ST. LANDELIN Amber Abbey Ale (France) ★★★
ST. LANDELIN Brown Abbey Ale (France) ★★★
ST. PAUL Triple Abbey Ale (Belgium) ★★★
ST. PAULI GIRL Pilsener (Germany) ★★★
ST. SEBASTIAN Dark Ale (Belgium) ★★★
SAMUEL SMITH'S Lager (England) ★★★
SAMUEL SMITH'S Winter Welcome Ale 1995–1996 (England) ★★★
SAPPORO Original Draft Pilsener (Japan) ★★★
SCHNEIDER Hefe-Weizen (Germany) ★★★
SCHNEIDER Aventinus Wheat Doppelbock (Germany) ★★★
SHEAF Stout (Australia) ★★★
SLEEMAN Cream Ale (Canada) ★★★
SPATEN Optimator Doppelbock (Germany) ★★★
SPATEN Ur-Marzen Oktoberfest Lager (Germany) ★★★
SPATEN Hefe-Weissbier (Germany) ★★★
STERKENS Bokrijks Kruikenbier Ale (Belgium) ★★★
STERKENS Poorter (Belgium) ★★★
TANGLE FOOT Ale (England) ★★★
THAMES Welsh Bitter Ale (Wales) ★★★
THOMAS HARDY'S Ale (England) ★★★
TUCHER Kristall Weizen Beer (Germany) ★★★
TUCHER Bajuvator Doppelbock (Germany) ★★★
TUSKER Premium Lager (Kenya) ★★★

WATNEY'S Red Barrel (England) ★★★
WICKULER Pilsener (Germany) ★★★
YOUNG'S Ram Rod Pale Ale (England) ★★★
YOUNG'S Old Nick Barley Wine Style Ale (England) ★★★
YOUNG'S Oatmeal Stout (England) ★★★
YOUNGER'S Tartan Special Ale (Scotland) ★★★

AVERAGE—NOT RECOMMENDED

ALGONQUIN Black & Tan (Canada) ★★
ALGONQUIN Dark Ale (Canada) ★★
AMSTEL Light Lager (Holland) ★★
ANDES Lager (Venezuela) ★★
BASS Pale Ale (England) ★★
BECK'S Oktoberfest Lager (Germany) ★★
BELLE-VUE Kriek/Cherry Ale (Belgium) ★★
BERLINER KINDL Pils (Germany) ★★
BODDINGTONS Export Ale (England) ★★
BREUG Lager (France) ★★
BUCKAROO Beer (Belgium) ★★
CALEDONIAN Golden Promise Ale (Scotland) ★★
CARLSBERG LIGHT Lager (Denmark) ★★
CARTA BLANCA Lager (Mexico) ★★
CREEMORE SPRINGS Premium Lager (Canada) ★★
DELERIUM Tremens Belgian Ale (Belgium) ★★
DE TROCH CHAPEAU Fraises/Strawberry Lambic (Belgium) ★★
DE TROCH CHAPEAU Exotic/Pineapple Lambic (Belgium) ★★
DOS EQUIS (Mexico) ★★
DUVEL Ale (Belgium) ★★
EDELWEISS Hefetrub Weizenbier (Austria) ★★
EDELWEISS Dunkel Weizenbier (Austria) ★★
EKU Hefe-Weizen (Germany) ★★
EKU Rubin Dunkle Lager (Germany) ★★
FULLER'S ESB—Extra Special Bitter Ale (England) ★★
GOSSER Export (Austria) ★★
HACKER-PSCHORR Original Oktoberfest (Germany) ★★
HARP Lager (Ireland) ★★
HEINEKEN Special Dark (Holland) ★★
HEXEN BRAU Dunkel (Switzerland) ★★
JOHN COURAGE Amber Lager (England) ★★
JUBEL (Germany) ★★
KINGFISHER Indian Lager (Brewed/Bottled in England) ★★
KIRIN Lager (Japan) ★★
KIRIN Dry (Japan) ★★
KRONENBOURG Pale Lager (France) ★★
KROPF Dark Draft Lager (Germany) ★★
LABATT 50th Anniversary Ale (Canada) ★★
LA TRAPPE Enkel Trappist Ale (Holland) ★★
LIEFMANS Kriekbier/Cherry Lambic (Belgium) ★★

Marston's Oyster Stout (England) ★★
Molson Ice (Canada) ★★
Molson Golden (Canada) ★★
Moretti Birra Friulana Pilsener (Italy) ★★
Niagara Falls Brock's Extra Stout (Canada) ★★
Oberdorfer Weissbier (Germany) ★★
Orval Trappist Monastery Ale (Belgium) ★★
Peroni Lager (Italy) ★★
Petrus Oak-Aged Dark Beer (Belgium) ★★
Presidente Pilsener (Dominican Republic) ★★
Razor Edge Lager (Australia) ★★
Red Stripe Lager (Jamaica) ★★
Rodenbach Red Ale (Belgium) ★★
Ruski Lager (Russia) ★★
St. Ambroise Oatmeal Stout (Canada) ★★
St. Paul Double Abbey Ale (Belgium) ★★
St. Paul Blonde Abbey Ale (Belgium) ★★
St. Sebastian Golden Ale (Belgium) ★★
Scaldis Noël Special Ale (Belgium) ★★
Staropramen Pilsener (Czech Republic) ★★
Tecate Pilsener (Mexico) ★★
Thomas Hardy's Country Bitter (England) ★★
Tolly Cobbold IPA (England) ★★
Tsingtao Pilsener (China) ★★
Tuborg Gold Label Pilsener (Denmark) ★★
Tucher Hefe Weizen Beer (Germany) ★★
Tucher Dunkel Hefe Weizen Beer (Germany) ★★
Weihenstephan Weizenbier (Germany) ★★
Wurzburger Hofbrau May Bok (Germany) ★★
Xingu Black Beer (Brazil) ★★

Poor—Not Recommended

Ba M'Ba BGI "33" Export (Vietnam) ★
Belle-Vue Gueuze Lambic Ale (Belgium) ★
Belle-Vue Framboise/Raspberry Ale (Belgium) ★
Bintang Pilsener (Indonesia) ★
Brasseurs Bière de Paris Lager (France) ★
Caesarus Imperator Heller Bock (Switzerland) ★
Clausthaler Non-Alcohol Brew (Germany) ★
Dentergems Wit/Wheat Ale (Belgium) ★
Dos Equis Clara Special Lager (Mexico) ★
Eku 28 Kulminator Uptyp Hell (Germany) ★
Elephant Malt Liquor (Denmark) ★
Fischer D'Alsace Amber Malt Liquor (France) ★
Fischer D'Alsace Bitter (France) ★
Foster's Light Lager (Australia/Canada) ★
Kaliber Non-Alcohol Brew (England) ★
Labatt Ice Beer (Canada) ★

LA CHOULETTE Amber Ale (France) ★
LINDEMANS Gueuze Cuvée René Lambic 1994 (Belgium) ★
MACANDREW'S Scotch Ale (Scotland) ★
MARSTON'S Albion Porter (England) ★
MEDALLA Pilsener (Puerto Rico) ★
MOLSON Light (Canada) ★
MOLSON Export Ale (Canada) ★
MOLSON EXEL Non-Alcohol Brew (Canada) ★
MOLSON Red Jack Ale (Canada) ★
MOOSEHEAD Canadian Lager (Canada) ★
MOUSSY Non-Alcohol Brew (Switzerland) ★
MURPHY'S Irish Stout Draught (Ireland) ★
NIAGARA FALLS Kriek/Cherry Ale (Canada) ★
NIAGARA FALLS Apple Ale (Canada) ★
NIAGARA FALLS Maple Wheat Ale (Canada) ★
NORDIK WOLF Light (Canada) ★
OBERDORFER Dark Weissbier (Germany) ★
OKOCIM O.K. Pils (Poland) ★
PACIFICO CLARA Pilsener (Mexico) ★
PETRUS Speciale Ale (Belgium) ★
PINKUS MULLER Ur Pils Organic Home Brew (Germany) ★
PORT ROYAL Export Pilsener (Honduras) ★
RED HORSE Malt Liquor (Philippines) ★
ST. PAUL Special Abbey Ale (Belgium) ★
SAKU OLLETEHAS Originaal Pilsener (Estonia) ★
SAKU OLLETEHAS Estonian Porter (Estonia) ★
SOL Especial Pilsener (Mexico) ★
SUNTORY Draft Pilsener (Canada) ★
SUPERIOR Clasica Pilsener (Mexico) ★
TAJ MAHAL Lager (India) ★
WURZBURGER HOFBRAU Bavarian Light (Germany) ★
WURZBURGER HOFBRAU Fallfest Beer (Germany) ★
WURZBURGER HOFBRAU Original Bavarian Holiday Beer (Germany) ★
WURZBURGER HOFBRAU Bavarian Dark (Germany) ★
ZIEGEL HOF Non-Alcohol Malt (Switzerland) ★

APPENDIX C

Complete Alphabetical
Domestic Beer Ratings Summary

ALASKAN Smoked Porter ★★★★
ALASKAN Amber Beer ★★★
ALASKAN Pale Ale ★★
ALMOND BROTHERS Amber Ale ★★★
ANCHOR Old Foghorn Barley Wine Style Ale ★★★★
ANCHOR Liberty ★★★
ANCHOR Porter ★★
ANCHOR Steam Beer ★★
ANDERSON VALLEY Boont Amber Ale ★★★
ANDERSON VALLEY Belk's Extra Special Bitter Ale ★★
AUGSBURGER Golden Lager ★

BADERBRAU Bock Beer ★★★
BADERBRAU Pilsener ★★★
BALLANTINE India Pale Ale ★★★
BELMONT Marathon Ale ★★★
BELMONT Strawberry Blonde Ale ★★
BELMONT Unfiltered Wheat ★
BELMONT Top Sail Amber Ale ★
BELMONT Long Beach Crude Nut Brown Ale ★
BERGHOFF Dark Beer / Dortmunder Style ★★★
BEVERLY HILLS Palimony Bitter Ale ★
BLUE MOON Nut Brown Ale ★★★
BLUE MOON Belgian White ★★
BLUE MOON Honey Blonde Lager ★★
BLUE MOON Raspberry Cream Ale ★★

BLUE RIDGE ESB Red Ale ★★★
BLUE RIDGE Golden Ale ★★
BOULDER Extra Pale Ale ★★
BREWER'S CAVE Black Barley Ale ★★★
BREWER'S CAVE Golden Caramel Lager ★★★
BREWER'S CAVE Amber Wheat Ale ★★
BREWERY HILL Cherry Wheat Ale ★★★★
BREWERY HILL Honey Amber Ale ★★
BREWERY HILL Pale Ale ★★
BREWERY HILL Raspberry Red Ale ★
BREWERY HILL Black & Tan ★
BREWSKI Bar Room Ale ★★★
BROOKLYN BREWERY Black Chocolate Stout ★★★★
BROOKLYN BREWERY East India Pale Ale ★★★
BROOKLYN BREWERY Lager ★★★
BROOKLYN BREWERY Brown Dark Ale ★★
BUDWEISER Lager ★
BUD Light ★
BUDWEISER Ice Draft ★
BUFFALO Lager ★★★
BUFFALO BILL'S Pumpkin Ale ★★★
BUNKER HILL Lager ★★
BUSCH Lager ★

CARLING BLACK LABEL Light ★
CATAMOUNT Bock ★★★
CATAMOUNT Porter ★★★
CATAMOUNT Christmas Ale 1995 ★★★
CATAMOUNT 10th Anniversary Ale Special Edition IPA ★★★
CATAMOUNT Amber ★★
CATAMOUNT American Wheat ★★
CATAMOUNT Pale Ale ★
CELIS White Hefe Weizen ★★★★★
CELIS Pale Bock ★★★★
CELIS Ale Grand Cru ★★★
CELIS Golden Ale ★★★
COLD SPRING Export Lager ★★
COLD SPRING Honey Almond Lager ★★
COLD SPRING Blackberry Bramble Ale ★★
COORS Winterfest ★★★
COORS Pilsener ★
COORS Light ★
COORS Cutter Non-Alcoholic Brew ★
COORS Red Light ★
CRESTED BUTTE White Buffalo Peace Ale ★★

DEVIL MOUNTAIN BREWERY Railroad Ale ★★★
DEVIL MOUNTAIN BREWERY Porter ★★★
DIXIE BLACKENED VOODOO Lager ★★★

DIXIE JAZZ Amber Light ★
DIXIE Slow-Brewed Lager ★
DOCK STREET Illuminator Bock ★★★★
DOCK STREET Bohemian Pilsener ★★★
DOCK STREET Philadelphia Amber ★★★
DORNBUSCH Alt Ale ★★★★
DOWNTOWN Brown Ale ★
DRYTOWN Susquehanna Gold Ale ★★★
DUBUQUE STAR Big Muddy Red Ale ★★★★

ED'S CAVE CREEK Original Chili Beer ★
ELK MOUNTAIN Amber Ale ★★
ELK MOUNTAIN Red Lager ★
ELM CITY Blackwell Stout ★★★★
ELM CITY Connecticut Ale ★★★
ELM CITY Golden Ale ★★
ERIN'S ROCK Stout & Amber Lager ★★★★

GEARY'S London Style Porter ★★★★★
GEARY'S Pale Ale ★★★
GEARY'S Hampshire Special Ale Winter 1995–1996 ★★★
GENESEE Cream Ale ★
GEORGE KILLIAN'S Irish Brown Ale ★★★
GEORGE KILLIAN'S Irish Red Lager ★★
GEORGIA PEACH Wheat Beer ★★★
GEORGIA Wild Raspberry Wheat Ale ★★★
GRAIL Amber Ale ★★★
GRANT'S Scottish Ale ★★★★
GRANT'S Perfect Porter ★★★★
GRANT'S Imperial Stout ★★★
GRANT'S Weis Beer ★★★
GRANT'S Celtic Ale ★★★
GRANT'S India Pale Ale ★★
GRITTY MCDUFF'S Best Bitter Ale ★★★★
GRITTY MCDUFF'S Best Brown Ale ★★★★
GRITTY MCDUFF'S Black Fly Stout ★★

HARPOON India Pale Ale ★★★
HARPOON Octoberfest ★★★
HARPOON Pilsner ★★★
HARPOON Alt Ale ★★
HARPOON Winter Warmer ★★
HARPOON Golden Lager ★★
HEARTLAND BREWERY Indiana Pale Ale ★★★★
HEARTLAND BREWERY Red Rooster Ale ★★★
HEARTLAND BREWERY Cornhusker Lager ★★
HEARTLAND BREWERY Harvest Wheat Ale ★★
HEARTLAND BREWERY Farmer Jon's Oatmeal Stout ★
HELENBOCH Holiday Ale ★★★

HEURICH'S Maerzen Lager ★★
HEURICH'S Foggy Bottom Ale ★
HUDSON Lager ★

IRON CITY Beer ★★

JACK DANIEL'S 1866 Classic Amber Lager ★★★★
JACK DANIEL'S 1866 Classic American Ale ★★★★
JACK DANIEL'S 1866 Classic Pilsner ★★★
JACK DANIEL'S Oak-Aged Winter Brew ★
JAMAICA BRAND Red Ale ★★★
J.J. WAINWRIGHT'S Evil Eye Raspberry Wheat ★★
J.J. WAINWRIGHT'S Evil Eye Ale ★
J.J. WAINWRIGHT'S Evil Eye Honey Brown Ale ★
J.J. WAINWRIGHT'S Evil Eye Oktoberfest ★
J.J. WAINWRIGHT'S Black Jack Black & Tan ★
JUAN PISTOLA'S Acapulco Gold Pale Ale ★★★★
JUAN PISTOLA'S Baja Tan Brown Ale ★★★
JUAN PISTOLA'S Sangria Ale ★★
JUAN PISTOLA'S Amber Ale ★

KATAHDIN Red Ale ★★★★
KOCH'S Golden Anniversary Beer ★★

LAKEFRONT BREWERY Riverwest Stein Beer Amber Lager ★★★★★
LAKEFRONT BREWERY Klisch Pilsner ★★★★★
LAKEFRONT BREWERY Cream City Pale Ale ★★★★
LAKEFRONT BREWERY ESB OCIA Certified Organic Ale ★★★★
LAKEFRONT BREWERY Eastside Dark Lager ★★★★
LAKEFRONT BREWERY Holiday Spice Lager 1995 ★★★★
LAKEFRONT BREWERY Fuel Café Coffee-Flavored Stout ★★
LATROBE Bohemian Pilsner ★★★★
LATROBE Bavarian Black Lager ★★★
LATROBE Pale Ale ★★★
LEINENKUGEL'S Red Lager ★★★
LITTLE KINGS Cream Ale ★★
LITTLE KINGS BRUIN Pale Ale ★★
LONE STAR Lager ★
LOWENBRAU Special Pilsener ★★

MAGIC HAT Irish Style Red Ale ★★★★
MAGIC HAT 9 Not Quite Pale Ale ★★★
MAGIC HAT Blind Faith IPA ★
MANHATTAN Gold Lager ★★★
McMAHON'S Irish Style Potato Ale ★
McSORLEY'S Ale ★★★
MEISTER BRAU Light ★
MICHAEL SHEA'S Black & Tan ★★★
MICHAEL SHEA'S Blonde Lager ★★★

MICHAEL SHEA'S Irish Amber Lager ★★★
MICHELOB Lager ★★
MICHELOB Dry Lager ★★
MICHELOB Amber Bock ★
MICHELOB Light Lager ★
MIDDLESEX Brown Ale ★★★
MIDDLESEX Raspberry Wheat ★★★
MIDDLESEX Porter ★★
MILL CITY Oatmeal Stout ★★★★
MILLER Reserve 100% Barley Draft ★★★
MILLER Reserve Velvet Stout ★★
MILLER Lite ★
MILLER Genuine Draft Cold-Filtered ★
MILLER Genuine Draft Light ★
MILLER ICEHOUSE Ice Beer ★
MOOSE Brown Ale ★★
MYSTIC SEAPORT Pale Ale ★★★

NAKED ASPEN Raspberry Wheat ★★★★
NAKED ASPEN Apricot Ale ★★★
NAKED ASPEN Pale Ale ★
NANTUCKET Island Amber ★★
NARRAGANSETT Lager ★★★
NEPTUNE Premium Ale ★★★
NEUWEILER Stock Ale ★★★
NEUWEILER Traditional Lager ★★
NEUWEILER Porter ★★
NEUWEILER Black & Tan ★★
NEW AMSTERDAM New York Amber ★★★★
NEW AMSTERDAM New York Ale ★★★★
NEW AMSTERDAM Black & Tan ★★★
NEW AMSTERDAM Winter Anniversary Dark Ale 1995–1996 ★★★
NEW AMSTERDAM Blonde Lager ★★
NEW AMSTERDAM Light Amber ★★
NEW ENGLAND Oatmeal Stout ★★★
NEW ENGLAND Atlantic Amber ★★★
NEW ENGLAND Gold Stock Ale ★★
NEW YORK HARBOR Amber Ale ★★★
NEW YORK HARBOR Dark Ale ★★★
NORTH COAST Ruedrick's Red Seal Ale ★★★
NORTH COAST Blue Star Great American Wheat Beer ★
NORTH COUNTRY Fat Bear Stout ★★★★
NORTH COUNTRY Whiteface Pale Ale ★★★
NORTH COUNTRY Maple Amber Ale ★★
NOR'WESTER Blacksmith Porter ★★★★★
NOR'WESTER Hefe Weizen ★★★★
NOR'WESTER Raspberry Weizen ★★★★
NOR'WESTER Best Bitter Ale ★★★

O'DOUL'S Premium Non-Alcoholic Brew ★★
OLD COLUMBIA Strauss Stout ★★★★
OLD COLUMBIA America's Finest Pilsener ★★★★
OLD COLUMBIA Karl Strauss' Amber Lager ★★★
OLD COLUMBIA ESB Ale ★★★
OLD COLUMBIA First National Bock ★★
OLD COLUMBIA Ed's Hoppy Birthday Pilsener ★★
OLD COLUMBIA Karl's Cream Ale ★
OLD COLUMBIA Karl Strauss' Light Lager ★
OLD PECONIC Hampton Ale ★★★
OLD SLUGGER Pale Ale ★★★
OLD THUMPER Extra Special Ale ★★★★
OREGON Nut Brown Ale ★★★★
OREGON Honey Red ★★★
OREGON ESB ★★
OREGON Hefeweizen ★
OREGON IPA ★
OREGON Raspberry Wheat ★
OXFORD Raspberry Wheat Ale ★★★
OXFORD Class Amber Ale ★

PERRY'S Majestic Lager ★
PETE'S Gold Coast Lager ★★★★
PETE'S Wicked Lager ★★★
PETE'S Wicked Winter Brew ★★
PETE'S Wicked Honey Wheat ★★
PETE'S Wicked Red Amber Ale ★★
PIG'S EYE Pilsener ★★★
PIG'S EYE Red Amber Ale ★★★
PIKE PLACE Pale Ale ★★
PINK TRIANGLE Light Beer ★★
PYRAMID Best Brown Ale ★★★

RATTLESNAKE Lager ★
RED BARON Cherry-Flavored Beer ★★
RED BONE Red Lager ★★
RED DOG ★
RED FEATHER Pale Ale ★★★
RED HOOK ESB ★★★★
RED HOOK Blackhook Porter ★★★★
RED HOOK Ballard Bitter India Pale Ale ★★★
RED HOOK Rye Ale ★★★
RED HOOK Wheat Hook Ale ★★★
RED TAIL Ale ★
RED WOLF Lager ★
RHEINGOLD Light ★★
RHINO CHASERS Dark Lager ★★★★
RHINO CHASERS American Ale ★★★
RHINO CHASERS Amber Ale ★★★

RHINO CHASERS Peach Honey Wheat ★★★
RHINO CHASERS Winterful ★★★
RIVERSIDE BREWING Golden Spike Pilsner ★
RIVERSIDE BREWING Pullman Pale Ale ★
RIVERSIDE BREWING Victoria Avenue Amber Ale ★
RIVERSIDE BREWING Raincross Cream Ale ★
RJ's RIPTIDE Oatmeal Stout ★★★★
RJ's RIPTIDE Original Honey Ale ★★★
RJ's RIPTIDE Two-Berry Ale ★★★
RJ's RIPTIDE Charger Gold Ale ★★★
RJ's RIPTIDE Dunkel Weizen ★★
RJ's RIPTIDE Red Ale ★★
ROCK ICE Amber Lager ★★
ROGUE American Amber Ale ★★★★
ROGUE Mogul Ale ★★★★
ROGUE Smoke Rauch Style Ale ★★★★
ROGUE Shakespeare Stout ★★★★
ROGUE Old Crustacean Barley Wine Style Ale ★★★★
ROGUE-N-BERRY Ale ★★★
ROGUE Dead Guy Ale ★★★
ROGUE Mexicali Ale ★★★
ROGUE Ale ★★★
ROGUE/ST. ROGUE Red Ale ★★★
ROGUE Maierbock Ale ★★★
ROGUE Golden Ale ★★
ROGUE Mo Ale Belgian Style ★★
ROGUE Mocha Porter ★
ROLLING ROCK Extra Pale Lager ★★
ROLLING ROCK Bock ★★
ROLLING ROCK Light Lager ★
RUFFIAN Extra Special Bitter ★★★★
RUFFIAN Copper Ale ★★★
RUFFIAN Porter ★★★
RUFFIAN Blonde Bock (Seasonal) ★★★
RUFFIAN Irish Red Ale ★★

ST. JAMES Ale ★
SAMUEL ADAMS Double Bock Dark Lager ★★★★★
SAMUEL ADAMS Honey Porter ★★★★★
SAMUEL ADAMS Dark Wheat ★★★★
SAMUEL ADAMS Triple Bock 1994 Brew Reserve ★★★★
SAMUEL ADAMS Scotch Ale Triple Malt ★★★★
SAMUEL ADAMS Boston Lager ★★★
SAMUEL ADAMS Boston Ale ★★★
SAMUEL ADAMS Boston Lightship Light ★★★
SAMUEL ADAMS Cream Stout ★★★
SAMUEL ADAMS Golden Pilsner ★★★
SAMUEL ADAMS Winter Lager 1995–1996 ★★★
SAMUEL ADAMS Cherry Wheat Ale ★★

SAMUEL ADAMS Wheat Brew ★
SARANAC Adirondack Amber Lager ★★★
SARANAC Chocolate Amber ★★★
SARANAC Season's Best Nut Brown Lager ★★★
SARANAC Golden Pilsener ★★
SARANAC Pale Ale ★★
SAXER Three Finger Jack Stout ★★★
SAXER Three Finger Jack Hefedunkel ★★
SAXER Three Finger Jack Amber Lager ★★
SAXER Lemon Lager ★★
SCHAEFER Pilsener ★★
SCHMIDT'S Light ★
SCRIMSHAW Pilsner ★
SEA DOG Riverdriver Hazelnut Porter ★★★★★
SEA DOG Old Gollywobbler Brown Ale ★★★
SEA DOG Windjammer Blonde Ale ★★★
SEA DOG Old East India IPA ★★
SHARP'S Non-Alcoholic Brew ★
SIERRA NEVADA Stout ★★★★★
SIERRA NEVADA Porter ★★★
SIERRA NEVADA Pale Ale ★★
SIMPATICO Amber Lager ★★
SIMPATICO Golden Lager ★
SLO BREWING CO. Cole Porter ★★★
SLO BREWING CO. Blueberry Ale ★
SLO BREWING CO. Brickhouse Extra Pale Ale ★
SPANISH PEAKS Black Dog Pale Ale ★★
SPANISH PEAKS Peaches & Cream Ale ★★
SPANISH PEAKS Black Dog Ale ★★
SPANISH PEAKS Honey Raspberry Ale ★
SPANISH PEAKS Black Dog Wheat Ale ★
SPORTS Light ★
STAR Raspberry Wheat Ale ★★
STEGMAIER 1857 Lager ★★★
STEGMAIER Porter ★★
STEELHEAD Extra Stout ★★
STOUDT'S Golden Lager ★★★
STOUDT'S Fest Marzen Style Lager ★★
STOUDT'S Honey Double Mai Bock ★

TELLURIDE Lager ★
THE SHIPYARD Longfellow Winter Ale ★★
THE SHIPYARD Export Ale ★
THE SHIPYARD Goat Island Light Ale ★
THE SHIPYARD Bluefin Stout ★

WEINHARD'S Red Lager ★★
WEINHARD'S Blue Boar Pale Ale ★
WHITE KNIGHT Light Ale ★★

WILD BOAR Special Amber Lager ★★★★
WILD BOAR Classic Pilsner ★★★
WILD BOAR Wild Winter Spiced Brown Lager ★★★
WILD GOOSE Porter ★★★
WILD GOOSE Amber Ale ★★★
WILD GOOSE India Pale Ale ★
WILD GOOSE Spring Wheat Ale '96 ★
WIT Amber ★★★★
WIT Black ★★★
WIT White ★★★
WOODSTOCK Arnold's Amber Lager ★★★

YUENGLING Porter ★★★
YUENGLING Lord Chesterfield Ale ★★★
YUENGLING TRADITIONAL Amber Lager ★★
YUENGLING PREMIUM Light Lager ★

ZIMA Clearmalt ★
ZIP CITY Vienna Amber Lager ★★★
ZIP CITY Oktoberfest Amber Lager ★★

APPENDIX D

Complete Alphabetical Imported Beer Ratings Summary

ADNAMS Nut Brown Ale (England) ★★★★
ADNAMS Broadside Ale (England) ★★★
ADNAMS Suffolk Extra Ale (England) ★★★
AECHT SCHLENKERLA Rauchbier (Germany) ★★★★★
AFFLIGEM Dobbel Abbey Ale (Belgium) ★★★★
AFFLIGEM Tripel Abbey Ale (Belgium) ★★★★
ALGONQUIN Special Reserve Ale (Canada) ★★★
ALGONQUIN Black & Tan (Canada) ★★
ALGONQUIN Dark Ale (Canada) ★★
ALTENMUNSTER Export Lager (Bavaria-Germany) ★★★
AMSTEL Light Lager (Holland) ★★
ANDES Cerveza (Venezuela) ★★
AYINGER Brau-Weisse Helles Hefe Weissbier (Germany) ★★★★
AYINGER Altbairisch Dunkel (Germany) ★★★
AYINGER Celebrator Doppelbock (Germany) ★★★

BA M'BA BGI "33" Export (Vietnam) ★
BASS Pale Ale (England) ★★
BATEMAN'S XXXB Ale (England) ★★★
BATEMAN'S Victory Ale (England) ★★★
BAVIK White Beer—Bière Blanche (Belgium) ★★★
BECK'S Dark Pilsener (Germany) ★★★★
BECK'S Pilsener (Germany) ★★★
BECK'S Oktoberfest Lager (Germany) ★★
BELHAVEN St. Andrews Ale (Scotland) ★★★★
BELHAVEN Scottish Ale (Scotland) ★★★★

BELLE-VUE Kriek/Cherry Ale (Belgium) ★★
BELLE-VUE Gueuze Lambic Ale (Belgium) ★
BELLE-VUE Framboise/Raspberry Ale (Belgium) ★
BERLINER KINDL Pils (Germany) ★★
BIG ROCK McNally's Irish Ale (Canada) ★★★
BINTANG Pilsener (Indonesia) ★
BODDINGTONS Pub Ale Draught (England) ★★★
BODDINGTONS Export Ale (England) ★★
BOHEMIA Pilsener (Mexico) ★★★
BRAKSPEARS Henley Ale (England) ★★★★★
BRASSEURS Bière de Paris Lager (France) ★
BREUG Lager (France) ★★
BROKEN HILL Lager (Australia) ★★★
BUCKAROO Beer (Belgium) ★★

CAESARUS Imperator Heller Bock (Switzerland) ★
CALEDONIAN Amber Ale (Scotland) ★★★★
CALEDONIAN Double Dark Ale (Scotland) ★★★★
CALEDONIAN Golden Pale Ale (Scotland) ★★★
CALEDONIAN Golden Promise Ale (Scotland) ★★
CANADIAN BREWING COMPANY Black & Tan (Stout and Lager)
   (Canada) ★★★
CARIB LAGER ★★★
CARLSBERG LIGHT Lager (Denmark) ★★
CARTA BLANCA Lager (Mexico) ★★
CERVEZA-AGUILA Pilsener (Colombia) ★★★
CHIHUAHUA (Mexico) ★★★
CHIMAY Grande Réserve Trappist Ale (Belgium) ★★★★★
CHIMAY Cinq Cents Trappist Ale (Belgium) ★★★★
CHIMAY Red Trappist Ale (Belgium) ★★★
CHIMAY Première Trappist Ale (Belgium) ★★★
CHRISTOFFEL Robertus Munich Lager (Holland) ★★★★★
CHRISTOFFEL Blonde Ale (Holland) ★★★★
CLAUSTHALER Non-Alcohol Brew (Germany) ★
COOPER'S Black Crow Ale (Australia) ★★★
COOPER'S Best Extra Stout (Australia) ★★★
CORONA Extra Pilsener (Mexico) ★★★
CORONA Light Pilsener (Mexico) ★★★
CORSENDONK Monk's Pale Ale (Belgium) ★★★★
CORSENDONK Monk's Brown Ale (Belgium) ★★★★
CREEMORE SPRINGS Premium Lager (Canada) ★★

DELERIUM Tremens Belgian Ale (Belgium) ★★
DENTERGEMS Wit/Wheat Ale (Belgium) ★
DE TROCH CHAPEAU Pêche/Peach Lambic (Belgium) ★★★★★
DE TROCH CHAPEAU Mirabelle/Plum Lambic (Belgium) ★★★★
DE TROCH CHAPEAU Framboise/Raspbery Lambic (Belgium) ★★★★
DE TROCH CHAPEAU Gueuze Lambic (Belgium) ★★★★
DE TROCH CHAPEAU Kriek/Cherry Lambic (Belgium) ★★★

DE TROCH CHAPEAU Fraises/Strawberry Lambic (Belgium) ★★
DE TROCH CHAPEAU Exotic/Pineapple Lambic (Belgium) ★★
DOS EQUIS (Mexico) ★★
DOS EQUIS Clara Special Lager (Mexico) ★
DOUBLE DIAMOND Burton Ale (England) ★★★★
DRAGON Stout (Jamaica) ★★★
DUVEL Ale (Belgium) ★★

EDELWEISS Hefetrub Weizenbier (Austria) ★★
EDELWEISS Dunkel Weizenbier (Austria) ★★
EKU Fest Bier Lager (Germany) ★★★
EKU Hefe-Weizen (Germany) ★★
EKU Rubin Dunkle Lager (Germany) ★★
EKU 28 Kulminator Uptyp Hell (Germany) ★
ELEPHANT Malt Liquor (Denmark) ★
ELEPHANT Red (Canada) ★★★
ERDINGER Weissbier Hefetrub (Germany) ★★★★★
ERDINGER Pikantus Dunkler Weizenbock (Germany) ★★★★★
ERDINGER Weissbier Dunkel (Germany) ★★★★
EUROPA Lager (Portugal) ★★★

FISCHER D'ALSACE Amber Malt Liquor (France) ★
FISCHER D'ALSACE Bitter (France) ★
FOSTER'S Special Bitter Ale (Australia/Canada) ★★★
FOSTER'S Lager (Australia/Canada) ★★★
FOSTER'S Light Lager (Australia/Canada) ★
FRAOCH Heather Ale (Scotland) ★★★
FULLER'S London Pride (England) ★★★
FULLER'S ESB—Extra Special Bitter Ale (England) ★★

GAMBRINUS Lager (Czech Republic) ★★★★
GOSSER Export (Austria) ★★
GRIFFON Extra Pale Ale (Canada) ★★★
GRIFFON Brown Ale (Canada) ★★★
GROLSCH Premium Lager (Holland) ★★★
GUINNESS Extra Stout (Ireland) ★★★
GUINNESS Gold Lager (Ireland) ★★★

HAAKE BECK Non-Alcohol Brew (Germany) ★★★
HACKER-PSCHORR Pschorr-Brau Dark Weisse (Germany) ★★★★
HACKER-PSCHORR Alt Munich Dark Ale (Germany) ★★★★
HACKER-PSCHORR Marzen Amber Ale (Germany) ★★★★
HACKER PSCHORR Weisse (Germany) ★★★
HACKER-PSCHORR Original Oktoberfest (Germany) ★★
HARP Lager (Ireland) ★★
HEINEKEN Lager (Holland) ★★★★
HEINEKEN Tarwebok Wheat Bock (Holland) ★★★
HEINEKEN Special Dark (Holland) ★★
HEXEN BRAU Dunkel (Switzerland) ★★

JOHN COURAGE Amber Lager (England) ★★
JUBEL (Germany) ★★
JULIUS ECHTER Hefe Weissbier (Germany) ★★★

KALIBER Non-Alcohol Brew (England) ★
KINGFISHER Indian Lager (Brewed/Bottled in England) ★★
KIRIN Lager (Japan) ★★
KIRIN Dry (Japan) ★★
KRONENBOURG Pale Lager (France) ★★
KROPF Dark Draft Lager (Germany) ★★
KWAK PAUWEL Ale (Belgium) ★★★★

LABATT 50th Anniversary Ale (Canada) ★★
LABATT Ice Beer (Canada) ★
LA CHOULETTE Amber Ale (France) ★
LA TRAPPE Quadrupel Trappist Ale (Holland) ★★★★★
LA TRAPPE Dubbel Trappist Ale (Holland) ★★★★
LA TRAPPE Tripel Trappist Ale (Holland) ★★★★
LA TRAPPE Enkel Trappist Ale (Holland) ★★
LIEFMANS Goudenband (Belgium) ★★★★
LIEFMANS Frambozenbier/Raspberry Lambic (Belgium) ★★★
LIEFMANS Kriekbier/Cherry Lambic (Belgium) ★★
LINDEMANS Pêche/Peach Lambic (Belgium) ★★★★★
LINDEMANS Kriek/Cherry Lambic (Belgium) ★★★★
LINDEMANS Framboise/Raspberry Lambic (Belgium) ★★★
LINDEMANS Gueuze Cuvée René Lambic 1994 (Belgium) ★

MACANDREW'S Scotch Ale (Scotland) ★
MACKESON Triple Stout (England) ★★★★
MAMBA Malt Liquor (Ivory Coast) ★★★
MARSTON'S India Export Ale (England) ★★★★★
MARSTON'S Pedigree Bitter (England) ★★★★
MARSTON'S Oyster Stout (England) ★★
MARSTON'S Albion Porter (England) ★
MCEWAN'S Scotch Ale (England) ★★★
MCEWAN'S Export India Pale Ale (England) ★★★
MEDALLA Pilsener (Puerto Rico) ★
MOLSON Ice (Canada) ★★
MOLSON Golden (Canada) ★★
MOLSON Light (Canada) ★
MOLSON Export Ale (Canada) ★
MOLSON EXEL Non-Alcohol Brew (Canada) ★
MOLSON Red Jack Ale (Canada) ★
MOOSEHEAD Canadian Lager (Canada) ★
MORETTI La Rossa Doppio Malto Lager (Italy) ★★★
MORETTI Birra Friulana Pilsener (Italy) ★★
MORRELL'S Oxford Castle Ale (England) ★★★★
MOUSSY Non-Alcohol Brew (Switzerland) ★

Murphy's Irish Amber (Ireland) ★★★
Murphy's Irish Stout Draught (Ireland) ★

Negra Modelo Dark Ale (Mexico) ★★★★
Newcastle Brown Ale (England) ★★★
Niagara Falls Eisbock Ice Beer (Canada) ★★★
Niagara Falls Brock's Extra Stout (Canada) ★★
Niagara Falls Kriek/Cherry Ale (Canada) ★
Niagara Falls Apple Ale (Canada) ★
Niagara Falls Maple Wheat Ale (Canada) ★
Noche Bueno Winter/Christmas Amber (Mexico) ★★★
Nordik Wolf Light (Canada) ★

Oberdorfer Weissbier (Germany) ★★
Oberdorfer Dark Weissbier (Germany) ★
Okocim O.K. Pils (Poland) ★
Old Growler English Ale (England) ★★★
Old Growler Porter (England) ★★★
Old Peculier Yorkshire Ale (England) ★★★★
Orval Trappist Monastery Ale (Belgium) ★★

Pacifico Clara Pilsener (Mexico) ★
Paulaner Salvator Doppelbock (Germany) ★★★★★
Paulaner Lager (Germany) ★★★★
Paulaner Oktoberfest Lager (Germany) ★★★★
Paulaner Bavarian Alpine Extreme Ale (Germany) ★★★
Paulaner Hefe-Weizen (Germany) ★★★
Peroni Lager (Italy) ★★
Peter's Brand Pilsener (Holland) ★★★
Petrus Triple Ale (Belgium) ★★★
Petrus Oak-Aged Dark Beer ★★
Petrus Speciale Ale (Belgium) ★
Pilsner Urquell Pilsner (Czech Republic) ★★★★★
Pinkus Home Brew Munster Alt (Germany) ★★★★
Pinkus Home Brew Wheat Beer (Germany) ★★★
Pinkus Muller Ur Pils Organic Home Brew (Germany) ★
Port Royal Export Pilsener (Honduras) ★
Presidente Pilsener (Dominican Republic) ★★

Radegast Original Lager (Czech Republic) ★★★★
Razor Edge Lager (Australia) ★★
Red Horse Malt Liquor (Philippines) ★
Red Stripe Lager (Jamaica) ★★
Rodenbach Red Ale (Belgium) ★★
Roman Dobbelen Bruinen (Brown) Ale (Belgium) ★★★★
Roman Ename Dubbel Abbey Ale (Belgium) ★★★★
Roman Ename Tripel Abbey Ale (Belgium) ★★★★
Royal Extra Stout (Trinidad, West Indies) ★★★★★

ROYAL OAK Pale Ale (England) ★★★
RUSKI Lager (Russia) ★★

ST. AMBROISE Pale Ale (Canada) ★★★
ST. AMBROISE Oatmeal Stout (Canada) ★★
ST. FEUILLIEN Blonde Abbey Ale (Belgium) ★★★★★
ST. FEUILLIEN Brune Abbey Ale (Belgium) ★★★
ST. GEORGEN BRAU Kellerbier Lager (Germany) ★★★★
ST. LANDELIN Blonde Abbey Ale (France) ★★★★
ST. LANDELIN Amber Abbey Ale (France) ★★★
ST. LANDELIN Brown Abbey Ale (France) ★★★
ST. PAUL Triple Abbey Ale (Belgium) ★★★
ST. PAUL Double Abbey Ale (Belgium) ★★
ST. PAUL Blonde Abbey Ale (Belgium) ★★
ST. PAUL Special Abbey Ale (Belgium) ★
ST. PAULI GIRL Pilsener (Germany) ★★★
ST. SEBASTIAN Dark Ale (Belgium) ★★★
ST. SEBASTIAN Golden Ale (Belgium) ★★
SAKU OLLETEHAS Originaal Pilsener (Estonia) ★
SAKU OLLETEHAS Estonian Porter (Estonia) ★
SAMICHLAUS Dark Lager (Switzerland) ★★★★
SAMUEL SMITH'S Oatmeal Stout (England) ★★★★★
SAMUEL SMITH'S Taddy Porter (England) ★★★★
SAMUEL SMITH'S Imperial Stout (England) ★★★★
SAMUEL SMITH'S India Ale (England) ★★★★
SAMUEL SMITH'S Pale Ale (England) ★★★★
SAMUEL SMITH'S Nut Brown Ale (England) ★★★★
SAMUEL SMITH'S Lager (England) ★★★
SAMUEL SMITH'S Winter Welcome Ale 1995–1996 (England) ★★★
SAPPORO Original Draft Pilsener (Japan) ★★★
SCALDIS Special Ale (Belgium) ★★★★
SCALDIS Noël Special Ale (Belgium) ★★
SCHIERLINGER Roggen Bavarian Rye Beer (Germany) ★★★★
SCHNEIDER Hefe-Weizen (Germany) ★★★
SCHNEIDER Aventinus Wheat Doppelbock (Germany) ★★★
SHEAF Stout (Australia) ★★★
SHEPHERD NEAME India Pale Ale (England) ★★★★
SHEPHERD NEAME Masterbrew Premium Bitter Ale (England) ★★★★
SHEPHERD NEAME Spitfire Ale (England) ★★★★
SINGHA Lager (Thailand) ★★★★
SLEEMAN Cream Ale (Canada) ★★★
SOL Especial Pilsener (Mexico) ★
SPATEN Lager (Germany) ★★★★★
SPATEN Dark Hefe-Weissbier (Germany) ★★★★
SPATEN Optimator Doppelbock (Germany) ★★★
SPATEN Ur-Marzen Oktoberfest Lager (Germany) ★★★
SPATEN Hefe-Weissbier (Germany) ★★★
STAROPRAMEN Pilsener (Czech Republic) ★★
STERKENS Bokrijks Kruikenbier Ale (Belgium) ★★★

STERKENS   Poorter (Belgium) ★★★
SUNTORY   Draft Pilsener (Japan/Canada) ★
SUPERIOR   Clasica Pilsener (Mexico) ★

TAJ MAHAL   Lager (India) ★
TANGLE FOOT   Ale (England) ★★★
TECATE   Pilsener (Mexico) ★★
THAMES   Welsh Bitter Ale (Wales) ★★★
THOMAS HARDY'S   Ale Vintage 1994 (England) ★★★★
THOMAS HARDY'S   Ale (England) ★★★
THOMAS HARDY'S   Country Bitter (England) ★★
3 MONTS   Flanders Golden Ale (France) ★★★★
TOLLY COBBOLD   IPA (England) ★★
TSINGTAO   Pilsener (China) ★★
TUBORG   Gold Label Pilsener (Denmark) ★★
TUCHER   Kristall Weizen Beer (Germany) ★★★
TUCHER   Bajuvator Doppelbock (Germany) ★★★
TUCHER   Hefe Weizen Beer (Germany) ★★
TUCHER   Dunkel Hefe Weizen Beer (Germany) ★★
TUSKER   Premium Lager (Kenya) ★★★

VELTINS   Pilsener (Germany) ★★★★

WATNEY'S   Cream Stout (England) ★★★★
WATNEY'S   Red Barrel (England) ★★★
WEIHENSTEPHAN   Weizenbier (Germany) ★★
WHITBREAD   Traditional Pale Ale (England) ★★★★
WICKULER   Pilsener (Germany) ★★★
WURZBURGER HOFBRAU   May Bok (Germany) ★★
WURZBURGER HOFBRAU   Bavarian Light (Germany) ★
WURZBURGER HOFBRAU   Fallfest Beer (Germany) ★
WURZBURGER HOFBRAU   Original Bavarian Holiday Beer (Germany) ★
WURZBURGER HOFBRAU   Bavarian Dark (Germany) ★

XINGU   Black Beer (Brazil) ★★

YOUNG'S   Special London Ale (England) ★★★★
YOUNG'S   London Porter (England) ★★★★
YOUNG'S   Ram Rod Pale Ale (England) ★★★
YOUNG'S   Old Nick Barley Wine Style Ale (England) ★★★
YOUNG'S   Oatmeal Stout (England) ★★★
YOUNGER'S   Tartan Special Ale (Scotland) ★★★

ZIEGEL HOF   Non-Alcohol Malt (Switzerland) ★

Suggested Reading

All of the following books and publications have assisted me in my beer education and in the writing of this book. I thank all of these beer experts and aficionados for their earnest contributions to the topic of suds. Likewise, I suggest that these books and publications be sought out.

Secret Life of Beer: Legends, Lore & Little-Known Facts, by Alan D. Eames (Storey Comminucations/Pownal, Vermont), 1995.

America's Best Beers, by Christopher Finch & W. Scott Griffiths (Little, Brown and Company/Boston, Massachusetts), 1994.

The Good Beer Book, by Timothy Harper & Garret Oliver (Berkley Books/New York, New York), 1997.

Michael Jackson's Beer Companion, by Michael Jackson (Running Press/Philadelphia, Pennsylvania), 1993.

The Simon & Schuster Pocket Guide to Beer, by Michael Jackson (Fireside/New York, New York), 1991.

The Beer Lover's Guide, by Bob Klein (Workman Publishing/New York, New York), 1995.

Beer Basics: A Quick and Easy Guide, by Peter LaFrance (John Wiley/New York, New York), 1995.

Beer: A History of Suds and Civilization from Mesopotamia to Microbreweries, by Gregg Smith (Avon Books/New York, New York), 1995.

The Beer Enthusiast's Guide, by Gregg Smith (Storey Communications/Pownal, Vermont), 1994.

The Beer Directory: An International Guide, by Heather Wood (Storey Communications/Pownal, Vermont), 1995.

The Ultimate Book of Beer Trivia, by Bill Yenne & Tom Debolski
(Bluewood Books/San Francisco, California), 1994.

MAGAZINES/NEWSLETTERS TO ENHANCE YOUR EVERYDAY BEER EXPERIENCE:

All About Beer—Published six times yearly
Beer, The Magazine—Published five times yearly
American Brewer—Published quarterly
The Malt Advocate—Published quarterly